Chanted Narratives

The Living 'Katha-Vachana' Tradition

Chanted Narratives

The Living 'Katha-Vachana' Tradition

Edited by
MOLLY KAUSHAL

Indira Gandhi National Centre for the Arts
New Delhi

D.K. Printworld (P) Ltd.
New Delhi

Cataloging in Publication Data — DK

Chanted narratives : the living 'katha-vachana' tradition / edited by Molly Kaushal.
Includes bibliographical references.

1. Indic literature — History and criticism. 2 Epic literature, Indic — History and criticism. 3 Oral tradition — India. I. Kaushal, Molly.

ISBN 81-246-0182-8

First Published in India in 2001

Publishers

Indira Gandhi National Centre for the Arts
Central Vista Mess, Janapath, New Delhi - 110 001

D.K. Printworld (P) Ltd.
Regd. office : '*Sri Kunj*', F-52, Bali Nagar, New Delhi - 110 015
Phones : (011) 545-3975; 546-6019; *Fax* : (011) 546-5926
E-mail: dkprint@4mis.com

Printed by: D.K. Printworld (P) Ltd., New Delhi

Contents

PART III

PERFORMERS, PERFORMANCE AND AUDIENCE

PART IV
REGIONAL AND CULTURAL DIMENSIONS

Introduction

The Indira Gandhi National Centre for the Arts (IGNCA) is actively engaged in research, documentation, publication and dissemination of knowledge. The conceptual plan of the IGNCA places the Arts within the integral framework of a cultural system. Integral to lifestyle, lifecycle and lifefunction, the arts find expression in a staggering multiplicity of forms and genres that combine within themselves the verbal, the visual, the kinetic and the aural. One of the aims of the IGNCA, through its programme under the *Janapada Sampada* division, is to re-establish these arts in their socio-economic context and underpin their contribution in shaping of Indian society and culture.

In the context of Indian cultures, it is impossible to speak of one monolithic tradition, given its cultural plurality and multiplicity of lifestyles. More so in the case of performing arts, which belie all categories in terms of folk-classic, oral-textual, sophisticated self-conscious individual artistic creativity and collective participative activity. Nothing elucidates this better than an epic performance. It combines within itself the word, the vocal and the instrumental music, the gesture and the mime, the dance and the drama, the decor and the costume. An epic performance in fact questions the very notion of a single genre existing in a state of isolation and exclusiveness. It has a coherent plot, but is capable of rendering an astonishing multiplicity of variants, styles and techniques. It is a medium of expression of self-identity and is yet most geographically wide spread, easily adopted and made own across and among regions by different social groups. It is a rich repository of mythical and historical past and yet provides rich role models for contemporary social order. It exemplifies and upholds social oganisations, religious practices, ethical values, customary law and yet its performers are the vehicles of expression of protest, dissent and reform, as also the articulators of satire and social comment.

Though already 'established epics' the *Mahabharata* and *Ramayana* have been objects of fascination and research among the scholars of South Asian art traditions, it is only recently that epic has been acknowledged as a living, vibrant phenomenon. These treasures of ancient history and collective memory are endangered in all areas of the world by more than one way. Today there is a strong need to gather, document and preserve this vanishing intangible heritage. It is only through a combined effort of linguists, anthropologists, folklorists, ethnomusicologists and humanists that a genuine attempt at documenting, transcribing, translating and establishing of texts of oral poetry can be made. Equally important is the task of comprehending and analysing the form and content of these narratives in relation to various socio-political and eco-cultural contexts.

With an aim of bringing together the individual efforts of scholars in the field, sharing and exchanging ideas, methodologies, experience and above all holding a dialogue among scholars coming from different and varied disciplines in order to deepen and broaden our understanding of different aspects of oral narratives and the complex nature of orality, IGNCA along with UNESCO organised a five day International workshop on '*Katha Vachana aur Katha Vachak* — Exploring India's Chanted Narratives' from 3-7 February, 1997. The workshop was linked to the UNESCO project 'Integral Study of the Silk Roads : Roads of Dialogue', which was part of its programme 'World Decade for Cultural Development'. This volume comprises papers presented at the workshop.

About thirty five scholars from France, Germany, Indonesia, Italy, Nepal, Srilanka, New Zealand, Britain and from different parts of India, belonging to various disciplines, age groups, specialisations and regions took part in the deliberations. For five days they delibrated on various issues beginning with the fundamental questions concerning definitions and terminologies, which led to a discussion on nature of orality, composition, performance, socio-economic context and the intense relationship that exists between the bard and his audience. All these fundamental issues concerning existing methodologies call for a paradigm shift in the academic discourse on orality and oral cultures. Rather than positing dichotomous relationship between oral and textual, folk and classic, dominant and marginalised, the process of simultaneity and complementarity needs to be taken cognizance of.

Very fundamental to the whole discourse on oral tradition is the question of the relevance of the nineteenth century terminologies developed in a specific socio-political context. Though their functionality for the purposes of a common nomenclature cannot be denied, the focus needs to be shifted to culturally embedded concepts and categories rather than trying to fit data belonging to a different culture into categories designed for socio-political management. If a genuine allowance is made for vernacular, there will be better integration of method and data.

The discussion on the nature of composition led to a review of both formal elements and contextual relevance which enables the text to originate and function. Understanding of both these levels is essential to grasp the meaning of the text and its performance.

Then comes the entire issue of modes of transmission of tradition, both at horizontal and vertical levels. In order to comprehend the nature of continual dialogue between classic and folk, written and oral, visual and aural, pan-Indian and regional, tradition and contemporaniety, the interrelationship and interlinkages at the level of themes, content and form across regions and among genres need to be understood and established. For a true comprehension of the nature of orality and processes of its creation from a different and more holistic perspective, it is essential to understand different levels at which transmission of ideas, forms and styles takes place simultaneously retaining their local distinctiveness.

The workshop was thematically divided into four sections: a) Nature of orality and methods of transmission; b) Composition and socio-economic context; c) Performers and audience performance; d) Regional and cultural dimensions.

The present volume retains this basic thematic structure and the papers have been grouped accordingly.

1. Nature of Orality and Methods of Transmission

This section deals with the complex nature of orality, ways and means through which it expresses itself, functions and gets transmitted. Baidyanath Saraswati puts forward seven *sutra*s or propositions that in his words "form a cohesive world of orality". These are: Word as world; Ritual as virtual reality; Knowledge as culture; Orality as transtemporal power; Orality as inverted flute; Oral transmission as grace; Oral epics as pre-text. The word is to be understood according to tradition as "primordial mystery combining in herself the three worlds of time: past, present and future". The word is sacred and powerful and linked with ritual. This link is the essence of a sacred performance. It is through this performance that "man steps towards transcendence". He further contends: "Forms of ritual vary, but the basic code remains the same in all cultures". In knowledge as culture he takes up different modes of transmission: oral, textual and transcendental and opines that depending on the predominance of one or the other, cultures themselves may be grouped into three basic types — oral, textual, and transcendental. Discussing various aspects of the word, he contends that it is the spoken word that unravels the mystery of *vac*, the sacred word and "[h]ence orality alone is the source of the vast and deep transtemporal power". However "[t]here is a constant passage from orality to textuality, as also a constant resourcing of the text in oral tradition. In India orality and textuality intertwine to reach its full reality". Coming back once again to ritual he contends: "Ritual has a central claim upon the construction and re-creation of oral epic....... As a historical myth oral epic is confined to a particular region and to a particular people. It becomes significant in and through ritual. Ritual provides transition from *historical myth to sacred myth*".

Nicole Revel sets out to explore "the complex and the subtle web uniting the subject and the world [which] involves all the senses and more particularly that of hearing and aural sensitivity". Here the emphasis is on capturing the essence of the language of the other: "One must ... acquire another language in all its phonological, morphological, grammatical, semantic, rhetorical, and symbolic complexity" in order to "become the interpreter of the interpretations of the other". She advocates a holistic approach to understand and analyse oral compositions. Here one needs to focus on the entire "space of orality", "the structures and formal principles", "the privileged moment of performance", "spatial-temporal and socio-cultural framework which stimulates it", and everything that constitutes the poet's life and only then can one "hope to gain access to the hidden meaning, to the features of identity exalted and sung by oral poetry". She then shifts her focus to relationship between epic and memory and contends: "the epic sings within the bard who hears it before he actually utters it". One among the many mnemotechnic devices the poet uses to convey his mental story are "melodic formulae". She elucidates it through the sound wave of the Palawan epic *Mamiminbin*. It is this tool that according to her helped her project the mental story of the epic on to space: "it is by listening to silence and intakes of breathing that I was able to find a way to project on space - the white page - this mental story performed by the bard..." She concludes: "in order to understand a myth, it is not enough to simply follow the narrative, as if this were a melody. The different variants have to be taken into consideration... as multilayered... in harmony... together these.... lead to the meaning."

Molly Kaushal's paper dwells upon the nature of orality as informed by the Gaddi discourse on oral tradition. She takes up the Gaddi sacred narrative *Saveen*. It belongs to that sphere of knowledge which the Gaddis recognise as *gandharav/gan vidya* (i.e. the knowledge encoded in and transmitted through the oral/sung word). Within the community there exist contesting views about the nature of orality. To some, the very fact of its transmission from generation to generation through the "heard" and "spoken" word makes it legitimate and authentic. To others its authenticity is relative and is legitimate only to the extent it upholds the text. She concludes: "Both practitioners and critics of orality dwell upon the mode of transmission of knowledge, thereby revealing the manifold and multilayered nature of orality... And orality gives in graciously to the will of all ... precisely because it is fluid, mobile, open and contextual".

Catherine Servan-Schreiber's paper looks at the conditions of transmission of Bhojpuri epics towards Nepal and Bengal and the role of oral performances and chapbooks in the spreading of narratives such as *Shobha Nayaka Banjara*, *Hirni-Birni*, *Gauraiya*, *Reshma-Chuharmal*, and *Bihula*. The paper focuses on the role of traders and merchant communities in spreading these epics. It also brings to the fore the role played by the printers and the "dynasties of printers" who have contributed to the spread of these *gathas*, under the forms of chapbooks (*chaupatiya*). She also looks in some detail at the role of "the public for these *gathas* — *riksha-valas*, coolies, boatman, baniyas, cattle-sellers... themselves wandering and moving people, listening to wandering and moving singers".

Khamba-Thoibi, a Manipuri folk epic has been part of the epic repertoire for hundreds of years and evidence to this effect is available in many historical documents. This epic is a "tragic drama of life and love" centring around its central male and female heroes, Khamba and Thoibi. S. Sanatombi looks at the origin and growth of this epic in the light of historical evidences. After giving a brief synopsis of the epic she moves on to discuss the various ways in which it is transmitted.

2. Composition and Socio-Economic Context

Papers in this section deal with the text and its context. Various aspects of the text such as its origin and development, composition and content are taken up here. Ritual, cultural and socio-economic contexts that define the narrative and its functioning at the level of expression, ideology and marker of identity are of major concern here.

A.K. Das, Desmond L. Kharmawphlang and KMA M. Usop's papers deal with the ritual context in which their narratives are embedded and which lends sacred essence to them. A.K. Das analyses the cultural dimensions of *Mopin* myth and ritual of Gallong group of the Adi tribe of Arunachal Pradesh. He gives a detailed description of the *Mopin* ritual and the associated myth and looks at them in their holistic framework which he points out: "is not a mere literary expression but an 'interactive institution', in which the sacred world and secular world of the Gallong coalesce. The sacred origin and the nature of society and its practices are reaffirmed through the 'institution'".

Desmond L. Kharmawphlang takes up a Bhoi myth of creation from Khasi hills and names it — 'The Golden Vine' — because of the dominance of this particular object throughout the myth, in its pictorial and symbolic aspects. Describing and comparing two different performance events, one of which was accompanied by the egg-divination ritual, he asserts: "It is during the performance of this ritual that the golden vine myth, narrated through chanting, emanates", and in order to understand its essence "one must accept it as basically religious and its subject matter as the ultimate questions of human existence: Where we and the things come from? Why we are here? And where we are going?" He also takes up the issue of translation of the myth and points out its inadequacies: "The translation of the text is far from being perfect due to some very obvious reasons. I find it impossible to match the interest of the original, as extending meanings into different language necessitates the throttling of the poet's/storyteller's voice. The translated text is also bereft of.... the drama that the performance veritably is."

KMA M. Usop's paper deals with the Dayak epics of second Burial from Borneo. He takes up Kaharingans' sacred myth of creation. Kaharingan are "registered and integrated under Hindu religion since 1980" and though he discusses the historical and cultural contacts that existed between the Dayaks and Indians, he does not take up the issue of Hindu influence on the Dayak oral epic. He instead focuses his attention on some compositional and stylistic elements of the epic that is performed during the second burial ritual of tiwah. "Its characteristic feature is depiction of *double-aspect God and Nature*, that is also reflected in the *semantic-parallelistic* or *semantic-integralistic nature* of its four lines of poems...." After discussing some linguistic and melodic components he takes up the ritual context of the performance and concludes that the insight one gains from tradition is that "[i]t is worthy to live rationally, beautifully and spiritually".

Sheila Asirvatham's paper is based on Tamil epics. After giving a brief introduction of Tamil epics and their thematic categorisation she moves on to discuss the epic of *Mathurai Veeraswami Kathai*, which is described as a sociological narrative. She takes up aspects of word power, pool of tradition, performance context and modes of transmission as informed by the epic. She also takes up the ritual and caste aspects of the narrative, that is mostly sung during the worship of its hero, Mathurai Veeran.

Both Mahendra Kumar Mishra and Bittu Venkateswarlu bring to focus caste legends and narratives of origin of Kalahandi and Andhra Pradesh respectively. Mishra explores the Kalahandi narratives that sing about origin of gods, castes, clans, and group identities. He categorises these narratives into 'sacred' and 'secular', throws some light on their composition, content and transmission and takes a detailed look at the singers of these narratives. Venkateswarlu on the other hand takes up the scroll narratives of Andhra Pradesh and the caste legends that the scroll depicts. He discusses their origin and development and throws important light on the relationship between the "dependent castes", who perform these narratives and "host castes", who organise and patronise these performances. Both these papers provide insight into the relationship of interdependence that exists between the performers and their patrons.

Daniel Neger's paper shifts the focus from ritual and religious context to socio-political context of the narratives. *Burrakatha*, a folk narrative prevalent in Andhra Pradesh is expressive of regional identity based on language and culture. Negers takes a detailed look at this narrative both from a historical perspective and its performative aspects. He also explores its cultural, political and literary background. The paper traces the relationship of *Burrakatha* with other narrative forms of Andhra Pradesh such as *Jamukulakatha*, *Tolu bommalata*, *Harikatha*, and *Natkam* among others. *Burrakatha*, that first emerged in 1940's under the influence of the communist party of India to give the nationalist and revolutionary message developed into "an artistic medium of regional significance in terms of (cultural and linguistic) group identity. This was done by gradually assimilating a large spectrum of story-telling and singing/acting traditions embedded in various specific art forms, borrowing either particular aspect in the mode of production/transmission or in inspiring new stories out of the repertoire of these forms". *Burrakatha* uses literary styles, codes and themes taken both from oral as well as written streams of traditional literature and theatre. Author takes up all these aspects of *Burrakatha* performance and after a detailed analysis makes the following observation: "*Burrakatha* today strongly appears as a unique and specific codified artistic folkform. Emerging out of a specific, much older folkform, in a new, modern and political context, it helps us to understand how tradition finds its way in redefining culture when the time comes to carry on a different message".

Ajay Dandekar brings in a different perspective and looks at the epic in terms of oral history. His concern with the epic is that of a historian. He ventures outside the text and contextualises it only to return back to it to locate "a more local, immediate and rooted context" that may provide important historical insight. He explores the oral narrative of *Kaba and Baji* belonging to the Dhangar community of the Western Deccan. Contextualising the epic in terms of its immediate ecological and changing socio-economic context, he discusses its relevance in understanding the interactions and intricate interrelationship between the nomadic pastoralist and sedentary agriculturist groups of Gavli Dhangars occupying the semi-arid tract of Deccan plateau.

Aditya Malik's concern is with various discourses that are available in the Rajasthani oral epic of *Devnarayan*. His focus here is primarily on representation of women in this "martial epic", that is primarily about heroes in a world dominated by "male values". The questions that he poses are: "How are women represented in this martial epic? Do women's voices express a `counter' system? Are women simple passive objects? Are they covert players or overt actors? What are the different contexts in which power issues from women?" He takes up different contexts in the narrative where women "appear either as" "anonymous" and "passive" figures or "emerge as immensely powerful, deciding over issues of life and death". Marriage, devotion and divinity are the contexts in which the identities of the women are formed as wives, mothers, devotees and goddesses. Taking up various episodes from the narrative to formulate his argument he observes that women's images in the epic of *Devnarayan* form a continuum: "On the one end of the continuum women's identities and power they wield are derived from their status as wives. On the other end of the continuum a woman's identity is derived from her divine origin. Midway between these two extremes is the figure of Sadu Mata, who represents a break from a complete identification with a human husband, to an identification with Bhagavan [God]. This identification characterises her both as a devotee and as a mother of Devnarayan. Whereas in the first case women wield influence in the domain of birth, in the second and third case, women wield power over both birth (life) and death".

3. Performers, Performance and Audience

The previous section focused on the text and its various aspects. The papers in this section shift focus from text to performance. In many ways this section is a logical and thematic extension of the previous one. The papers in these two sections overlap and interact in term of issues they explore. The text lives through performance and both are governed by the same socio-historical and cultural context. Text of oral narratives and its performance are inextricably linked together, a fact brought out by many of the papers above. Performance can not be discussed without taking into account its performers and the audience who together generate both the text and the performance in an appropriate socio-cultural milieu.

William Sax's paper discusses two kinds of texts of the epic. One is written and available through classical sources, other is oral, in the vernacular and generated through its performance. He looks at the relationship between these two texts through a study on the *Pandav lila* of Uttarakhand, an amateur village dramatisation of the *Mahabharata* epic in a ritual context involving dance, drumming, dramatisation and competitive bardic recitation. Comparing the two, he observes that "the *Mahabharata* is something other than what we normally think it is, and .... *Pandav lila* is something other than what we would normally understand as 'folk drama'". Through his discussion on the performance he demonstrates that "this ritual dramatisation of the epic is not a secondary derivation from a more fundamental source, not a vulgarisation of the Sanskrit text, but is itself an authentic, primary expression of the epic.." He further notes that "the *Mahabharata* is first and foremost an oral tale, a bedtime story, or a performance seen by the flickering firelight; and to think of it as a book is a monumental distortion, an artefact of the academic mode of production... In Garhwal, the *Mahabharata* is an ancestral tale periodically enacted as a form of ancestor worship, and one that provides a basic — probably the basic — paradigm for what it is to be a Rajput. It proves that the *Mahabharata* is alive and well, a living tradition and not a frozen text in a dead language".

Pandav lila is also the concern of Richa Negi's paper, where it figures as *Pandava* dance. She looks at it in terms of a ritual performance and explores the nature of performance, performer-performance, audience-actor relationship, as well as the social and emotional response of the community to it. She writes: "An actor here is a performer for life and not just a one-show man momentarily satisfying his artistic urge." The performance itself is "a theatre of reality... not a mere enactment of the *Mahabharata* lore, but a sacred history re-actualized and re-lived through performance." Commenting on the audience-actor relationship she notes: "the relationship of the actor and the audience is not that of the observer and the observed. It is ... a relationship of the performer and participatory audience". The response to the performance is emotional. She concludes: "*Pandava* dance... acts as a locus of human expression. It reveals, moulds and transforms the personal as well as cultural identity individually and collectively, preserving the living continuance of a tradition."

S.M. Pandey's paper takes a detailed look at the singers of the oral epic *Loriki*. He profiles eight singers, whose versions he collected and who are mostly Ahirs, traditionally a community of milkmen and cowherders. He begins by summarising the basic story line of the epic and then comes to the issue of relationship of the epic with the Ahir community. He notes: "It is important to notice the fundamental association of this text with the ethnic and social group called the Ahirs. The important characters in the story are Ahirs, and it is they who transmit this material from generation to generation and form its audience." The main body of his paper however concerns the singers of this epic, their social background and more importantly their different styles of singing the epic. The reasons for the emergence of different styles are manifold as he elaborates: "Disciples learn in the company of their teachers when they are performing, but in their free time they try to perfect it in their own way, exercising their originality and talents..." and that the "singers do not have a fixed text.... they produce different texts each time they perform, and though most of the singers claim that they are faithfully reproducing the versions of their respective teachers, in fact all of them use different styles of singing and different sets of descriptions. They never follow a single tradition." He further points out: "The most important thing about the singers is that they are creative composers as well as singers. They can compose while singing." He notes his disagreement with some of the formulations of A.B. Lord's theory and demonstrates that his singers use different meters for the same kind of formula, which is contrary to what Lord has to say about formulae and meters.

Mohan Upreti, whose untimely passing away we deeply bemoan, in his paper deals once again with the singers of the narratives. *Rajula Malushahi* is a narrative about love and honour, sung in Kumaon hills. Through the study of its text, music and style of narration the author explores the dominant role played by the singer, "who with the main story line and musical form gives a free reign to his imagination in depicting the events and characters, his socio-cultural background determining his approach".

Sabir Badalkhan in his paper on *sher* singing tradition among the Baloch, highlights the role of the audience in the transmission and preservation of an oral poem. Through his discussion of various performance events he demonstrates that it is the performer-audience relationship that determines the quality of the performance as well as the continuity of tradition. The paper takes up both the traditional setting of this art of minstrelsy as well as its place in the modern world. What helped preserve the tradition and high quality of performance was non-tolerance of any attempt to improvise the text of the poem on the one hand, and total identification of the performer and listeners with the times and characters of the poem, on the other. He laments the gradual fading away of this tradition under the changing socio-economic and cultural milieu of Baloch society, for whom *sher* singing was at one time considered "a noble action" and a "prestigious pastime".

Both Nabin Chandra Sarma and T.N. Shankaranarayana explore the aspect of gender in the narrative and performance, taking A.K. Ramanujan's well known categories of *akam* and *puram* as point of departure. Sarma bases his enquiry on the oral epic of Assam, the *Padma Purana* and Shankaranarayana discusses the *Junjappa* epic of the Kadugollas of Karnataka. Both the papers after discussing the text of the narratives and their socio-cultural and ritual context move on to the singers and performance. Exploring both male and female performances of their respective narratives they come to similar conclusions that may be summerised as follows: female performances are for women and centre around them; male performances are for both men and women but are centred around men. The female performance belongs to *akam* genre and male performances are traditionally a *puram* genre.

M. Mani Meitei's paper on the *Khamba-Thoibi* folk epic of Manipur also discusses the gender aspect of the narrative performance and points out the role of "male-constructed ideology and social code" in a performance situation and shows "the extent to which gender ideas govern a performance". However the main body of his paper deals with a specific performance event, through which he explores different factors that govern a performance situation. He observes that text and context are "welded together" and "[t]ext alone without the contextual background is a soulless body". Of equal importance is the singer-audience relationship which "takes precedence over most other related issues and questions". He also discusses various narrative techniques used by the singer to enhance the performance.

4. Regional and Cultural Dimensions

The two papers that have been grouped here deal with the classical epic, the Ramayana and its spread to neighbouring countries. Whereas C.M. Bhandhu looks at the oral narratives of *Ramayana* such as *Chait*, *Dhamari*, *Nachari*, *Sorathi*, *Balun* and their performance style in Nepal, H.M.D.R. Herath discusses narratives associated with Sita in the central hills of Srilanka. He also explores many historical sites associated with these narratives. Both the papers give insight into how a text travels to distant lands, is adopted and made own. Existence of a text in its various oral and written versions that fulfill the contemporary aesthetic and moral objectives in regions other than the land of their origin brings us back to Sax's observations about the relationship between the book and its oral versions.

Other papers that were presented under this section have been published in a separate volume in Hindi. These papers deals with the epic traditions of northern, central and western India.

The workshop that had throughout stressed the need for preserving, through collection, documentation and archiving this intangible heritage, passed a resolution addressed to UNESCO and Government of India to this effect.

An appeal to UNESCO : to consider the oral Wisdom Tradition as World Heritage; and to Constitute a Commission to carry out a study of the cultural dimension of a creative orality and balance transformation which would give traditional culture all the force it needs — a renewed sense of pride, and a new deal in development.

An appeal to the Government of India: to recognise the importance of orality in cultural development: to document oral traditions which are characterised not only by their diversity but also their richness; and to promote oral education through performing arts, oral literature, oral history and indigenous worldview alongwith the modern system of education, specially at the primary stage.

Molly Kaushal

Part I

Nature of Orality and Methods of Transmission

1

Orality and its Complexity

Baidyanath Saraswati

THIS paper is written in the spirit of those who are unlettered. It is not written in the way of anthropology. Nor is it in symphathy with history and folklore. It is also not aimed at constructing a new model. A set of seven propositions has been plucked from the tradition of India, but not adequately developed. Evidently, this is an unfinished paper aimed at making the oral tradition transparent. Of the seven *sutras*, or propositions, presented in this paper each has an *ontonomy* of its own. Together they form a cohesive world of orality.

Word as world

Tradition tells us in innumerable ways that the Word is the world. The Word, imperishable, is the Firstborn of Truth.[1] This (in the beginning), was only the Lord of the Universe. His Word was with him. This Word was his second. He contemplated. He said, "I will deliver this Word so that she will produce and bring into being all this world."[2] The Word is infinite, immense, beyond all this. . . . All the Gods, the celestial spirits, men and animals, live in the Word. In the Word all the worlds find their support.[3] The Word makes known the Vedas, the ritual, knowledge of all kinds. It also makes known heaven and earth, wind, space, the waters, fire, the Gods, men, animals, birds, grass, and trees, all animals down to worms, insects, and ants. It also makes known what is right or wrong, truth and untruth, good and evil, what is pleasing and what is unpleasing. The Word makes all this known.[4]

The Veda is not the Word of God. Nor is it inspired or authored by God. It is simply the primordial Word of which no human being is the author: *apaurusheya*. This Word is the consort of Prajapati, the creator of the world. She was at the beginning. She is the whole of the *shruti*, the source of human knowledge. She is the primordial mystery combining in herself the three worlds of time: past, present, and future.

No wonder, then, that every Word is sacred and powerful.

Ritual as virtual reality

A classic question found in practically all traditions is: What is the furthest limit of the earth, the centre of the world, the high heaven where abides the Word? The Vedic answer is extremely concise: "The altar is the furthest limit of the earth, the sacrifice is the world's centre, prayer is the highest heaven where abides the Word."[5]

Sacrifice (ritual) is a four-fold code[6] which points beyond what cannot be expressed in human language. It is in and through ritual that man deciphers the meaning of his existence and creates a world where the Spirit, man and matter meet, that is, the divine, the human, and the material. Forms of ritual vary, but the basic code remains the same in all cultures.

(i) *Mantra*: The Word as God, composed of *akshara*, imperishable letters, is uttered by mouth, heard by the ear and apprehended by the mind. *Mantras* are those particular sounds which are used in worship and practice. The *mantra* of a deity is intoned in the proper way according to *varna*, letter, and *svara*, rhythm. Hence, a *mantra* when translated ceases to be a *mantra*. The *mantra* is not the same thing as prayer or self-dedication. Prayer is conveyed in what words the worshipper chooses, and bears its meaning on its face.

(ii) *Mudra*: The hand-gestures and bodily positions, are the constituent of performance. In worship, *mudra* is performed by pronouncing a *mantra*, generally for the fruition of the *mantra*. Hence, *mudra* is a *mantric* sign. In dance, *mudra* means subtle hand-gestures representing specific feelings. As ritualistic gesture, *mudra* is of several kinds, each having a name.

(iii) *Dhvani*: The world is pervaded by the power of sound, *dhvani*, *nada*, or *prana*. Sometimes a distinction is made between the articulate sound associated with gross matter and the sound sorted and extracted by the listener from the gross matter. The first is called *dhvani*, the second *sphota*. Certain forms of *dhvani* are considered inauspicious such as hooting of an owl, the cry of a dog or a jackal, and so on. There are ways of producing auspicious sound. At the time of marriage and worship women produce a sound by twisting their tongue. To please Shiva the worshipper produces a peculiar sound with his mouth, imitating the babbling of a he-goat. Shiva is pleased by the sound of *damaru*, Visnu by the conchshell, and Shakta deities by drums and gongs. All Gods and Goddesses are propitiated by bells and cymbals.

(iv) *Vyavahariki*: The most common constituent of a ritual is the everyday language of interaction. The priest is the knower. As a ritual specialist, he instructs the performer to follow the prescribed way. For example: Bring the Cow! Chant the *mantra*! Look at the pole-star!

It is through ritual that man steps toward the transcendence. At the early stage of every civilization the thirst toward transcendence was linked with an action. Ritual action is both simple and complex. It creates a 'virtual reality' of the original sacrifice of Prajapati by which the world came into being. Creation is sacrifice. It embodies (a) *solitude* or self-awareness: the performer taking cognizance of himself; (b) *sacrifice* or making a person: performance of life-crisis rituals; and (c) *integration* or unity of all: man, animal, nature, the earth, and the sky.

Knowledge as culture

Anthropologists posit the proposition that man is the creator of knowledge, he is the measure of all, he has invented culture. This is wholly untenable in a worldview which holds that knowledge precedes man, just as a mother's breast is filled with milk before the child is born. Primeval knowledge is self-existent. Only one-fourth of it is revealed. As commonly understood, human knowledge has multiplied in time and space. The Sanskritic cultures claim that their deposit of knowledge consists of eighteen classes of the basic scriptural texts which are the perennial source of practically all the learned traditions. Of these the Veda is the root of knowledge; it revealed itself to the ancient seers who possessed infinite wisdom and truth.

Culture[7] may be conceived as a deposit of knowledge accumulated in time. The deposit of each culture is made up of two parts: the manifest and the unmanifest. The manifest part contains the knowledge of things divinely revealed and humanly discovered, interpreted. The unmanifest part contains the beliefs and hopes of what is yet to be revealed or discovered. Divine revelation and human discoveries keep the manifest part of the deposit in a state of flux. The unmanifest part remains in a perpetual state of mystification. Hence, any classification of culture, based on content and form, that is, the manifest part of the deposit, is bound to be partial and tentative. A relatively more enduring and valid classification can be sought in terms of the modes of transmission of tradition.

There are three principal modes of transmission: oral, textual, and transcendental. Adopting one of these as the *essential* mode of survival, all cultures may be grouped into three basic types namely oral, textual and transcendental. Using Sanskrit terminology, these may be called *laukik*, *shastriya* and *naivrittika*, respectively.

(i) *Oral Culture*: The entire way of life of peasant potters is guided by the verbal testimony and collective memory of their elders. Their productive techniques of selecting suitable clay, throwing, processing, beating, enlarging, painting and firing are based upon the oral sources. Their productive organisation also operates on an oral mechanism. The price of each of the pottery goods is fixed in divine consultation. The marketing of products is determined by contractual relationships with the *jajman*, the client. The contract is unwritten, unrecorded, and yet faithfully honoured and renewed, or carried on from one generation to the next. In matters of social organisation and religious performances they fall back upon the memory of their elders. The entire code of their behaviour, *lokachara*, is orally transmitted. And yet they function efficiently, and beautifully, in this turmoiling universe.

(ii) *Textual culture*: In contrast to the pottery-making culture, Brahmanic culture is based *essentially* on the reliance in and the authority of the *shastra*, that is, the codified knowledge revealed and subsequently interpreted and enlarged. In the beginning the scriptural text was transmitted orally. But later, the method of oral transmission changed in a fundamental way, perhaps to ensure that the revealed Words maintain their proper orthodoxies. The Vedic hymns are recited in eight different ways of ordering the Words, called *ashtavikriti*. The *shastra* was illumined by a highly developed grammatical tradition. All this made it different from the normal transmission of tradition followed in oral culture. Brahmanic culture is a textual culture because its primal source of knowledge, both theoretical and applied, is the *shastra*, the omnibus scriptural text. In this regard it is important to bear in mind that there are subtle differences between the *shastra* and the 'text'. The cultural meaning of *shastra* is: 'that which governs thought and behaviour'. Thus, what the *shastra* stands for is not necessarily the 'text' as meant and interpreted in modern discourse. However, as a body of codified Sanskritic knowledge, Brahmanic culture is a textual culture. The connection between the 'text' and the *shastra* is, therefore, a logical one.

(iii) *Transcendental culture*: The people involved *exclusively* in the cultivation of excellence in transcendence are distinguished by their *nivritta karma*, disinterested act. They are different from those who act with *pravritt*, or *kamya karma*, the object of attaining worldly gains. Their distinction lies in the renunciation of the householder's life. They perform all acts of subsistence disinterestedly. The fact that they are not a part of the householder culture becomes self-evident at the time of the initiation ceremony. The novitiate shaves his head and face, which is symbolic of his leaving the householder's life and ushering into spiritual culture. Performance of funeral rites signifies the 'ritual death' of this-worldly individual and a 'new birth' for spiritual life. At one stage in initiation the novitiate walks seven steps stark naked, which suggests that he has wiped off his worldly impurities. The Guru offers him the Word (*mantra*) in a low voice, bows down before him and gives him a new name. The preceptor's bowing down to his disciple symbolises the latter's entry into a new world of enlightenment, that is, joining the fraternity of transcendental culture. All the three forms of culture allow orality at different levels of existence, and in varying degrees of celebrations. However, the orality of oral culture has an esoteric flavour of its own.

Orality as transtemporal power

The Vedic conception of the Absolute, the Brahman, as eternal and unidentified *shabda-tattva*, Word Principle, has influenced the entire grammatical and linguistic tradition of India. Bhartrihari,[8] the great grammarian, mentions three aspects of the Word, the three stages through which it passes whenever one speaks, that is, when the Word, which is at first quite internal, is externalised for the purpose of communication.

(i) *Vaikhari*, the intoned Word. The most external stage when it is uttered by the speaker and heard by the hearer. It is closely related with *prana*, life-force, which is what strikes against the organs of articulation at the time of utterance and brings about its temporal sequence. *Vaikhari* is not merely the name of the fully externalised form of speech. Such sound as that of a drum, of a flute, of a lute are also included in it. In this way *vaikhari* is said to have infinite varieties. Its chief characteristic is that it has a fully developed temporal sequence.

(ii) *Madhyama*, the middle one. Going inward, this stage is associated chiefly with the mind, the intellect, and not with the organs of articulation. It is the Word conceived by the mind before its actual utterance. There is no real temporal sequence in *madhyama*. But it is not absolutely without it. It is there in a subtle form.

(iii) *Pashyanti*, the seeing one. The next and the innermost stage is said to have infinite varieties. It is also described as being of a lower and a higher kind. The higher kind is *param rupam*, beyond the range of verbal usage; it is *para*, the highest dimension of Word.

What has been shown in this classification is the human consciousness of the Word's totality. Man cannot grasp the whole; he can grasp only a part of it. The Veda reveals only one quarter, one out of the four, the spoken portion. The four feet express the wholeness. Thus man speaks intelligibly one-fourth of the Word. The fourth that beasts and bird speak is not intelligible. But the wise who possess insight know all these four divisions. The mystery of *vac*, the sacred word, is unravelled by the spoken word. Hence, orality alone is the source of the vast and deep transtemporal power. Man can free himself from the bondage of language. Ritual is the mother of reality. It is through ritual that man moves from the level of *vaikhari* to *madhyama*, and ultimately, to *pashyanti* too.

The movement from 'oral' to 'textual' to 'transcendental' appears simple and self-evident anthropologically; but it is not so. The 'oral culture' moves through the spoken word because of 'memory', from the past to the present. The 'textual culture' moves not, because the text of the manifest knowledge is codified and bounded. New texts are created, new ideas are born and differentiation is also made, but in each case knowledge is essentially dialectical or codified. The 'transcendental culture' moves and it moves not, because there is a logical continuity between *vaikhari* and *madhyama*. But once it leaps to *pashyanti*, the 'seeing' of reality, the wholly transcendent, there is no movement. In the *pashyanti* stage there is a discontinuity with reference to *vaikhari* and *madhyama*, and there is no *vibhaga*, actual split. Hence, it is said that a *brahmajnani*, the knower of the Absolute, becomes speechless.

Orality as inverted flute

The Word, as expressible experience, originates in the twilight of the non-manifest. The saints of India have developed *sandhyabhasha*, a 'twilight language', a language of light and darkness — partly light, partly darkness. The Tantric texts are frequently couched in 'intentional language' — a secret, 'virtual language' obscure with double meaning. For example:

ravi, surya, the 'sun' = *rasana, pingla*, 'the right artery' in the yoga body.

shashi, chandra the 'moon' = *lalana, ida*, 'the left artery' in the yoga body.

bodhichitta, 'the bodhi mind' = *shukra* 'semen verile'

karin 'elephant' = *chitta*, 'thought', 'mind'.

These illustrations[9] show the paradoxical aspect of *sandhyabhasha*.

Kabir, a medieval saint poet, used obscure language. Here is an example:[10]

The bees have flown, the cranes have settled;
Night is gone, day also will pass.
The maiden jiva shivers and shudders with fear;
She knows not how her lover will receive her.
An unbaked pot retains not water.
When the swan departed, the body withered.
My arms are aching with scaring the crows.
Kabir says, Now this tale is ended.

According to the tradition, in this poem 'bees' and 'night' both mean 'youth'; 'cranes' and 'day' both mean 'old age'; the 'lover' is God; the 'swan' is the soul and 'scaring the crows' means 'opposing ceremonial rules'. Kabir was an unlettered man. As he says,[11]

I am not skilled in book knowledge,
Nor do I understand controversy.
or again:[12]
I touch not ink nor paper, nor take pen in my hand;
Of the greatness of the four ages
Kabir has given instruction with his lips.

The non-literate Kabir expressed his 'experience' in a technical language, giving ultimate significance.[13]

Kabir, when the Sabda has entered the body,
The lute resounds without strings.
Inside and outside, it pervades all
And all wanderings are over.

The saints in the north Indian tradition have widened the narrow lane of language. They spoke a language called *ulatabamsi*, 'the inverted flute', for which Kabir was particularly famous. The songs of saint Paltu Sahib were composed in the enigmatic, 'turned around', *ulta* language. Paltu's name derives from a verbal form *palatna* which itself means 'to be inverted or changed' and which often appears together with *ulta* as a popular colloquialism: *ulta-pulta*, mixed up, turned around.

Oral transmission as grace

The doctrine of the power of the *shabda*, spoken word, is evident in the verse of Kabir, Nanak, and other saints. Without *shabda*, as expressed through the Guru, salvation cannot be obtained. The *shabda* is complex. Behind this is also the conception of God as the 'Letterless One'. Says Kabir:[14]

In the one Sabda are thirty-six melodies;
It makes the music that is infinite.
The mouth is the neck, the ears the shell;
The True Guru has set the frets.
This is the property of the thirty-four letters;
That a thousand names are to be seen in them.
Everything connected with the three words
Is contained in the fifty-two letters;
These letters shall perish,

But he who is beyond letters is not in them.
Where there is speech, there letters are used;
Where there is no speech, there no mind abideth.
God is contained both where there is speech
And where there is not;
Nobody appeareth like unto Him.
Make thy body the churn,
Thy heart the churning-staff;
Into the churn (put) the Word instead of milk;
Make hearty meditation on God thy churning;
Pour the Guru's favour into it as thy cold water.
He in whose heart God hath planted
His word hath ceased to thirst.
Kabir, slight is the stroke of a lance;
Though struck by it man may breathe (for a time);
But he who can endure the stroke of the Word is a Guru,
And I am his slave.

One with the idea of *nama* (name like Rama and Krishna) is that of Word, *shabda*. As often as *nama*, *shabda* also occurs in the songs of the saints. It is one of the concepts whose correct understanding and identification is not easy. It is used both as being one with God and also as a means of gaining that state. On the other side, it occurs as a compound with Guru, *Guru-shabda*, and sometimes as Guru's *shabda*, the former signifying an identity. In answer to the question of a *yogi*, as to who his Guru was, Nanak replied: 'The Word is the Guru and the mind attuned to the Word is the disciple.'

The *sant* literature is replete with analogies describing the transformative power of the Guru. Kabir describes the transformation, stressing the universal effectiveness of the *bhrangi-Guru's* transforming power:[15]

My Guru's a great bhrangi
When kits come near, that bhrangi
Gives them colour like himself.
Their legs become different;
Their wings become different,
He colours them a different colour.
He doesn't look at rank or origins
For the devotee is an outcaste.
When it flows into a crossing channel
The Ganges water itself is called a little stream
But someone who has thus become the river

No longer has to jump across it.
He stopped the crooked
Movements of my mind
To show that beyond the essence in essentials
And the companion in companionship.
He unbound my bonds
And tore through what was pressing me;
He gave Kabir an access to the Lord beyond all reach
And dyed him in Rama's colours.

Transformation from a lower to the higher state of knowledge is possible by 'oral transmission' as the *bhrangi Guru* does. The process of transformation has been explained by the analogies of *bhrangi*, the bumblebee, and *kit*, the bug. As widely believed, the *bhrangi* makes the *kit*, the most ordinary insect, like himself. The process of transformation is explained this way:[16] when the *bhrangi* approaches the *kit* he buzzes loudly in his ear, causing him great anxiety. The *kit* then retreats into himself, leaving his outside to harden while his inside softens. Eventually the *kit* becomes soft and light enough to fly away from within, leaving an outer shell behind.

Within the world of orality, a complex channel of Grace and power is formed. Guru is for his disciple a channel of wisdom easily accessible and trustworthy. Guru, God and *Mantra* form a continuous universe. They are one and the same just as the words *ghata, kalasha* and *kumbha* designate the same thing, a pot.

Oral epic as pre-text

Oral and textual cultures differ due to causes acting in the modes of transmission of knowledge. Differences[17] are physiological rather than morphological, as illustrated in Table 1. One curious result of the distinction is this. Differences are caused by 'cultural selection' acting mainly by substituting one element for another. Thus, one may find differences between corresponding elements of different cultures like those found within a culture complex. For instance, what consists of orality and textuality in the culture complex of India is the same, arranged in the same structure, in Australia, Europe, or America.

However, it needs to be clarified that the transforming principle in this case is quite unlike the Darwinian theory of evolution in the vertical direction. There is also a horizon on the horizontal plane. Orality and textuality are the sublime pair lying in horizontal position. The text of the Vedic hymns revealed itself. This revelation was not the voice of a human revealer. The Veda is *shruti*, that is that which is 'heard' (rather than 'seen'). What the sages 'heard' was transmitted orally from one generation to the next. Oral epic is a pre-text. It does not belong to the Vedic tradition of *shruti*. It is a human document of events and characters which were 'seen' (rather than revealed). What was 'seen' by a human ancestor is still remembered (*smriti*) and orally transmitted without interruption.

There is a constant passage from orality to textuality, as also a constant resourcing of the text in oral tradition. In India orality and textuality intertwine to reach its full reality. The texts of the *Ramayana* and the *Mahabharata* have been effectively transmitted at the synchronic-diachronic cross-cultural level in and outside India. The characters of these two great epics constitute an aspect of truth. For those who believe in them, it is a sacred history. It is history, so it is true. It is sacred, so it transcends both time and history; that is, it refers to a transhistorical truth.

Table 1: Physiological differences between 'oral' and 'textual' cultures

Oral	*Textual*
1. Experiential, empirical: sanctity and authority ascribed to human memory and experience	1. Expressional, theoretical: sanctity and authority ascribed to written or unwritten codified Words and experience
2. Direct, personal: man to spirit interaction, informal system of learning	2. Indirect, impersonal: man to word interaction, man replaced by linguistic code
3. Creative: uncodified context created afresh on each occasion of transmission	3. Repetitive: codified content repeated on each occasion of transmission
4. Primary knowledge: *mythos* the essential mode of consciousness, spiritually derived knowledge	4. Secondary knowledge: *logos* essential mode of consciousness, subject to induction and deduction
5. Unbounded, immeasurable: flow of thought uninterrupted, spontaneity the dominant feature	5. Bounded, measurable: thoughts codified or put to writing, become structurally fixed, dialectics the dominant feature
6. Unity of expression: collective memory, anonymity, concreteness	6. Uniqueness of expression: individual memory, uniquely identified statements, conceptual abstraction
7. Primacy of *praxis*: knowledge and behaviour closely interlinked	7. Primacy of *theoria*: knowledge independent of behaviour

In a deep intercultural communication, as evident in India, it is no wonder, then, that textual epics have inspired several of the oral epics. But no oral epic is a pale imitation of the *Ramayana* and the *Mahabharata*. The hero of the *Lorikayan*, an oral epic of eastern Uttar Pradesh, is an incarnation of Hanuman or Krishna. But in no way is he tied to a particular understanding of any of these two characters. The *Salhesa*, an oral epic of Mithila, does not even mention a single character of the *Ramayana* or the *Mahabharata*. The hero Salhesa is deified. He rides a terracotta horse and his adventures are narrated scrupulously at the shrine, generally under a fig tree dedicated to him. Epics are 'cultural markers'. For that reason no culture would like to distort its epic.

Oral epics are much more alive than we tend to think. Each one of them is a living world in itself, a complete tradition. Every character represents a new type. And thus it contains all conceivable characters, both good and evil, expressing human emotions of various kind. Ritual has a central claim upon the construction and re-creation of oral epic. It intends *alaukik upaya*, a transcendental way, to mirror the whole range of human experience. Ritual is a kind of re-enactment, or commemoration, of an authentic act by which man keeps his link with the transcendence alive and effective. As a historical myth oral epic is confined to a particular region and to a particular people. It becomes significant in and through ritual. Ritual provides transition from *historical myth* to *sacred myth*.

Oral culture has a good deal of 'openness'. Its existence is simple but essence is complex. It is sustained by transtemporal power. The language of the 'inverted flute' is complex and unintelligible to those who do not belong to that tradition. It can be grasped only by Grace. It is transmitted through a variety of channels: myth, ritual, music, dance, drama, for instance. Trance as a way of 'verification' is often associated with oral performance. At the human level, it is the 'memory' of a *sacred historical* event which is faithfully followed. That 'memory', or 'multisensory communication', taken absolutely, coincides with omniscience. It is the 'memory', not the narrative, that makes oral epic unique and 'self-reflective' in the mystery of a pre-given cosmos.

Yet one cannot deny that there is a certain continuity between orality and textuality which is far more important than their physiological differences. The *Ramalila* and the *Krishnalila*, though of recent origin, have inspired and increased the richness of oral performances. Recitation (*parayana*) of the *Ramayana* and the *Mahabharata* as a ritual act, has integrated India's timeless oral and textual traditions. Both the traditions work in the spirit of the whole. Both sustain themselves by sacred performance. Ritual is a universal form of celebration. Without ritual there is no living tradition, no normal civilization.

Notes

1. *Taittiriya Brahmana*, II.8.8.5 (cf. Panikkar, 1977).
2. *Tandya Maha Brahmana*, XX.14.2 (cf. Panikkar, 1977).
3. *Taittiriya Brahmana*, II.8.8.4 (cf. Panikkar, 1977).
4. *Chandogya Upanisad*, VII.2.1 (cf. Panikkar, 1977).
5. *Rgveda*, I.164.34-35 (cf. Panikkar, 1977).
6. See Saraswati, 1982.
7. See Saraswati,1988.
8. Cf. Saraswati, 1982.
9. Cf. Saraswati, 1982.
10. Cf. Keay, 64.
11. Cf. Keay, 39.
12. Cf. Keay, 39.
13. Cf. Gold, 122.
14. Cf. Keay, 87-8.
15. Cf. Gold, 23.
16. Cf. Gold, 22.
17. See Saraswati, 1992.

References

Gold, Daniel, 1987, *The Lord as Guru: Hindi Sants in North-Indian Tradition*, New York, Oxford University Press.

Keay, F.E., 1931, *Kabir and His Followers*, Calcutta, Association Press.

Mishra, Manoj Kumar, 1997, 'Maukhika mahakavya ke sahityika-o-sanskritica tattva: Lorikayan-o-Salhesha ka tulanatmaka vishlesana', paper presented at the Workshop on "Katha Vachana aur Katha Vachak: Exploring India's Chanted Narratives", New Delhi: Indira Gandhi National Centre for the Arts.

Pandey, Shyam Manohar, 1987, *The Hindi Oral Epic Lorikayan* (*The Tale of Lorik and Canda*), Allahabad, Sahitya Bhawan Pvt. Ltd.

Pannikar, Raimundo, 1977, *The Vedic Experience: Mantramanjari*, London, Darton, Longman and Todd.

Saraswati, Baidyanath, 1982, *Ritual Language: a Transanthropological Perspective*, Varanasi, N.K. Bose Memorial Foundation.

———, 1988, *Thinking About Tradition: the Indian Vision*, Varanasi, N.K. Bose Memorial Foundation.

———, 1992, 'Textualizing Tribal Tradition2, *Journal of Indian Anthropological Society*, 27, 209-17.

Vatsyayan, Kapila, 1996, *Bharata*: *The Natyasastra*, New Delhi, Sahitya Akademi.

2

The World of Orality

Nicole Revel

If the senses give us access to the world and if the world seems to profile itself spatially, then we tend to grant primacy to visual perception and descriptions of the real. However I would also like to show that a complex and subtle web uniting the subject and the world involves all the senses and more particularly that of hearing and aural sensitivity.

Like a bird, the ethnographer descends into a landscape, listens to the music of the world and of all things, rhythms and melodies. His many travels, across forests and seas, take him to communities. There he begins to capture the music of the languages, of the many ways to be in this world — chats exchanged in daily life, laughter of children, play on words, power of words, pleasure of words and all their magic spells. His sound experience is open, and drives him always further, even tempting him to project the beauty of a song onto the space of a white page. Little by little, and as a gift in return, he captures the meaning that the Other gives to his own world.

The object of the analysis is rather a set of shared values of representations of a human society, the *doxa* of a particular culture. Language plays a primary role in this perception of the other. One must also acquire another language in all its phonological, morphological, grammatical, semantic, rhetorical, and symbolic complexity.

Each language says the world through words, immediate constituents, logical and abstract orders. Each language captures the world, seizes it and reconstructs it by thought and the mediation of symbols. Then, and only then, can one hope to become the interpreter of the interpretations of the other.

For each society has an interpretative presence in the world, a particular world that empirically and intellectually the people try to make their own, in order to ensure their survival. In other words, it centres around understanding collective and cultural representations, not mental representations or mental images which psychologists try to apprehend. It focuses upon an ensemble of ideas and values specific to a society and partially and semi-consciously present in the minds of individual people.

The interplay of perception, discriminations, denominations, categorisations, taxonomies — these hierachised structures — and other ways of ordering the data of observation and experience, all representations of thought, manifest the intellectual and spiritual attitude of the group under consideration.

In the specific space of communication, we focus upon the space of orality, the structures and formal principles underlying the semantic fields and narratives must be brought to light. Each has its own unique systematic organisation and reveals an interpretation of life according to an aesthetics, a rhetoric and an ethic.

To go intelligently to the heart of a story, is also to go to the heart of things, exploring all the latitudes of meaning. Through the analysis of an oral/aural composition, through the relationships of the chanted story and the spatial-temporal and socio-cultural framework which stimulates it, one would hope to gain access to the hidden meaning, to the features of identity exalted and sung by oral poetry.

The bard sings in a living context, amidst a very present community. It is a privileged moment of performance, this complex action through which "a poetic message is simultaneously transmitted and perceived, here and now. That instant where speakers, listeners, and circumstances are concretely face to face." (P. Zumthor, 1983) Then something very special brings the community in togetherness. There is no more rupture between the self and the world; empathy prevails.

In our work as the interpreter of the interpretations of the other, nothing of the poet's life can be overlooked, neither him as a person, nor the society and the circumstances inviting him to sing, to perform. This holistic approach seems to me to be the minimal way to access this complexity.

Let us shift to the relationship between epic and memory, for I have some notions I would like to refer to and propose as an instigation to our joint effort to understand and share in the process of analysing these long chanted narratives.

Everything begins within the singer of tale and some kind of a negative image inside his mind anticipates his *proferatio* in Latin, according to my tradition, by the oral chanted narrative. One could say that the epic sings within the bard who hears it before he actually utters it.

In order to be able to convey in an intelligible way this immense mental story, the bard has several devices that he uses consciously or semi-consciously. This is the strength of his tradition within himself, within his memory, within his body, within his hearing, within his heart. For he is also emotionally involved.

We are aware of 'poetic formulae' since the work of M. Parry and A. Lord and I will not enter into this subject for this is familiar to most of us. But I would like to show you what are 'melodic formulae' in Palawan tradition.

Melodic formulae

Let me illustrate with the sound wave of *Mamiminbin*, an epic of 3 h 30' which I subtitled: *His quest of a wife.*

The illustrations here reveal the transcription of the beginning of the epic in Palawan, with a new tool that I discovered when I donated my collection to the National Library of France, to be preserved for the future, and when it was dubbed on compact disk. The technicians showed how they work and proceed visually.

Illustration 01

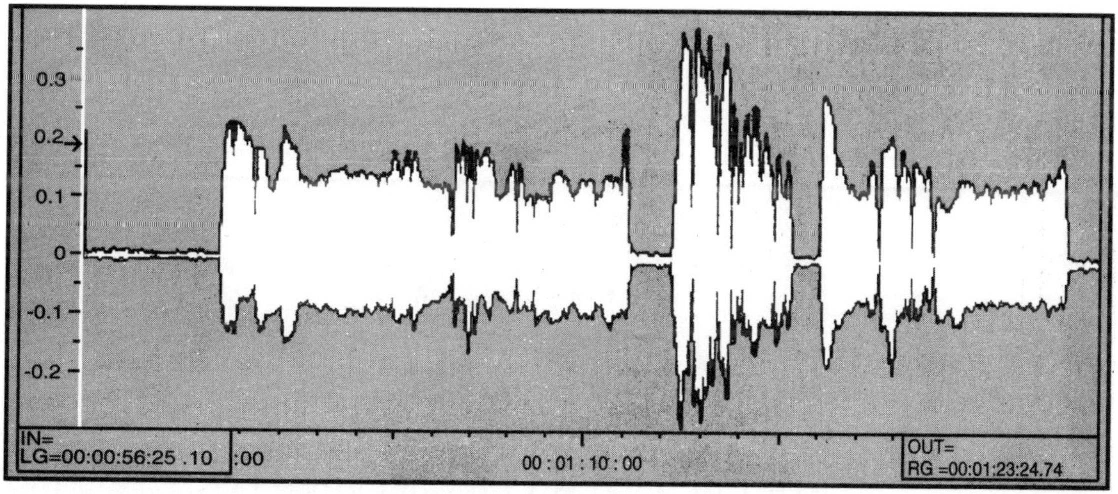

CD 37 de 54" à 1'16"

M.-B. *Hin atin kwan yä Balud maya lamang bäräsän ku dimyu bä.*
Hin sabab kwan yä näkwit nä dag päsäsanang ku atwä ät lungsud
Sälus kayang ga pägbäräsän ku dimyu bä

Illustration 01.1

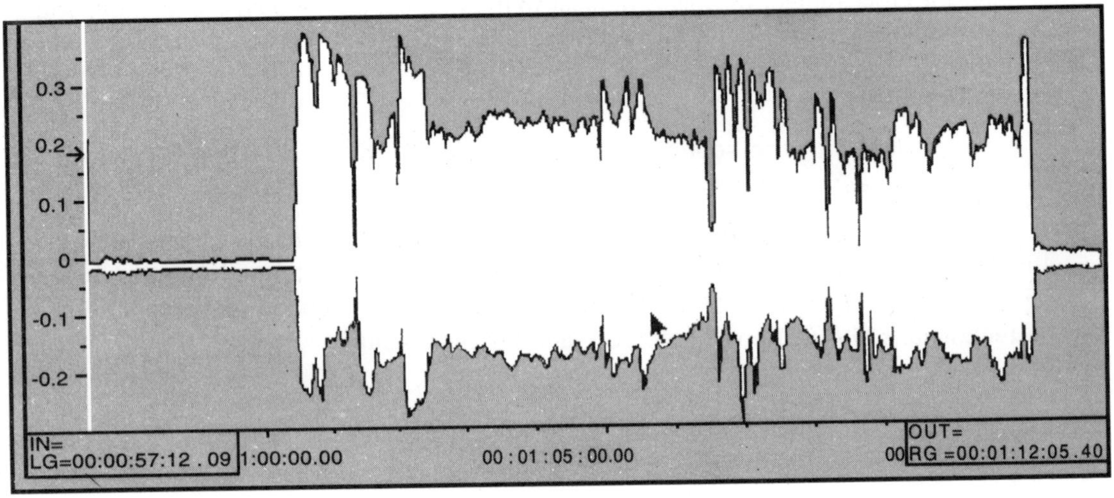

CD 37 de 54" à 1'05"

Hin atin kwan yä Balud maya lamang bäräsän ku dimyu bä.

Illustration 01.2

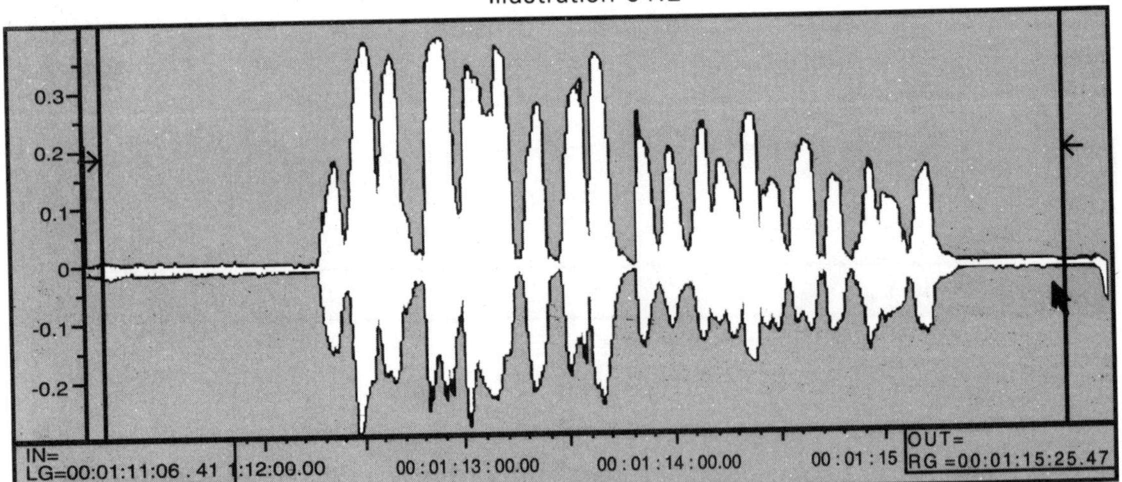

CD 37 de 1'06" à 1'09"

Hin sabab kwan yä näkwit nä dag päsäsanang ku atwä ät lungsud.

Illustration 01.3

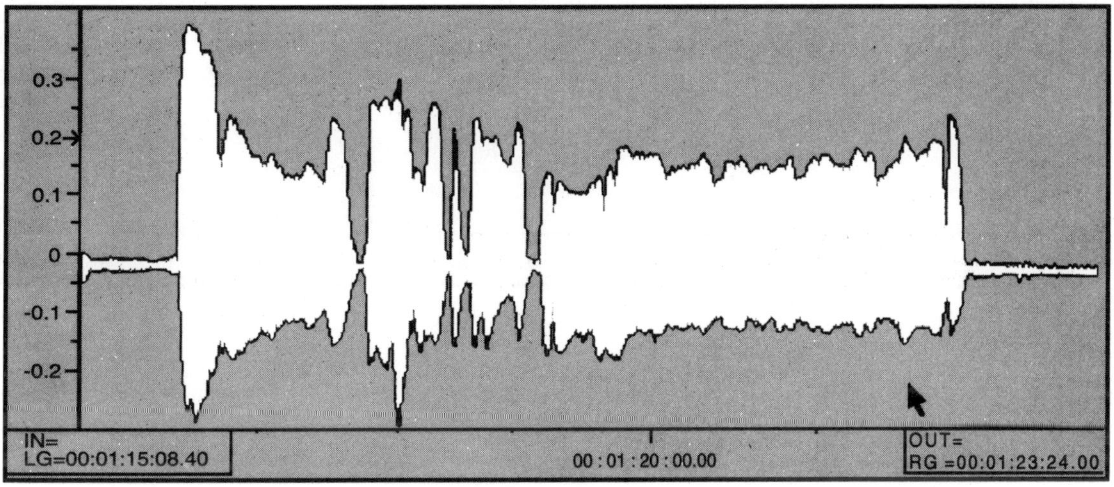

CD 37 de 1'09" à 1'16"

Sälus kayang ga pägbäräsän ku dimyu bä.

You can see here images in two dimensions – amplitude on the vertical axis and time on the horizontal axis. The voice develops with intakes of breathing and pauses where the line stretches. The sound wave is produced here for the first three blocks or breathing groups of phrases and sentences.

Illustration 1, 2, 3

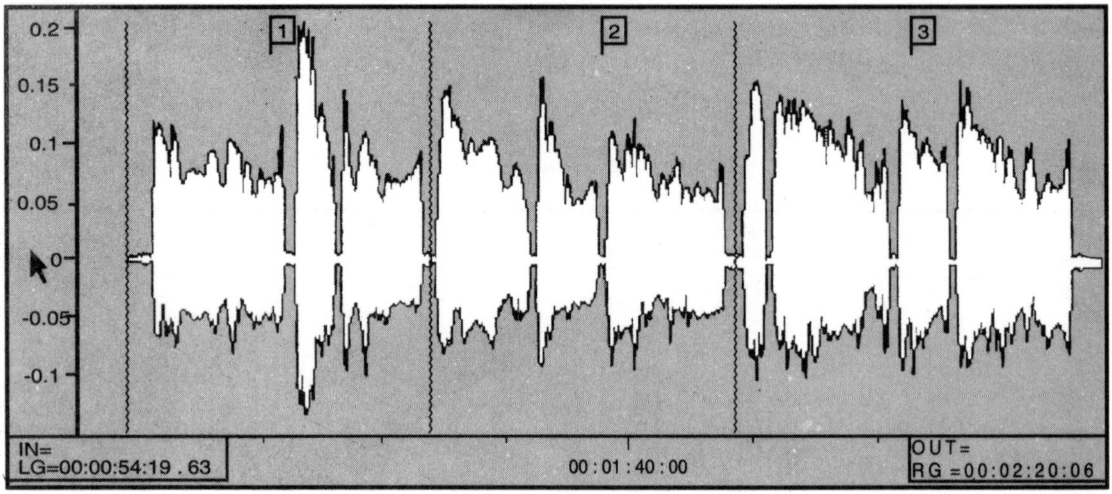

CD 37 de 54' à 2'09'-'

M.-B. *Hin atin kwan yä Balud maya lamang bäräsän ku dimyu bä.*
Hin sabab kwan yą näkwit nä dag päsäsanang ku atwä ät lungsud
Sälus kayang ga pägbäräsän ku dimyu bä.

Hin sägwaq kwan yä baqatinsi dakän bäpaq diki
Hin nä längku mäsändalan ät säläd atäy ku bä.
Mänunga kwan yä ipuhun ku dimyu mängäbyaq ku nä ät
mänduruk ät däpugan ku bä.

Hin sabab kwan yä
Ha dakän päguliqan ku manäv duqut märayuq mäkabiq atin aku nga mäsusa
täyan atin
Hin mägkäradya kunuq bä.
Hin mänunga nä dakän maya nä ät käradya ät bänwa ku atin
kaya nä pikirän ku batän kunuq bä.

I would like to point out that the sound image duplicates the transcription I made by the ear. I mean to say that it is by listening to silence and intakes of breathing that I was able to find a way to project on space — the white page — this mental story performed by the bard in 1971.

If we take the second image, the first block that was transcribed with three *alineas*, it makes up a block, that is, a breathing group of words that sets the song into motion. Here there is no metric form. We are in prose, but an opening formula (*Hin*) and a closing formula (*bä*) which functions as a prosodic device, a substitute for a rime. Hence the visualisation allows a perfect 'montage' indeed, and could be of great help to the transcriptor. It only helped me *a posteriori* to verify the accuracy — or eventually the non-accuracy of my transcription.

I can make a zoom on each of the lines 1 and 2. You can visualise the totality of an epic or progressive details of the singing in various sound waves fixed by a picture of it, by transforming the sound into an image of sound. When I transcribed for the first time epics among the Highlanders of Palawan, I had no model whatsoever to be influenced by, and this was a privilege. Not all epics are in verse and metric form, but breathing techniques and breathing groups of words can be the relevant rhetorical unit.

I would like now to introduce another notion, the notion that was given to me by a very knowledgeable and talented scholar, who has been my predecessor in Great Britain, Professor Arthur Hatto. I would like to convey to you the notion he formulated as 'Epic moments'.

Epic moments

Dr. Hatto convened a seminar on 'Heroic and Epic Poetry' between Oxford-Cambridge and London from 1969 to 1972. Dr. J. Smith, has applied the notion of epic moments to Pabuji epic. I have tried to apply it to *Mamiminbin* epic and found that we are probably dealing here with a universally operative notion. I quote Professor Hatto:

> Epic poetry is apt to condense long drawn tensions into brief scenes of dramatic power enhanced by visual magnificence, that is *epic moment*.
>
> Epic moments are highly charged narrative ganglia and it is suggested — as one of the fruits of comparative studies — that possession of them in memory, confers power upon the mature bard to build up an episode or even a string of episodes.

In other words, and thanks to the comparative method in a vast area of literature he has been dealing with, in togetherness with many other scholars,

> it is suggested that epic moments, in addition to being great poetry, are mnemotechnic elements of epic and an order, altogether superior to that of theme or formulae now so well discussed and that they will therefore mark, or help to mark, the structure of an epic.

I applied to the *Mamiminbin* epic, this notion and observed a crescendo of epic moments to the climax of the story, all built up through a mirror image in the quest of a wife, namely all actions are wrong in the first half of the epic with a crescendo of negative epic moments. Then all actions turn right and positive after the cure by Master Thunder in the middle space, and the shamanic Voyage of the two heroes. Then the good behaviour is conveyed up to the end to a perfect alliance. Affinity links are set up in the best possible way, namely sisters' exchange which is perfectly relevant in this society, through a crescendo of positive epic moments going towards an unfolding of the plot.

I would like you to remember this triangular pattern which drives to the end of an epic and their notion of crescendo of epic moments which I find absolutely operative; then the 'narrative structure' in the way we dig it up in my tradition of France, with Professor Claude Levi Strauss's guidance.

As Georges Dumezil was looking for constants, we now look for contrastive differences, the one that bears distinctive features. This is of course under the influence of structural linguistics.

Hence, I have brought to surface the relevant oppositions, in geographical spaces, flora, fauna and the various levels of contrast between characters which build up a very constant scheme. And I had the joy to be able to record again the same bard twenty-five years later, in August 1996. When he was about to sing, an enlightenment occurred to me. Usually, I never interfere with his choice because he has a very wide repertoire. Not only him, but each of the singers of tales in this area has various epics in his memory. But this time I said to him before he started, "Could you not sing *Mamiminbin* once more tonight?" He agreed to my request and in a matter of a second he shifted from one mental story to another mental story and started the song of *Mamiminbin* taking leave of his pet birds, the Nutmeg Pigeons and going in a quest for his wife.

At this point, I would like to say that in order to understand a myth, it is not enough to simply follow the narrative, as if this narrative were a melody. The different variants have to be taken into consideration and the version I laid down on paper is not the canonical version because it is written; it is one — but only one — among all the possible variants and versions. I wrote down the first leaflet of it. However, the different variants must be taken into account as multi-layered, as if they were in harmony; together these multiple variants will lead to the meaning.

There is a dynamics in the long string of sung narratives transmitted from generation to generation. Epics do circulate as speech circulates. As the singer of tales performs and captures his audience, there are various processes at work simultaneously, producing in a reiterative and creative way, understanding and interpretation.

These are the extensive and complex arrays of mnemotechnic devices. However, the rigour of the narrative structure, its clarity together with the power of poetic formulae, repetitive segments fix in the people's memory, the sequence of the episodes and related utterances basic to the plot.

Still innovations are possible and do occur, giving an oral performance of an epic this fresh, fluent movement which manifests creativity at work.

3

Saveen: Singers and Performance Context

Molly Kaushal

THE Gaddis are a north-western Himalayan semi-nomadic community, inhabiting the Dholadhar mountain range in the Chamba district of Himachal Pradesh. They have a rich repertoire of epic-lore, with their own local plots, styles and techniques of delivery of popular epics such as: *Ramayana* (*Rameen*) *Pandavvani* (*Pandveen*), *Prem Sagar* and *Sukh Sagar*, besides *Gugga Mandlik* and *Saveen*.

It is unfortunate that most of the cantos of *Gugga Mandlik* are now forgotten. It is hard to come by a bard who can sing this epic beyond one or two episodes. However, *Saveen* is still a living and vibrant tradition among the Gaddis. There are several reasons for this, the foremost being the direct relationship that exists between the Shiva mythology and the Gaddi interpretation of their lifestyle and patterns of livelihood.

The most fascinating aspect of *Saveen* is its ability to adapt itself to different contexts and styles of rendering. Three distinct styles of singing *Saveen* can be discerned here. Each is associated with a specific caste and professional group, context, function and musical accompaniment. The most popular is the *ainchali*, sung mostly by Brahmanas (though Rajputs sing it too) during the *nuala* ceremony, held in honour of lord Shiva at the time of entering a new house, marriage, birth of a male progeny, etc. The singers of *ainchali* are called *bande*. At the time of *nuala*, it is mandatory to have four *banda*s. One of them is the lead singer and the others are his vocal support. Two *dholki*s and a *dhanthal* are the essential musical instruments. The singing is accompanied by a male dance, *dandara*s on single beat in the beginning and on double beat later. Besides the singers, this performance requires a *jogi*, who is a silent witness to the whole ceremony. A group of female singers is also a must at the time of *nuala*. They provide a much needed rest to the bards during their night long performance. These women singers are ordinary invitees to the ceremony and have no claim to being bards or professional singers. Whenever the bards stop to have their *chilam* and *chai*, the female guests start singing hymns to Shiva. These hymns are also called *ainchali*. They are short lyrical poems in praise of lord Shiva and his consort Parvati. The performance of the epic at *nuala* requires not only a group of singers and a set of musical instruments, but also an auspicious moment and a consecrated sacred space. It requires a priest to conduct the ritual and a shaman to establish contact with the gods and pronounce their will. It needs the sacrifice of a ram either to appease the *navagrha*s or to show gratitude to Shiva. The stage for the performance is set by cleaning one of the corners of an east-facing wall with cowdung and then drawing a *mandala* of the earth containing 32 squares. In the centre of the *mandala* is erected the *Sumeru Parvat Kailash*, upon which fall nine streams of celestial Ganga from above, in the form of 9 woollen threads. Shiva is invited to come and reside on the top of this Kailash till the ceremony lasts, after which he is given a ritual farewell. While the stage is being set, the *banda*s and ladies sing various hymns describing the entire process of drawing the *mandala* and the reason for which it is being drawn.

Once the ritual sacrifice of the ram is carried out, *banda*s take their seats and formal singing of the *Saveen* starts. One of the cantos is chosen for the night either by the singers themselves or at the request of the guests or the host. The most popular is the *Shiv-vivah*.

One of the best known singers of the *Saveen* in *ainchali* style is Nanku, who is held in high esteem throughout Bharmour. It was not easy to persuade him to sing for me. He emphasised the music; I wanted the text. He said he had never sung alone, never during the day time, and never without the ritual. And of course there was no such thing as a complete version of the *Saveen*. It was endless like Shiva's own *maya*, (play/*lila*) and at *nuala* one barely manages to complete one canto. Several visits later after much explaining and cajoling, Nanku agreed to sing alone, during the day, without the ritual and with just one *dholki*.

Nanku's version of *Saveen* consists of four cantos: *Anaj guru*, *haran-shikar*, *Shiv-vivah*, and *gardreen*. The *kali* (canto) of *Anaj guru* starts with his birth, creation of the earth, the female counterpart of *Anaj guru* – *Manasa*, birth of Brahma, Vishnu and Shiva. It ends with the death of *Anaj guru*, his last rites and coronation of Shiva as the Lord of the three worlds. *Haran-shikar* describes Shiva's battle with various demons. It ends with his first encounter with Parvati. *Shiv-vivah* is a detailed discription of Shiva-Parvati marriage. It ends with Parvati coming to live with Shiva at *Mani-Mahesh Kailash* in Chamba. *Gardreen* contains a fascinating account of Parvati casting a magic spell on Shiva in order to make him reveal his liaison with Ganga. It narrates the birth of *kalkutia zehr* (poison) – the illegitimate son of Parvati from Brahma, churning of the ocean by Shiva and other gods in order to reveal the secret of this birth. *Gardreen* provides us with glimpses of Shakta-Shaivism conflict in the form of *Kamakhya* acting as *badi mohini* – the great temptress in direct conflict with Shiva for supremacy. *Gardreen* ends with the battle between *naga*s and *garuda*s. Interestingly, here the *garudas* are Shiva's helpers, whose leader, *Totala Rani* sends Dhanvantri *vaid* to cure Shiva of the magical spell.

According to Nanku and many others, the Gaddi *Saveen* has no other *kali* apart from the above-mentioned four cantos and if any singer adds to them, which many do, it is taken from the textual, literary tradition and can by no means qualify as authentic rendition of the Gaddi *Saveen*. However, other singers like Roomi Ram (70 years old, village Chaurasi) feel that orality is fluid; it cannot claim to have one fixed text or form, the singer may exercise his right to include or exclude episodes and no one version can be termed authentic or not-authentic; each singer has his own repertoire of episodes which another singer may not be aware of. However, most of the *ainchali* singers and common people agreed that main cantos of the Gaddi *Saveen* are basically the ones sung by Nanku.

Before I discuss the second style of delivering the *Saveen*, I would like to dwell a little more on the *bandas* as a special category of bards. The narrative chanted by them is more or less a fixed text, memorised by the bards, who make an extra effort to recite and pass it on with as little innovation as possible at the level of the thematic content. The charm of their individual performance lies in the use of elaborate descriptions, laced with beautiful similes, metaphors, and selection of appropriate formulae from the rich repertoire of poetic language, and of course, their voice. The personal character of the individual bard is a very important criterion for his performance to be generally accepted as an authentic account of the Gaddi history and tradition. This category of singers are the acknowledged custodians of that stream of knowledge which is encoded in and passed on through the oral and the sung word, the *gandharav vidya* or *gan vidya*. But increasingly they are being sidelined and the authenticity of their narrative is being questioned. If epic was 'True History' once, it is now taken as quasi-history only. However, even the die-hard critics of this tradition are defensive about directly challenging its authenticity. The critics of the *gan vidya* are that class of people who have had some kind of access to what is perceived as scriptural knowledge, which is Sanskritic and literary, and hence it has more accountability. The bards on the other hand question the accountability of the written word, which is "scripted by one person, and who is bound to commit errors". Orality to them is authentic and legitimate, for a written word can be wrong, but not the one that has been 'heard' and 'spoken'.

The second class of singers are the traditional healers. They manipulate the healing power of the chanted word. Their rendering of the epic is different from that of the *bandas*, not only at the level of style, but also at the level of the selection of the formulaic language and the usage to which it is put. The musical instrument used by the healer-chanter is *dopatra* — the original healing instrument created by Parvati with different organs of her own body and given to the first healer-chanter, Sumala *jogi*, in order to put into trance the first victim of the act of sorcery — Shiva himself. This episode forms part of the last canto, *gardreen*. The hearing of *gardreen* from a *gardi* — the healer chanter — on *dopatra* is enough to expel the evil influence of sorcery from within the body of the victim and thereby cure him. If the *banda*s recreate the original drama of creation through *nuala*, the *gardi* re-enacts the original healing seance. He takes recourse to *gardreen* when everything else in his repertoire fails. The victim is covered from head to toe and is made to sit with hands and feet dipped in water in front of the healer. The rendering of *gardreen* is interspersed with other healing chants, the secret *mantra*s, which I was not allowed to record for the fear that they may lose their efficacy once revealed.

The third category of singers are those bards for whom the singing of the epic is an economic pursuit. This class of bards are called *ghurai*, and the instruments they use are *rubana* and *khanjari*. Their style of singing the *Saveen* is called *musade*, which means singing accompanied by explanation of verses in prose. The *Saveen* here becomes Shiv-*katha*. A *ghurai* is often invited to render his *katha* on such occasions as *chaubarkhi* — *shraddh* ceremony performed after four years of death when the deceased person ceases to be a *pret* (ghost) and becomes a *pitar* (ancestor). Very often *ghurai*s go from village to village in the month of *Magh* to perform Shiv-*katha* at night in the houses of devout patrons. A *ghurai* may be invited to perform at a thanksgiving ceremony after a wish-fulfillment. Unlike the singers of *ainchali*, or *gardreen*, a *khanjari* player is more inclined to increase his repertoire by means of inventing his own new episodes, new details and descriptions, by adapting, to his style of singing, episodes he may have heard elsewhere or read in some locally available popular print versions of the *Shiv Puran* text.

One of my informants Kirpa Ram, a 60-year-old man, turned out to be a very innovative and talented bard. He wove into the main plot of the *Saveen*, the local history of Bharmour as perceived by him, his three years of experience in the army, his knowledge of places like Mehrauli in Delhi, Kashmir, Kedarnath, Amarnath and even Kabul, which figures in his narrative as *Kabuldesh*—an underground kingdom of the artisans, though often overlapping with *piyal-lok* or *naglok* (the nether-world). He thus rendered a version lasting up to 34 hours. He divided his narrative into two parts: the early childhood of Shiva as *Saveen*; and episodes, that he believed to be from the written text, as *Shiv Puran*. His version includes episodes like *Sati bhasm*, *Bhasmidant*, creation of Kedarnath, etc. Another *ghurai* ended his version of the *Saveen* with the coronation of Ganesha, turning of Karttikeya into a snake and the birth of Krishna heralding a new *yuga* (age). Interestingly, even in the *nuala* ceremony, at day-break, *ainchali* singers sing about the birth of Krishna, thereby indicating the next stage in the cosmic cycle, having its own deities and ethical norms.

For a *ghurai*, it is imperative to have his repertoire ever-increasing. He is in competition with other *ghurai*s. His popularity depends on his capacity to make his rendition as exciting and as fresh as possible. For him, it is also important to stress that his narration is an accurate account of the *Shiv Puran* text. Reasons for this are manifold. The *ghurai* belongs to the Hali-caste, which forms the lowest rung of Gaddi social order. He, in present times at least, is not automatically looked upon as a custodian of Gaddi culture and history in the manner, say, the *banda*s are. His area of influence within the Bharmour sub-tehsil seems to be marginal. His clientele comes mainly from the low-lying area, called *bhunchakha* which is closer to Chamba and Kangra and is perceived by the Bharmour Gaddis as closer to Panjabi culture than to Gaddi culture. For him, it is essential to stress the pan-Indian nature of his narrative rather than to stress the uniqueness of his tradition in the way that Nanku does. However, in spite of his vociferous claim to a verbatim narration of the *Shiv Puran*, he is not acceptable to that group of people who are actively engaged in a discourse on orality *vis-a-vis* textuality, because of his caste affiliation. Very ironically his own penchant for innovation becomes his undoing, for many people tend to mistrust him. According to some, a *ghurai* stretches his narrative so as to be paid more, adds frivolous details and anecdotes in order to humour his audience, thereby compromising the purity and originality of both the textual and the oral traditions. However outside Bharmour, *ghurai* is a revered and a much sought after bard for his rendering of the *Shiv-katha*, *Rameen*, *Pandveen*, *Sukh Sagar* and *Prem Sagar*.

By way of concluding, I would like to say that the *banda* in the Gaddi society is seen as a custodian of oral history, culture and tradition; his narration is sacred history; his performance, a re-creation of the sacred past through ritual and chant. He is revered and respected for this, and also at times challenged. The *gardi* has access to the healing power of the chanted word, and he uses this power for the good of the people. The *ghurai* is a skilful artist, who manipulates the power of the spoken and sung word to weave beautiful narratives and thereby earn a livelihood. He is acceptable to some, appears frivolous to others, but remains an integral part of the Gaddi epic tradition, ever renewing it, enriching it and carrying it across the region. He is the one who is responsible for the mobility of genres, ideas, forms and techniques, lending as well as borrowing them. He is a recognised artist, else I would not have been led to him.

Both practiotioners and critics of orality dwell upon the modes of transmission of knowledge, thereby revealing the manifold and multilayered nature of orality. The orality of Nanku as well as of the healer-chanters belongs to the realm of the transtemporal, transcendental reality—the realm of 'truth-revealed' and thereafter preserved. In this sense it is 'frozen in time'; it cannot be played around with. The orality of Kirpa Ram belongs to the realm of 'truth-discovered' and thereafter put to an artistic and creative use. It is ever changing and ever renewing itself. To the supporters of textuality, orality is relevant only if it upholds the text. And orality gives in graciously to the will of all the three, precisely because it is fluid, mobile, open and contextual.

4

The Transmission of Bhojpuri Epics Towards Nepal and Bengal
Oral Performance and Selling of Chapbooks Editions

Catherine Servan-Schreiber

Introduction

According to linguists such as George Grierson or Uday Narayan Tiwari, the borders of the Bhojpuri language are mostly located in the western part of Bihar and the eastern part of Uttar Pradesh. In fact, the range of the Bhojpuri-speaking region is not only far wider than what the maps drawn by these linguists show, but it covers a very large area of northern India and of the Nepali Terai, stretching from Allahabad to Calcutta as well as from Kathmandu to Ranchi.

Bhojpuri literature, possessing a rich but little known *Sant* poetic tradition, is mainly oral, and remains an inheritance of the medieval repertoire of the ancient bards. The impressive spread of the Bhojpuri language is due to the great popularity and literary achievement of a rich epic literature, not only still orally performed, read, sold, and known, but also used for promoting Bhojpuri's claim for recognition under Schedule VIII of the Indian Constitution.

What we refer to as 'epic literature' in Bhojpuri are long versified archaic texts of the medieval period, which are sung and recited by a bard, whether he is professional or not, and whether he sings a *chappella* or with an instrument. The genre is unanimously called *gatha* (narrative song), or less often *geet* (song) or *panvara* (ballad). If it is orally performed, it is sung by male singers only (with a single exception), for an exclusively male audience. If it is printed and sold on the pavements or in the small shops of the bazaars, it is both sold and bought most exclusively by men. Not only are the agents of transmission of these texts of a low social status, if not extremely low, but the public of these texts are mainly *rikshaw-vala*s, coolies, Ahir, Dusadh, Noniya, Teli (oilmen) and small traders. The question of the audience and patrons of this literary genre in the modern context of urbanisation will be referred to a little later.

Leaving the *Ramayana* and the *Mahabharata*, and considering more geographically located *gathas*, we can say that four main categories of epics co-exist in northern India:

(a) The *gathas* linked with the cycle of king-renouncers belonging to the Shaivaite Nath sect and disciples of Gorakhnath, like *Gopichand*, *Bhartrihari*, *Rani Saranga-Sadabrij*, *Sorthi-Brijabhar*, *Gugga*, *Raja Rasalu* or *Malushahi* and *Rajula*[1], sung by wandering ascetics with a *sarangi* musical accompaniment.

(b) The Rajput epics sung by pastoral and martial castes who were linked to Rajputs for service (mainly Ahir, Nat, Dusadh or Noniya), such as *Lorik*[2], or the famous *Alha-Udal*, *Nihal De*.

(c) The epics which were brought by traders and reflect, like the Rajput epics, the migration of population from western India towards the east. They are sung by Teli, Baniya, Nat or Noniya.

(d) The Muslim *kissas* of Arabo-Persian origin, which are very close to the Indian epics, such as the story of *Hatim Tai* or the famous sufi *premakhyan* inspired by Indian *gathas*.

For a long time, I have been working on the Bhojpuri king-renouncers cycle of *gathas* of the Nath, whose particularity was to be sung by Muslim wandering *jogis* (Champion 1991, 1995a; O Henry 1988; Servan-Schreiber 1995). At present, I am focusing more on the contribution of the traders to the transmission of Bhojpuri epics in northern India. The transmission of four main Bhojpuri *gathas*: *Shobha Nayaka Banjara, Hirni-Birni, Reshma-Chuharmal* and *Bihula* can be considered to be linked with the trading castes. Whereas the first three are transmitted from the Bhojpuri region to the Nepalese Terai, the fourth one is connected to the migration of traders between the Bhojpuri-speaking belt and Bengal.

Before inquiring into the content of these epics, and their impact on Bhojpuri culture, the question of the methodological approach to the study of these epics has to be considered. Though every scholar of epics and chanted narratives is deeply aware of the importance of their oral transmission and of the symbolic and emotional impact of the voice of the bard, he should not separate the oral transmission of the epics from the printed one. Therefore, four approaches should underline the study of Indian chanted narratives:

1. The identity, story of life, geographical itineraries, halting places and webs of relations of the agents of transmission of the oral performance of the *gatha*,

must be carefully noted. I have given great importance to the drawing of maps of the places where the wandering singers would go and perform, and have endeavoured to follow their routes from Allahabad to Kathmandu or Calcutta, from Mirzapur to Biratnagar. Very often, it happens that a singer of tales has a double occupation, whether he be a professional singer or not. For instance:

(a) An oilman and a singer of epic

(b) A Kevat (boatman) and a singer of epic

(c) A Dusadh (who takes care of the cattle) and a singer of epic

(d) A Julaha (weaver) and a singer of epic.

2. I give great importance to the printers and the dynasties of printers who have contributed to the spread of these *gatha*s under the form of chapbooks (*chaupatiya*). For instance, the main Bhojpuri printers of *gatha*s are Thakur Prasad, in the Kachauri Gali of Varanasi bazaar, Jamb Press in Varanasi, Narayan and Co. in Patna (Salimpur), Jaya Durga Press of Nagendra Prasad Singh in Patna (Naya Tola), and Chauhan and Co. in Gorakhpur. For the Maithili *gatha*s, the main printers are Urvasi Prakashan (Patna and Darbhanga), Janaki Prakashan (Patna), Janaki Press of Janakpur (Nepal) and Morang Pustakalaya of Biratnagar (Nepal). Outside the Maithili and Bhojpuri belts, two famous printers of Calcutta, Loknath Pustakalaya and Bholanath Pustakalaya, both on Mahatma Gandhi Road, can be considered as among the oldest dynasties of printers of Bhojpuri and Maithili chapbooks. Thakur Prasad of Varanasi also has a branch at Mahatma Gandhi Road in Calcutta. As to the run of copies, it starts from 5,000 to 10,000 for the most popular *gatha*s, and they are reprinted every two years in the presses of Varanasi, Bombay or Calcutta. The importance of the study of the printing of chapbooks of *gatha*s in India, and the importance of this literature often called 'pavement literature', must not be overlooked and the idea that the existence of chapbooks is harmful to the oral performance should not be entertained. Moreover, quite often, the material support of orality is not only the voice of the bard, and one has to explore also the role of images in the transmission of orality. As shown by Mr. Venkateswarlu in his paper — an image on the wall is also a story.

3. I also endeavour to follow the web of sellers and of small pedlars selling chapbooks (*paikar*) and images of the heroes of the *gatha*s, and establish maps of their itineraries.

4. I try to determine the public for these *gatha*s. Most often, they are *rikshaw-vala*s, coolies, boatmen, Baniyas, cattle-sellers . . . themselves wandering and moving people, listening to wandering and moving singers.

As to the location where these *gatha*s are most often both heard and sold, one can rely on the *maidan* (ground) of the great cities, the stations, the gates of the cities, the bazaars, the temples, the tombs of the Muslim saints and the great fairs (*hat* or *mela*). This is also to break with the idea that the *gatha* is the product of the village. It is an urban product and it is the sign of vitality of an urban culture which has kept its specificity and strength.

It would not be possible to speak about the transmission of the Bhojpuri epic repertoire without mentioning the role played by the merchant communities, whether flourishing or quite modest, in spreading these texts. The Bhojpuri-speaking belt is an Indian region leading to Bengal towards the East and to the Himalayan Terai towards the North. Through this region goods were circulating from Iran, Trans-oxus, Syria, Iraq and Turkey. Its economy was prosperous, owing to the products it was producing, among which were cotton, opium, indigo, sugar, saltpetre, mustard oil, varnished pottery of Sivan, blankets from Shahabad, perfumes from Ghazipur, tobacco of Gorakhpur and of Mithila, knifework, basketwork from Muzaffarpur, brass and copper utensils, small carpets from Mirzapur, stone pestles and mortars from Chunar, rice from Patna, and silk and muslin sarees from Varanasi. Iron and salt were exploited. After bringing these goods up to Tibet, through the Terai roads, the merchants would bring back musk, saffron, honey, woollen clothes and Tibetan carpets. The importance of the great Bihari markets is also to be mentioned. One of the most famous cattle fairs of northern India is the Sonepur *mela*, near Patna, which provides elephants, camels, sheep, buffaloes, horses and birds. But there are many others: Brahampur, Buxar, Sirpaul, Ekawana, Karaghar, Kulharia in the district of Shahabad; Arreraj, Bettiah, Madhuban, Rajpur and Gobindganj in the district of Champaran, and Sahodra where the Tharu population of Nepal come for their shopping needs. These fairs are the starting points of many a caravan going to Nepal or Bengal. Concerning the medieval period, the works of R. Choudhary (*History of Muslim Rule in Tirhut*) and J.N. Sarkar (*Glimpses of Medieval Bihar Economy*) allow us to reconstitute the roads and itineraries, and identify the main categories of merchants. Concerning the exchanges of goods between India and Nepal, the study of Jahar Sen, *Indo-Nepal Trade in the Nineteenth Century*, shows well the rivalry between the Newar traders and their Indian neighbours. Among the Indian traders of the cities of the Terai and the Kathmandu valley, the Sikhs of Punjab and the Marwaris of Rajasthan have become quite famous (Gaborieau 1978, 184). Much more modest, and less showy, the Bhojpuriya have nevertheless been able to take advantage of their geographical position and their spirit of enterprise, to play a role of 'passeurs' between India and Nepal. The most intense places of exchange have been in Bengal, along the Ganges, and Nepal, through the Terai. One can consider a triangle linking Calcutta, Biratnagar and Patna. Even though Birganj is now challenging Biratnagar for the trade with Calcutta, the main jute factories of Biratnagar are slowly closing and many official personalities of the city have been transferred to Dhankuta. Biratnagar is still one of the main halting-places in the itinerary of the Bhojpuri merchant. But a distinction must be made between the opulent Baniyas and Telis, mostly grain-traders and oil-traders, who quite often run two shops, one in Bihar, and one in Nepal or Bengal, and can afford to have a *bhainsaha* to carry their goods on the back of a buffalo, and the small pedlars who walk along the roads with their goods in their *jholi* (bag): mirrors, combs, needles, handkerchiefs, fancy jewels, ribbons and candles.

The transmission of *Shobha Nayaka Banjara* and *Hirni-Birni* and the glorification of the *bhainsaha* merchant's migration from the Bhojpuri region to Mithila and Morang by Teli and Netua storytellers

Of all Bhojpuri castes of traders involved with the trade between India and Nepal — Teli, Vaishya, Suri, Kayasthas, Halvai, Agarvala, Rajput, Khatri, Kalvar or Brahman, that of the *bhainsaha banjara*, wandering traders who go along roads with their goods on their buffalo's back, is the one whose 'epic story' is narrated in greatest detail in the oral tradition. The word *banjar* itself is confusing. In Bhojpuri, it is the equivalent of the Sanskrit *vanij*, and must not be taken for the 'Labana *banjara*' caste, coming from the West, though their occupations have been and are still quite similar: in the medieval past, they were in charge of supplying the armies with food and arms and they transported and sold goods, grains and cattle on horses and caravans, a work they are nowadays doing with lorries and vans. But though the train system has improved a lot, and the number of colourful vans is quite visible on the border between India and Nepal, there are still narrow roads that can be burrowed only by the Bhojpuri *bhainsaha*. The figure of the merchant as a hero of the oral tradition in India is not an isolated phenomenon. The *Manasa Mangalkavya* of Bengal shows the community of the *gandhavanika*, who sells spices and perfumes. The Sanskrit literature gives an important place to the merchant in texts such as *Mahabharata*, the *Katha-Sarit-Sagara* and the *Jataka* (Bhattacharya 1989, 302-5), but in the Bhojpuri area, not only singers of tales or chapbooks glorify the figure of the *bhainsaha*, but a whole independent flowering of pictures and small images reinforces its popularity.

The *gatha*s related to the merchant Bhojpuri epics have the particularity of being a part of the repertoire of a certain category of story-tellers who belong to the Teli or Netua castes and who are specialised in showing dressed animals, like deformed buffaloes, monkeys, snakes or sheep, and in selling talking birds that they carry in cages from *mela* to *mela*. Many of them rear and sell cocks for cockfighting, a pastime and game very much appreciated in the Terai region, and their wives are often specialised in tatooing and selling of talismans, which gives them a great freedom of movement, coming and going from house to house, and narrating on these occasions the stories of *Shobha Nayaka* or *Hirni-Birni*. Their status, very near that of the wandering beggar, is much lower than the one of the higher Telis or Vaishya who patronise them. These people can be heard in public places like *melas* or *maidans*, and can also perform for private audiences, for the pleasure of Telis or Vaishya who like to hear the epic of *Shobha Nayaka Banjara*. It is also a custom that on the occasion of *Divali*, the festival of the Vaishya and of Lakshmi Devi, once the shop has been repainted in a fresh blue colour, and the new records books have been opened, Teli or Netua singers are called in the courtyard of the trader's house to perform these two *gathas*. Among the caste of merchants who are still very attached to the literary value of these *gathas*, the Kanu, both sweet-makers and sweet-vendors, have to be mentioned.

SHOBHA NAYAKA BANJARA

Oral performance

The *gatha* of *Shobha Nayaka*, though issuing from a merchant tradition, is built like the *gathas* of the king-renouncers, with episodes of the quest for a spouse and the ordeals that are undertaken by the heroes for the fulfilment of their mission. It shows the webs of alliances which have formed between the Bhojpuriya communities in Mithila and in the Nepalese district of Morang, to resist the several dangers of these adventurous seasonal migrations. Shobha is the chief of a caravan, coming from the city of Belupur (district of Saran). He is the leader of six hundred fellows, with a caravan of six hundred bullocks. He is married to a merchant's daughter of Mithila, called sometimes Bari, sometimes Jasumati, but his duty compels him to leave his nuptial house on the very day of the wedding, like the king-renouncers stories of *Sorthi* or *Saranga-Sadabrij*. The itineraries covered by the caravans of Shobha Nayaka are quite vast. They go from Varanasi to Patna, halting at the Sonepur *mela*. Then, from the Bandih fair (in Ballia District), they go to Barhaj Bazaar (District of Gorakhpur). They go from Patna to Mithila, then either to Morang, or to Calcutta. The kind of goods sold by Shobha are of several kinds: some jewels from one part, and turmeric, betel-nuts, cloves and pepper and some buffaloes from another. Many dangers await the Bhojpuri *bhainsaha* merchant on his way to the border of Nepal: the presence of the police and customs which compels them to long halts in their *chauki*, the exorbitant taxes that the Indian and Nepalese governments try to impose on them, the covetous highway robbers who often compel them to hire the services of armed soldiers called *burkundaze* to protect them and their goods, and, last but not least, the dangers of paludism and malaria in these insalubrious hills of the marshy Terai. The oral performance of this *gatha* can last from one to three nights. The men gather in the courtyard of a merchant's house, while the women listen from upstairs, or a balcony, or from behind *zharokhas*. In their patronising of low-status singers of their caste's epics, the merchants remind one of the Rajputs of the medieval period, who would entertain singers and genealogists for the glorification of their deeds, the prestige of their community, and the collective memory, through a tradition that only the magical spell of the singer of tales can provide.

Chapbooks of Shobha-Nayaka Banjara

Though the epic of *Shobha* presents all the characteristics of the Bhojpuri medieval *gatha*, it is difficult to evaluate its medieval origin. The oldest form available to us is that collected and printed by George Grierson and given as a 'specimen' of the Bhojpuri language. He collected it from a wandering singer of the Shahabad district in 1885. The versions available nowadays bear the sign of modernity as long as allusion to transport of goods by train are included. But the frame of the plot and the archaic and versified language gives the impression of belonging to the same literary trend as the great Bhojpuri medieval *gatha* tradition. Each of the great dynasties of Bhojpuri printers has edited one or several versions of the story of Shobha the merchant. The version printed by Loknath Pustakalaya around 1930, under the title *Asli Shobha Nayaka Banjara biso bhag*, indicates the fourteenth printing of it, and 5000 copies of it were published. Thakur Prasad of Varanasi has printed two different versions; one, *Shobha Nayaka Banjara*, the second one, *Bari Banijarva ka geet chauviso bhag*. It has been collected by Mahadev Prasad Singh, the most famous chapbook collector of the Bhojpuri-speaking belt, and, as the title indicates, it takes the merchant's wife as the heroine of the story. Anyway, the most popular of them is the one published by the Jamb Press of Varanasi. The printed versions are much more developed than the oral ones, and the great difference lies in that they focus less on the heroism of the wandering merchant leading his caravan in marshy lands, and more on the drawbacks created by his absence in the Bhojpuri society: feeling of abandonment by the wife, birth and hiding of illegal children, cruelty of the in-laws towards the lonely spouse, or, on the contrary, 'sexual' relations between the merchant's wife and her brother-in-law, whether younger or older than her, and sometimes, with both.

As in the oral versions, the episodes of the printed versions are linked together without any transition. The chronology of events is seldom respected, and unexpected 'flashbacks' intervene without any warning. Disjointed as it is, this break of linking *d'enchainements* reinforces the idea of the wandering Bhojpuriya, who is not liable to be sedentarised by any event, whether his own marriage or the birth of his child.

HIRNI-BIRNI

Oral performance

Together with the story of *Shobha Nayaka Banjara*, the Teli and Nat (or Netua) singers also tell the narrative song of two Bhojpuri heroines of the Netua caste. These daring, quarrelsome, and not very commendable creatures, have also the habit of practising their trade along the roads leading from Bihar to the Terai. One can see them often dancing while their husband is singing or playing the drum, and they are specialised in tatooing, as a famous Bhojpuri song reminds us:

> *Two* Natini *in Patna city*
> *Whose turn is it for being tatooed?*
> *There's a threat over Patna, there's a panic over Ballia*
> *The whole of Bhojpur is panic-stricken*
> *They will tatoo all Gangotri*[3]*, they will tattoo all Sitamarhi*[4]*, they will tatoo all Janakpur*
> *They will tatoo all Baidyanath Babadham*[5]
> *They will tatoo all Jhariya, all Dhanbad and all Bokaro*[6]
> *They will go where jewels and gems are abundant*
> *They will tatoo Jagjivan Ram.*[7] *They will tattoo Kunvar Singh, the man who sacrificed himself for the country*[8],
> *They will tattoo Vidyapati, Bhikhari and Mahendra*[9],
> *They will engrave a sun or a moon on their arm.*
> *From the top of their houses, the inhabitants of Chapra are spreading the news.*
> *In Azamgarh, they have a bad reputation.*

One of the lesser known activities of the Nats is to have followed the armies in the medieval period. They were in charge of bringing and protecting the convoy of ammunitions. Though they are not considered as belonging to the martial castes, they are also well-trained in martial arts, and lots of *pahalvan*s belong to their caste. Among their other activities, the making and selling of cords meant for keeping the loads on buffaloes securely tied, provided an incentive for them to go to Nepal to buy the special *bunku*s herb, which is used for making these cords. This activity brings them to the *mela*, where they take care of the transport and indulge in the trade of animals also. One of their most famous and spectacular activities is the taming and selling of birds, and they are masters in organising the cock-fights that the Bhojpuriya are so fond of. The itineraries of the Nats are even wider than those of the Telis. They say they come from Gujarat. As their reputation suffers from the suspicion of prostitution of their women, they often refer to the *gatha* of *Hirni-Birni* to assert their link with the Rajput castes. This famous epic relates the story of two Natinis, Hirni and Birni, their migration from Gujarat to the Bhojpuri region with their buffaloes and their cocks, their wedding with a Kshatriya *pahalvan*, named Posan Singh, and the establishment of their progeny through prestigious alliances concluded with a branch of Bhojpuri Rajputs from Mirzapur, and Maithili Rajputs from Tirhut. The eventuality of a matrimonial alliance between Nats and Kshatriyas is dubious, as the Bhojpuri Rajput clans of Mirzapur, the Chandelas and the Kharwars, were among the elitist and most isolated clans of the region, and were not used to patronising mercenary army men coming from the lower pastoral or trading castes, as other Rajput clans would quite often do in the centre of the Bhojpuri-speaking belt (Downs 1992, 45). But in praising, in their oral tradition, an alliance between Kshatriyas and Nats, the Bhojpuri bards were not so far from reality. Some roads taken by goods caravans between Mirzapur, Darbhanga and Nepal were clandestine roads through which the great traders of Mirzapur and Kharwa would hire the services of Nats for the protection of their goods. Wandering, travelling acrobats with many a facet, the Nats are much less marginalised and modest than one could think. Nevertheless, the oral performance of *Hirni-Birni* is only to be heard on the occasion of *melas*, on the great urban *maidans* or in the streets of a city, or in the proximity of an *akhara*, but not in the respectable houses of Teli or Baniya traders.

Chapbooks editions of Hirni-Birni

Three different editions of this *gatha* exist: one by Thakur Prasad, one by Loknath Pustakalaya, one by Bholanath Pustakalaya. That of Thakur Prasad is much more detailed than the two others, and includes 'Rajput-like marriage episodes' with battles and descriptions of the sons of Posan Singh, the low status degraded Kshatriya. That of Bholanath Pustakalaya insists on the importance of an urban martial culture, describing many Bhojpuri *akharas*, and giving details of wrestling only with bare hands by *pahalvans*. As to the cover of the chapbooks edited by Loknath Pustakalaya, it suggests more obviously the link with Nepal, the two Natini sisters being there dressed much more like Nepali women than Indian women.

Transmission of *Gauraiya gatha* and *Reshma-Chuharmal* towards Mithila and Nepal and the glorification of the honourable bandit and cattle-stealer by Dusadh bards

Very near to the Ahirs, the pastoral caste Dusadh has a much lower social and economic status than the Yadavas. Though they take care of cows and buffaloes as well as the Ahirs, their breeding of swine gives them an impure status in the Indian hierarchy. They have other 'polluting' or unpleasant duties, such as taking care of corpses or announcing bad news in the good status families. They have attempted, as the other low status castes, to rise in the hierarchy, by assimilating themselves with the Kshatriyas as often as they could, but they have not really succeeded, and their status remains quite low. They have, unlike the Yadavas, not produced major political leaders, with the exception of Bhola Paswan Shastri, who was the Chief Minister of Bihar for a short time. Rather, they have been incorporated in the gangs of more than one Bhojpuri landlord or political leader (Frankel 1989, 60). Though they are cattle-breeders and sellers, the Dusadh are also counted among the martial castes of India. Many a sepoy recruited in the battle of Plassey, for instance, belonged to the Dusadh caste (Crooke, 1974, 346). Both their martial abilities, and the breeding and selling of cattle, gives them great mobility. And they have a great role in the transmission of the oral tradition in the Bhojpuri-speaking belt, by spreading a repertoire which glorifies the honourable bandit, a very appreciated theme relevant to the universe of violence so deeply rooted in the Bhojpuri society.

GAURAIYA, THE BHOJPURI 'ROBINHOOD'

The character of the low caste bandit who steals goods, destroys the wealthy merchants' shops, destroys their registers, redistributes their wealth to the poor Bhojpuriya and hides himself in the swine stables, is as beloved in the Bhojpuri-speaking belt as were, in Italy, the famous Tempratino or the fearsome Musolino. Highway bandits who attack the travellers with their single *lathi*s are the heroes of more than one *gatha*. The best example is that of Gauraiya. The etymological origin of this name is double, *goru*, meaning 'which pertains to the cattle', and *gor* meaning the place where dead people are cremated or buried. This 'deified bandit' is not only mentioned in the *gatha* of *Gauraiya* widely spread and sung by Dusadh singers but he also has a cult in Patna, where he has two sanctuaries, and towards the Champaran region. He has priests (*ojha*s), oracles who interpret his messages, and the devotees who sacrifice cocks, swine or he-goats to him. He is very often requested to cure leprosy, diseases, natural catastrophes, and to protect the villages or the *muhalla*s of a city. That cult of the deified bandit is found not only among the Dusadh but also among the Bhojpuri Brahmans who revere him and associate his cult with that of the dead spirits. But the story of *Gauraiya* is only to be heard from the Dusadh non-professional singers, and no chapbook of it is, so far as I know, available.

CHUHARMAL, THE BHOJPURI DEIFIED CATTLE-STEALER

Oral performance

Whereas Gauraiya kidnaps travellers or the rich merchants for ransom, Chuharmal braves the landlords by stealing their lands and cattle, and contributing to the expansion of the Bhojpuri conquest towards the East. The *gatha* of *Chuharmal* is in many respects one of the most enlightening sources for the reconstitution of the history of the region. It enables one to understand the scheme of migration of pastoral and martial populations coming from Uttar Pradesh and Bihar, going to Magadha or Mithila, and up to the Nepalese Terai. A very popular version of the story of *Chuharmal* is to be found among the Tharu community of Nepal (Maun 1968, 62; Champion 1995b), which shows the continuation of the Bhojpuri-speaking belt influence. The story of *Chuharmal-Reshma* is to be heard only by non-professional Dusadh singers, inside their community, on recreative or festive occasions such as *Dasehra*. The singer also plays on a *dhol*, and is accompanied by a band of eight percussionists, seven on cymbals and one on *khartal*. The story is to be heard in the districts of Mirzapur, Patna, Gorakhpur, Ballia, Ghazipur, Azamgarh and Basti, and also in southern or eastern parts of Bihar where Bhojpuri is spoken as well as Maithili or Magahi.

The *gatha* of *Chuharmal* is considered to be originally 'Magahi' *gatha,* and not a 'Bhojpuri' one, on account of Chuharmal having come from Mokama, a small city of Magadha, but it has become extremely popular in the Bhojpuri-speaking belt, and is printed much more in Bhojpuri than in Magahi. In the Bhojpuri *gatha* of *Chuharmal*, the hero is a Dusadh, well known for his bravery, and he is coveted by a beautiful princess, daughter of a landlord, called Reshma, who dies of love for him. But their love is forbidden for several reasons. Reshma is of a much higher status, and there is an 'incestuous' relation among them according to the Indian tradition, as long as they belong to the same village and are '*guru bhai* and *bahan*' — that is, they have shared the same teacher. Not only does he disregard her and despise her, but also his main aim is to conquer the kingdom and lands of the father of Reshma, in order to gain more pasture for his cattle to enable his cattle to migrate eastwards, and promote the welfare of the poor Dusadh community. Inspired by the Bhojpuri and Magadhi stories of *Reshma-Chuharmal*, the Maithili *gatha* of *Salhes-Chuharmal* is among the most popular Maithili *gatha*s. There are many similarities between the story of *Salhes-Chuharmal* and that of *Lorik*. Both of them come from a martial and pastoral caste, both of them are loved by a lower status princess, and both of them are in charge of lands and cattle. But there are many differences between the Maithili '*Salhes* story' and the Bhojpuri '*Chuharmal* story'. The Maithili text respects the Indian order and hierarchy, while the Bhojpuri *gatha* of *Chuharmal* is very subversive. Chuharmal is perceived as a very popular Bhojpuri figure, who has been able to fight against the oppressive landlord families, and it exalts the virtues of robbery, treachery, violence and brutality. The Bhojpuri *gatha* of *Chuharmal* reminds also very much of the Bhojpuri epic of *Alha-Udal*. Chuharmal is not only a brave regional hero but he is also a truly sadistic character, who co-operates with *jogini*s for the death of Reshma: she is burnt alive with his complicity because of her love for him. In the same way, Sonva, the Bhojpuri heroin of *Alha-Udal*, kills her brother herself, in front of their own father, in order to have no obstacles in the way of her marriage with Alha. Such an outburst of sadistic violence is not to be found in Maithili *gatha*s.

Chapbooks of Reshma-Chuharmal

Two editions of the *Reshma-Chuharmal gatha* are circulating in the Bhojpuri-speaking belt. One, in twelve parts, bears the name of *Rani Reshma Chuharmal ka geet,* and is edited by Thakur Prasad, from Varanasi; the other, under the same title, is much longer, and is edited by Loknath Pustakalaya of Calcutta. Both are widely sold in the regions of Varanasi, Calcutta, Mirzapur, Patna, Monghyr, Fatuha, Mokama and Darbhanga.

Even more than *Lorik,* the *gatha* of *Chuharmal* reflects the ambiguity of the relationship that existed between the Rajput castes and the pastoral and martial castes they were using for their services, and patronising as bards. This situation, typical of the medieval period, is still to be observed in contemporary Bhojpuri society. In the Bhojpuri-speaking part of Western Champaran, where the sugar-cane barons are very tempting targets, and where more than forty gangs of kidnappers are at work, most of the gangs assert that they are acting "to eliminate some social inequalities, to deprive only the wealthy people to give to the poor ones" (Ali 1994). Ancient owners of the land and chiefs of kingdoms, nowadays deprived of their rights to landed property, the Dusadhs have become the most eloquent apostles of violence and of banditry as acts of honour. It is to the singing of their bards, as well as to the spread of small edited chapbooks of their repertoire, that the image of the Bhojpuri bandit owes a great part of its popularity.

The transmission of *Bihula gatha* by Teli, Noniya, Nat, Kevat and Dom bards along the Ganga

The Ganga River, which crosses and then surrounds the Bhojpuri-speaking belt from Mirzapur to Bhagalpur, and links it to the rest of India, has created a way of access and a privileged commercial relation between that area and Bengal. Though Bengal is nowadays one of the greatest producers of tobacco, rice, sugar-cane, tea and jute, it was not so in the medieval period. At that time, not only did the Bhojpuri country supply it with its goods, but it was quite superior to Bengal owing to the variety of its products and the power of its output. The fact that urban life was much more developed there than in Bengal (Marshall 1987, 38), reinforced the trading vocation of this region. Rice from Patna, opium, timber, sugar, ginger, saltpetre, pepper, betel and cereals were among the most popular imports into Bengal. Potteries and glassworks of Bihar, textile, paper from Rajgir that was used for manuscripts, were also exported to Bengal. Later, optical and scientific instruments — optical glasses, astrolabes and telescopes — were sent. Some products came from Bengal in return, but in smaller quantities. That was mainly copper, lead and silk. The most intense traffic was that between Patna and Calcutta, and included several halts such as Phatua (Fatwa), Bhagalpur, Colgong and Marich (Mircha). The boats sailing the Ganga could carry up to three hundred passengers. The most common boat for carrying goods was the *patela* (or *patera*). A very large military labour force from various low castes was recruited on these boats in order to maintain the safety of the journey. Most of these men were called *Buxariya*, after the name of the Bhojpuri city of Buxar, where most of them were recruited.

Parallel to the selling and transport of these goods, other types of trades were carried out along the fluvial way, and most of the wandering castes of story-tellers and singers were fully involved in these activities: from one part, the trade of cattle, and from another part, the trade of arms. The Bhojpuri country specialised in the making of arms, from the most simple types – bows, arrows, *lathi*s (wooden sticks) – to the most sophisticated ones (rifles, guns, pistols), which was in fact a direct extension of saltpetre extraction. The Noniyas, who specialised in the extraction of saltpetre and the making of arms, could accompany these convoys, but the boldness and mobility of the Nats made them the best partners of the merchant castes for an often dangerous, if not clandestine, trade. As for Bhojpuri cattle, it was so robust that the inhabitants of Bengal wanted them for their ordinary carriages as well as for drawing artillery carts on battle-fields. On those boats going along the Ganga river were also carried all sorts of birds captured in Nepal by Bhojpuri bird catchers for sale in Bengal. These were mynah, parrots, and above all, the famous cocks trained for cock-fighting. For all these purposes, the Nats were much more skilled and freer than the Ahir to come and go. Introduced, through their itinerary, in the literary universe of Bengal, the Nats have borrowed, recomposed and spread, for the sake of the merchants who were patronising them, the story of *Bihula Lakhindar*, which they have mostly spread along the Ganga river and in the eastern part of the Bhojpuri-speaking area.

The story of *Bihula*, which is very famous in Bengal, belongs to the cycle of *Manasamangal*, long poems or versified stories in praise of the female deity of the snakes, Manasa (Sen 1911, 257-76; Dimock 1963, 196-294; Smith 1980; Bhattacharya 1995 and 1996).

According to the original plot of the *Manasa* story, the Devi, born out of Shiva's semen, wants to have her cult honoured by mortals. She reigns over snakes, whose venom she can induce or retrieve, and hence her name *Vishahari* or *Bishahari*, remover of venom. She is much offended in the story for not receiving the cult worship from the Bengali merchant Chando, and so she uses all her forces to destroy the family and wealth of the man who remains Shiva's devotee. After destroying his ships, and having managed to kill his sons, she uses a snake's help to bite the youngest son of the merchant, Lakhindar, who dies on his wedding day. His wife, Bihula, is brave enough to take her husband's corpse on a raft along the Ganga, and gain entrance into Indra's paradise, where she succeeds in having her husband resurrected from the dead. Chando forgives the Devi when his sons come back to life, and her cult is established among the mortals.

ORAL PERFORMANCE OF *BIHULA*

The peculiarity of the *gatha* of *Bihula*, in the Bhojpuri-speaking area, as in the case of the Assamese version of this text, *Padma Purana* (Padma being the name of Manasa) analysed by Nabin Chandra Sharma in this volume, lies in the fact that women can also be the performers of the *gatha*. This is a complete exception in the Bhojpuri oral epic literary field, where the performers are strictly masculine bards. Therefore, not only do the versions differ according to the caste of the singer, but they also differ when the 'feminine' version interferes.

THE TEXT OF THE ORAL PERFORMANCE AMONG THE NAT (OR NETUA) BARDS

When listening to the oral performance of the story of *Bihula* by Netuas, who are the bards of the rich Teli and Baniyas, one realises that it has been completely changed from the original Bengali written text of the *Manasamangal*, or from the Assamese *Padma Purana* and it altogether excludes the presence of the goddess Manasa. It is a story meant to glorify the deeds of a wealthy Bhojpuri trader of Surujpur and his victory over a vicious and jealous Brahman who, being childless, and feeling humiliated by an allusion to this misfortune by the merchant, plans his ruin and the death of his children. But then the story of the saving of her dead husband by Bihula remains quite similar to that of the *Manasamangal*, except that Indra is the only deity involved in Lakhindar's resurrection. Many other differences occur in the text. Neto (Netiya in Bhojpuri) is a man-eating demon, whereas the Bengali Neto is a friend of Manasa created by Shiva. And at the end, the merchant becomes a king. As to Bihula, she is shown more as a trader's wife than as an Indian *pativrata*. As Manasa is totally absent from the plot of the *gatha* of *Bihula* of the Bhojpuri Netua, its performance is not necessarily associated with the cult of Manasa, or the celebration of the *Nag Panchami* festival, as it is in Assam or Bengal. It is sung in the houses of merchants, in open air, on maidans or in the streets of a city.

THE TEXT OF THE ORAL PERFORMANCE OF *BIHULA* AMONG THE KEVAT AND THE DOM

At the time when the means of transporting goods were more limited, the Kevat of Mirzapur were transporting timber and stones from Chunar to Assam and Calcutta and bringing from there coconuts and bamboos to Mirzapur. As with all the mobile castes whose double and eventually triple vocation has already been mentioned, the Kevat also have a role to play in the transmission of oral tradition. The communities of Kevat of Varanasi and Mirzapur specialised in the singing of a genre of song called *kajri*, and in performing the *Bihula*. In their story, Bihula's father is a Bhojpuri trader, whereas Lakhinder's father is a trader from Delhi. The performance of *Bihula* can be heard during the festivals of oral competitions which are organised several times a year on the *ghats*. As can be expected from the occupation of the Kevat, it focuses mainly on the story of the journey of Bihula on her raft along the Ganga.

With the modernisation of boats, and the change in the nature of the goods exported, the profession of the Kevats is deeply threatened. The singing of *Bihula* is a way for them to express their relation to the river and to share it with the public, and to express pride at the knowledge they are transmitting about the taming of the current, about removing the obstacles. It gives them the illusion that at the end of the twentieth century, which marginalises them, they are still the masters of the river.

Also very familiar with the river through their presence on the cremation grounds, are the Doms, who work on the banks of the Ganga and the Gandaki, and have their own tradition of singing *Bihula* with the *ektara*. Here the story focuses on the Dom couple who help Bihula, and in the final episode in which Bihula disguises herself as a Dom. The Doms of the eastern part of the district of Champaran also sing *Bihula*, but they have replaced the character of the wicked Brahman by a witch who harms Lakhindar and Bihula through her evil spells.

THE SINGING OF *BIHULA* BY WOMEN

As already mentioned, *Bihula* is the only Bhojpuri *gatha* to be sung by women. They sing it in groups, calling themselves *nagin* (or wives of the snakes), on the day of *Nag pancami*, while Manasa Devi and the *naga*s are honoured through the selling of popular images, and offerings to the real *naga*s which are captured for the occasion and then released, or to the clay *naga*s which are often placed under sacred trees. On this occasion women go from village to village, from sanctuary to sanctuary, and sleep in the open. It deserves to be mentioned that in the same manner as discussed by Nabin Chandra Sharma in his article on *Padma-Purana, Bihula* can be heard in Muslim sanctuaries, and is common to both Hindus and Muslims. The best example is that of the *Miranji ki dargah* of Vaishali (Bihar), where the festival of *Nag pancami* is celebrated collectively in the presence of a Muslim *pir* as well as that of a Hindu *pujari*, and during which are present all castes including the highest (Champion, 1992).

CHAPBOOKS OF THE STORY OF *BIHULA*

There are three printed versions of this story circulating in chapbooks. One named *Asli Bihula Bishahari sampurn aur khand* is devoted to the cult of Manasa, but it is not so popular in the heart of the Bhojpuri area and is more spread on the eastern border of it. The only really representative versions of the Bhojpuri culture are *Satya Katha Bala Lakhandar* by Thakur Prasad of Varanasi, and *Bihula Bala Lakhandar solho bhag*, published by Loknath Pustakalaya from Calcutta. They are much more detailed than the oral versions regarding the cult of the river and the young merchant Lakhinder, the journey of the raft from *ghat* to *ghat*, and the previous births of the characters.

THE STORY OF *BIHULA* AND THE BHOJPURI IDENTITY

The Bhojpuri story of *Bihula* differs greatly from the Bengali one. First, the interpretations of the *gatha* differ, and the occasions of singing it also differ. Rather than a celebration of Manasa, it is a literary way of linking together the community, territory and all those castes whose occupation is related to the Ganga River and whose income depends on this, a fact which remains as one of the most characteristic ways of life of a great part of the Bhojpuri speakers.

CONCLUSION

It should not escape our mind that the people of Bihar and Uttar Pradesh who are very much attached to the singing and reading of *gatha*s in Bhojpuri or Maithili, are also fighting against the 'imperialism' of Hindi. There is a saying in Bhojpuri that the *Ramlila* of Ramnagar is for the boorish people, but those who are true connoisseurs, true *rasika*s, will listen to *Lorik, Alha-Udal* or *Bihula*. As for the *gatha*, it is much more powerful, according to them, than the simple popular song, because it contains the memory of the past, and the collective memory of a region. And there is another saying in Bhojpuri that:

> The song is nothing to the soul. The *gatha*, and the *gatha* only, is powerful, because it contains the memory of the past, and the glory of the regional heroes. It has a historical dimension, and yet, it transcends time and space.

Now to come to the *gatha*s related to the traders' itineraries from the Bhojpuri and Maithili belts, one can say that they follow the pattern of the Rajput medieval migrations from western to eastern India. We know that between India and Nepal, products such as silk from Varanasi or rice from Patna were exchanged. From Nepal, came yak tails, blankets, wool, herbs and drugs. With Bengal, the trade was mainly concerning timber, glasswork and potteries of Bihar, together with salt and saltpetre. The castes that have transmitted these epics were mainly the *bhainsaha* people, that is to say, people who were bringing packed bullocks on the roads to Nepal, and Kevat (boatmen), who were bringing goods from Mirzapur to Calcutta. In the same way I have stated that epics were not the result of an oral village tradition, but the product of an urban culture. One must also be aware of the fact that along with the silk roads, two other kinds of roads were very important for the penetration of epics towards Bengal and the Nepali Terai:

(a) the roads of the traders of cattle, buffaloes, horses, and also often of the traders of trained birds which could speak, and cocks, famous for cock-fighting.

(b) the roads of the trade of arms. Bihar was well-known for its salt and saltpetre production, and all those castes linked with saltpetre production, the sale of gun powder and the traffic in arms, produced great singers of *gatha*s, and have given birth to a tradition of *gatha*s which is still alive.

One of the most important contributions of the Bhojpuri *gatha*s to the comprehension of Bhojpuri history and culture, is to show the character of the *bideshiya*. That term, so deeply-rooted in the Bhojpuri pathos, refers to the wandering or migrant lonely Bhojpuriya, outside the Bhojpuri-speaking belt not only, in fact, on the roads of *Terai* or Bengal, but outside the Indian subcontinent itself, in the context of the Bhojpuri diaspora in Trinidad, Mauritius or Surinam. Going deeper into the study of *gatha*s I have oriented my inquiry to Mauritius, where there is a concentration of Bhojpuri population. Though the presence of the bard seems to have disappeared there in the modern scenario, possibilities remain of listening to a performance of *Lorik* or *Alha-Udal* by elderly people, and on the stalls of the market of Port-Louis, I saw chapbooks of *Lorik, Alha-Udal* and *Sorthi-Brijabhar* by Loknath Pustakalaya of Calcutta and Thakur Prasad of Varanasi.

Notes

1. *See* Mohan Upreti's contribution in this volume.
2. *See* Shyam Manohar Pandey's contribution in this volume.
3. The source of the Ganga River.
4. The Indian city of Mithila which is a parallel to the Nepali city of Janakpur, and where Sita is supposed to have been born.
5. Very famous place of pilgrimage located in Deogarh and consecrated to Shiva, in the north-eastern part of Bihar.
6. Dhanbad and Bokaro are very important industrial complexes of Bihar.
7. Political leader from an untouchable community. He was the president of the Congress Party from 1969 to 1971 and a long serving minister in the central government.
8. Kunvar Singh is the famous Bhojpuri hero of the Mutiny, who resisted British power in 1857, lost his life in this fight, and has become one of the most popular incarnations of Bhojpuri identity.
9. Vidyapati is the famous Maithili poet of the fifteenth century; Bhikhari is Bhikhari Thakur, very popular Bhojpuri playwright in the 1950s; and Mahendra is Mahendra Mishra, Bhojpuri poet and writer of *purvi songs*. We can therefore notice the anachronic fantasy, gathering in a single song the most favourite personalities of Bhojpuri country.

Bibliography

Ali, Shaqfat, 1994, 'Au Bihar, la police protège les kidnappeurs', *Courrier International*, n° 180, 14-20 avril, p. 26.

Bhattacharya, France, 1986, 'A propos d'une représentation du *Candi Mangal* au Bengale occidental', *Adyatan*, n° 3, pp. 7-26.

———, 1989, *Etude comparée des Mangal Kavya bengali Manasa et Candi*, Thése pour le Doctorat d'Etat es Lettres, Université de la Sorbonne Nouvelle, Paris III, 3 vol.

———, 1995, 'La secte des *Nath et le Manasa Mangal', in* Catherine Champion, ed., *Traditions orales dans le monde Indien. Purusartha*, n° 18, Paris, Editions de l'EHESS, pp. 315-25.

Champion, Catherine, 1991, 'Une approche du soufisme médiéval au Bihar, à travers une etude de litterature orale bhojpuri', in Françoise Mallison, ed., Littératures médiévales de l'Inde du Nord, Paris, Ecole française d'Extrême-Orient, pp. 81-113.

———, 1992, 'Remarques sur l'implantation de la confrèrie Shattari à Vaishali, Bihar', in Alexandre Popovic, ed., *La Transmission du savoir dans le monde musulman périphérique*, Lettre d'information n° 12, mars, pp. 28-38.

———, 1995a, 'Entre la caste et la secte. Un *kissa* du repertoire des *Bhartrihari jogi* musulmans de la region de Gorakhpur', in Marie-Louise Reiniche et Henri Stern, eds., *Les ruses du salut. Religion et politiques dans le monde indien. Purusartha*, n⁰ 17, Paris, Editions de l'EHESS, pp. 25-41.

———, 1995b, 'La geste de Salhes-Cuharmal au Bihar. Problemes de composition', in Nicole Revel et Catherine Champion, eds., *Les litteratures de la voix: les Epopées*. Actes du seminaire 1993-94: Interaction oral/ecrit, Paris, INALCO, Centre de Recherche sur l'Oralité, pp. 49-51.

Choudhary, Radhakrishna, 1970, *History of Muslim Rule in Tirhut,* Varanasi, Chowkhamba Sanskrit Series Office.

Crooke, W., 1974, *The Tribes and Castes of the North-Western India,* Delhi, Cosmo Publications (1st edn. 1896).

Dimock, Edward C., 1963, *The Thief of Love. Bengali Tales from Court and Village*, Chicago, University of Chicago Press.

Downs, Troy, 1992, 'Rajput Revolt in Southern Mirzapur, 1857-58', *South Asia*, vol. XV, n° 2, pp. 29-46.

Frankel, Francine, 1989, 'Caste, Land and Dominance in Bihar. Breaking down the brahmanical order', in M.S.A. Rao and Francine Frankel, eds., *Dominance and State Power in Modern India*, Delhi, Oxford University Press. Vol. I, *Decline of Social Order*.

Gaborieau, Marc, 1978, *Le Népal et ses populations*, Bruxelles, Editions Complexe.

Grierson, George, 1889, 'Selected Specimens of the Bihari Language, Part II, The Bhojpuri Dialect. *The Git Naika Banijarwa', Zeitschrift der Deutschen Morgenlandicher Gesellschafgt*, vol. XLII, part II, pp. 468-524.

Marshall, P.J., 1987, *The New Cambridge History of India. Bengal: the British Bridgehead. Eastern India 1740-1828*, Cambridge, Cambridge University Press.

Maun, Prafulla Kumar Singh, 1968, *Tharu Lok Git*, Varanasi, Deepak Press.

O'Henry, Edward, 1988, *Chant the names of God. Music and Culture in Bhojpuri-speaking India*, San Diego, San Diego State University Press.

Sarkar, Jagadish Narayan, 1978, *Glimpses of Medieval Bihar Economy,* Calcutta, University of Calcutta.

Sen, Jahar, 1977, *Indo-Nepal Trade in the Nineteenth century*, Calcutta, Firma K.L. Mukhopadhyaya.

Sen, Dinesh Chandra, 1911, *History of Bengali Language and Literature,* Calcutta, University of Calcutta.

Servan-Schreiber, Catherine, 1995, *La Transmission du répertoire médiéval bhojpuri. Chanteurs-conteurs ambulants et livrets de colportage: une frontiére de l'identité régionale*. Mémoire presente dans le cadre de l'Habilitation a diriger des recherches, Paris, Ecole des Hautes Etudes en Sciences Sociales.

Smith, William L., 1980, *The One-eyed Goddess. A study of the Manasa Mangal*, Stockholm, Almqvist & Wiksell International, Acta Universitatis Stockholmiensis (Stockholm Oriental Studies, 12).

Tiwari, Uday Narayan, 1960, *The Origin and Development of the Bhojpuri Language*, Calcutta, The Asiatic Society.

5

The Manipuri Folk Epic Khamba-Thoibi
Origin, Growth, Transmission, and Customary Laws

S. Sanatombi

Origin and growth

MANIPURI oral tradition is enriched by the presence of the folk epic *Khamba-Thoibi*. It has been part of the epic repertoire for hundreds of years which can be judged by the fact that King Chingkhu Telheiba of Moirang, who is mentioned in the sung folk epic, was a contemporary of Meidingu Thangbi Lanthaba of Kanglei[1] (Manipur). Meidingu Thangbi ruled in Kangla from 1302 to 1324 according to *Cheitharol Kumbaba* (Court Chronicle) (Ibungohal and Khelchandra 1989:16). However, presence of historical figures does not necessarily make the epic a document of histroy. At best it can be called quasi history. Chingkhu Telheiba, Chingkhu Akhuba (the king's brother) may be historical figures but Khamba and Thoibi are mythological heroes. Both Thoibi and Khamba were sent by God Thangjing[2] (the God of Moirang, and also the guardian of the western part of Manipur) to act out the tragic drama of life and love centering round Moirang. They were not ordinary human beings, and at crucial moments they showed their divine attributes. However, popular belief gives these characters historical credibility. It is believed that the clothes worn by the characters of the epic are the same as preserved in the shrine of Thangjing at Moirang. Besides there are many places in Manipur which are held to be associated with the epic. It is also held that Khamba and Thoibi belonged to the sixth part of the epic cycle known as Moirang *Shaion* stories[3].

The *Khamba-Thoibi* epic was sung, as reported in the *Moirang Kangleirol*,[4] during the time of King Chingkhu Telheiba (Mangoljao 1979:14). It was then customary to sing any eventful happenings during the king's time almost contemporaneously. The *Khamba-Thoibi* epic which was originally a "family or 'closet' tale" (Sanatombi & Meitei 1996:134) had undergone many changes in due course of time in both size and singing style. With the fall of Moirang at the hands of Kanglei King Ningthoukhomba

(1432-67) the story might have migrated to Kangleipak and through it to other states of Manipur[5]. Social, historical and cultural factors have been responsible for the growth of this epic in Moirang. Besides, factors such as topography, location and natural environment have played a significant role. The Loktak Lake, revered as the benign mother, has provided the people of Moirang with an endless supply of food, fish, *heikak, yelang* and rice. It is also responsible for the growth of the epic lore and romances.

In its infant stage the *Khamba-Thoibi* epic might have been sketchy and much shorter than its present size and probably did not undergo much change till Moirang became a part of Kangleipak. A significant change in the growth of the epic took place in 1874, the year in which King Chandrakirti (1850-86) of Manipur made his famous political visit to Silchar to attend a meeting at the invitation of the British Government. That trip is known in Manipuri history as '*Chandrakirti jila changba*' (the State visit of Chandrakirti to Silchar). In those days whenever the king made an outing or went on a tour, *pena* (an indigenous musical instrument of the Meiteis) singers used to accompany him, singing songs[6]. When King Chandrakirti went to Silchar he was accompanied by the royal court *pena* singer, Chanambam Bapu Hanjaba (known as Chanambam Oza), whose job was to please the king by his sweet songs on the *pena*. In fact, the journey was long and mountainous, and the singer ran short of songs as he went on presenting them day and night. Being a man of wit and wisdom he obtained the king's permission to apply the story of *Khamba-Thoibi* to *pena*. The task was successful, and the story grew into a full epic, consisting of over 34,000 lines under the patronage of King Chandrakirti. Since then *pena* has become a popular instrument that always accompanies this epic song. Another remarkable musical change took place during the time of King Churachand Singh (1891-1941) with the introduction of the musical instrument *dholak*. *Dholak* is currently used for the Khongjomparb songs, which are dedicated to the Khongjom War hero, Paona Brajabasi, under whose leadership a fierce battle was fought against the mighty force of the British at Khongjom in 1891. The first application of this instrument on experimental basis was by a singer whose name was Nongthombam Chaoba Singh (also known as Kulijaoba). But the use of the same instrument does not put the two song forms, *Khongjomparb* and the *Khamba-Thoibi* epic under one category, the first being nurtured in the style of classical Hindustani music, *Nata Sankritana* and traditional folksong, and the second derived from the original *pena* style.

Thus it is evident that the growth and development of this oral epic of Manipur from its budding stage to full flowering have been solely due to the creative vision, imaginative faculty and improvisation skill of the bards, both known and unknown. Their ability to collate, expand, interpolate and embellish cannot be questioned, and this ability varies from singer to singer. Ultimately this becomes the deciding factor of the many versions of the epic *Khamba-Thoibi* available today.

There is another development, introduced by a few Britishers posted in Manipur in the nineteenth and twentieth centuries, that can be witnessed at the level of the written text. The earliest ever known written record of this story appeared in Major W. McCulloch's book, *Account of the Valley of Munnipore and of the Hill Tribes* (1859). He writes thus:

> The tale of Khamba and Thoibee, sung by their [Meiteis] eesiesukpa or bards, never fails, with a popular singer, to rivet attention. The scene of this tale and the place where it was originally sung is Moirang. The hero and heroine are persons said to have flourished hundreds of years ago. . . . Thoibee is regarded as a goddess, and that Khamba was a man of giant proportion, is held to be incontestable. . . . The singers of the adventures of Khamba and Thoibee accompany their songs with the notes of the pena, the solitary musical instrument of Munnipore. . . .
>
> – McCulloch 1859:26-7

From what McCulloch has written it is confirmed that this epic has been sung with the accompaniment of *pena* for centuries. After McCulloch, we only find some sketchy references to the epic made by R. Brown and E.W. Dun in their books, *Statistical Account of the Native State of Manipur* (1874) and *Gazetteer of Manipur* (1886) respectively. Another Englishman who made a notable introduction of the story to the English speaking world is T.C. Hodson. He not only gives the full text of the story in prose stretching over 18 pages but also includes 53 notes and explanations in his book, *The Meitheis* (1975:134-54). Among the Manipuris who presented the story of *Khamba-Thoibi* in prose form in Manipuri was Haodeijamba Cheitanya. His book entitled, *Masina Khamba Thoibigi Warini* (this is the story of Khamba Thoibi) (1899) was published in Calcutta because he was exiled from Manipur for his radical outlook. However, the real monumental work of high poetic quality appeared only in 1964, the year in which Hijam Anganghal Singh's *Khamba-Thoibi Sheireng* (The poetry of Khamba-Thoibi) came out posthumously. Anganghal (1892-1943), a court scribe, took about five years to transcribe the *Khamba-Thoibi* oral epic set to *pena* rhythm. He accomplished the herculean task of writing down the story in actual *pena* style, each line having seven iambic heptameter. He wrote down over 34,000 lines heard by him from his Guru Chungkham Manik Singh, a court singer of great repute. The epic poetry, thus, in its written form, consists of 43 cantos and 1270 pages covering the story from the birth of Khamba to his wedding. It reminds one of the Finnish national poets, Elias Lonnrot who created the *Kalevala* "epic cycle from a mass of scattered folk verses" (Dorson 1978:2). Anganghal too, can be called the Lonnrot of Manipur who could place a folk version of the "National Romantic Legend of Manipur" (Chatterji 1974:159), that is the *Khamba-Thoibi* epic, before the public in a formidable form and style.

All this reflects the development of the Manipuri oral epic *Khamba-Thoibi* over the years. Furthermore, in the recent years academic interest in this oral epic has been aroused adding another dimension to the epic in question. This helps in the interpretation and exploration of different perspectives of the epic using modern canons of literary criticism.

A brief synopsis of the epic

The action of the epic centres round the characters of Khamba and Thoibi. Khamba is an orphan; at his birth his father, Puremba beat the war drum out of joy, and that cost him his life. Ngangkhaleima, his mother, too, died of sorrow at the death of her husband. Khamba now had no one but his sister Khamnu by name to look after him. Their childhood days were a long tale of sorrows, suffering, poverty and humiliation, though they were helped at times by their father's friends, Thonglen and Kabui Salang Maiba. In his adolescent period Khamba met Thoibi, a girl of unparalleled beauty, the daughter of Jubaraj Chingkhu Akhuba, who was the younger brother of Chingkhu Telheiba, king of Moirang. Their meeting crystallised into true love, that was tested time and again through many ordeals. The affair invited the jealousy of Nongban, a nobleman's son, who had an overwhelming influence on Thoibi's father. Nongban's image as a champion of Moirang was considerably effaced due to the sudden rise of Khamba. He was defeated by Khamba in all open contests and national games thereby making his chances of getting Thoibi as a prize retreat in the background. He knew that he could not defeat his rival, Khamba by fair means. So he resorted to evil designs. He tried to get Khamba killed by making him catch a dreaded bull, followed by a foot race competition and an arrow shooting game. Khamba was tied to the foot of an elephant and dragged, thereby putting his life in peril. However, through the intervention of gods, goddesses and Thoibi, Khamba came out victorious each time. This shocked and angered Nongban and Chingkhu Akhuba, whose mind was poisoned by the villain against Khamba. Though Thoibi's father knew the real worth of Khamba's virtues, but much as he liked them, he could not think of Khamba marrying his daughter because he was conscious of the social position he enjoyed and Khamba's lack of it. However the Last Judgment was yet to arrive: It was the verdict of God Thangjing. A man eating tiger appeared from nowhere at the crucial moment. It was decided that the one, who among these two killed the tiger would be married to Thoibi. In the last trial Nongban was defeated. Khamba killed the tiger. He and Thoibi were united. However their earthly union was short. An error of judgement brought their earthly existence to an end.

Transmission of the epic

An examination of the process of transmission of the Manipuri oral epic *Khamba-Thoibi* sheds a good deal of light on the various ways in which this epic is/has been transmitted. The whole process of transmission may be grouped as under: verbal, non-verbal, and cultural memory. Bards, singers, folk plays, and recently radio, T.V., films, cassettes, dance, painting, serials in daily papers, and the particular places with which the epic events and characters are associated directly or indirectly serve as tools of transmission of the epic. Of these the role taken by the bards for hundreds of years is of prime importance. This epic occupies a distinctive place in Manipuri folklore so far its transmission is concerned. It is seldom narrated in prose as is done in the case of other folktales. It is sung, and singing is done by trained and professional singers. The transmission through the singers is not necessarily vertical, that is from father to son or/and within the family. Nor is there a special caste or clan which carries the story as is done in some parts of India, for example, the epic of Koti and Chennaya (Tulu) "is sung by members of the Parva caste, a low untouchable caste of sweepers." (Claus 1981:15-16) In Manipuri society any member can become a singer of the epic if he or she so desires. To become a professional singer, however, one has to learn from a Guru. The training period often lasts about ten years, and the apprenticeship is marked by austerity. There is another kind of restriction also: women as per social custom do not sing the story on *pena.* They use *dholak* instead. A clear picture of this method of transmission is shown in the table on page 68.

The transmission of the epic has taken a new turn in the recent times with the advancement of electronics media, like the radio and the T.V. The All-India Radio Imphal Station broadcastes a programme on the epic song almost every evening for half an hour or so either with the accompaniment of *pena* or *dholak*. Similar programmes are shown on television also occasionally. These programmes along side the real singing performance by a number of bards have popularised the epic story among the masses. Besides, the epic has been filmed very recently based on Anganghal's epic poetry, *Khamba-Thoibi Sheireng*. This, along with audio-taped cassettes and folk plays especially the *jatra*s, enhances the transmission process. Further, the *Khamba-Thoibi* dance in the *Laiharaoba* festival of the Meiteis, and the renewed interest in the areas and places where Thoibi went and left her imprint do certainly act as reminders of the cultural past of which this epic forms an important component. Thus, the transmission of a folk epic takes place in many forms, shapes and versions, depending on how the narrative exists in a culture. Dorson says: "The narrative may be sung, chanted, recited, acted out, danced, or presented in a combination of these ways." (Dorson 1978:4)

Mobility of the bards

There is a widespread mobility of the epic singers from one place to another, and from one village to another in Manipuri society. The popular singers get invitation on all days of the week or month. About twenty years ago *Pena* and *Khongjom-parba* songs were the very items for recreation. At times at a particular place singing session

SL. No.	Name of singer/ Professional Name	Sex	Date of birth/death	Place of (1) birth (2) settlement	Father-son transmission	Trained by professional singer	Literate/illi-terate	Instrument held: pena/ dholak	Singing the epic in full or not	Remarks
1.	Shvi Chungkham Koireng (Chungkham Manik)	M	b. 1875-1958	(1)Charangpat (2)Khurai, Imphal	Father, a court *pena* Singer	Trained by his father, Ch. Tondra, a *pena* singer in the court – at a young age	Illiterate	pena	In full	Could sing other ballads
2.	Heisnam Ibomcha Singh (Uyan Ibomcha)	M	b. 1931-1989	(1) Uyan	Father, a *pena* singer	Trained by his father, Oza Parijat, Koijam Chaoba & age of Ch. Manik – from the age of 10	Semi-literate	pena	In full	Awarded by (1) Dr. Rajendra Prasad, President of India (2) Pt. J. Nehru, PM, India.
3.	Ningthoukhongjam Khunjao	M	b. 1915-1992	(1) Pheiyeng	No	Trained by Angom Udoi Singh, Angom Lolei, Rupo Singh Nungoi Mera & Uyan Ibomcha – at the age of 15	Semi-literate	pena	In full	
4.	Wangkheimayum Thambalngou Singh	M	b. 1926	(1) Lamdeng	No	Trained by Y. Kanhai, Oza Gopal, Y. Tombi	Semi-literate	pena	In full	Presently Asstt. Visiting guru, J.N. Dance Akademi, Imphal
5.	Heisnam Iboton Singh (Thanga Mangoljao)	M	b. 1911	(1) Thanga (2) Imphal	No	Apprenticed to N. Kulijaoba, Kh. Deva Singh, M. Chaoba Singh – at 8 years	Semi-literate	dholak	In full	Can sing all Moirang Kanglei stories
6.	Smt. Thangjam Ibeni Devi	F	b. 1927	(1) Wangkhei Leikai	No: father was a famous singer, but died young	Trained by Th. Krishnamohon, T. Tombi & Tona	Semi-literate	dholak	In full	Historical ballad singer, Leirol, *Ramayana*, *Maha-bharata* singer
7.	Smt. Mani Devi	F	1932	(1) Lilong Chajing	No	Apprenticed to Smt: Th. Ibeni Devi	Semi-literate	dholak	In full	Can sing other ballads, *Ramayana* and *Maha-bharata*

continued for 5/10 days. Twenty days', or a month long performance was also a regular phenomenon. Singing was mainly done in the evening for four or five hours, and since the singing session came to an end at 10 or 11 pm generally the singer spent the night at the place of the performance if the distance between his house and the place of performance was considerable. Singer's entire responsibility was borne by the host family, which invited him. However, singer made his own arrangements for travelling to and fro from the place of the performance. The singer not only went to the Meitei villages in Manipur but also served people outside the state in the Meitei inhabited areas in Assam and Tripura.

Customary laws

The singing of the epic involves certain laws of its own. As the epic is very long the person or family or audience, according to the taste, chooses an episode or episodes to be sung. The choice of the narrative part(s) rests with the one who invites the singer, but even then the singer has some say in it. Each singing session normally lasts 3 to 4 hours.

There are no hard and fast rules regarding the occasion or time of performance. Performance on such occasions as birth (the sixth day *swasti puja* after the birth of a child), marriage and marriage related events, family rites, community and seasonal festivals, after harvesting of crops can take place. There is no restriction on the nature of the occasion on which this epic may be sung. In this regard it is closer to other epics like the Yugoslav than to some typical Indian epics like the *Siri*. "Epic poetry", says A.B. Lord, "in Yugoslavia is sung on a variety of occasions" (Lord 1981:14). Whereas the *Siri* epic singing strictly observes a particular time of the year. Lauri Honko in his "Studying Oral Epics" writes: "There is no doubt that the annual Siri festival arranged during the full-moon nights in March constitutes an authentic context for the Siri epic" (Honko 1993:196). However, the performance is governed by some norms and social customs. The singers do not come to a place on their own to perform, entertain and collect money from the audience. A singing performance is the outcome of a formal invitation by a responsible person. Invitation is sent on three pieces of *pan* (betal leaf) placed on a round banana leaf. The date and place of performance, the cash payment to be made are discussed at the time of the invitation. Presently the fee demanded per performance ranges from Rs. 500 to Rs. 600 depending upon the distance.

Often the place chosen for the performance is the outhouse in front of a traditional Manipuri house facing east. The outhouse is called *shangoi*, and it faces the house. The singer sits facing the house or the north. The seat he occupies is slightly raised, and is often a cot or a table covered with a white cloth. Before he sits he prostrates before his seat, and repeats the same before the audience, who also reciprocate in the same manner.

The kind of dress the singer wears depends on the kind of instrument he uses, *pena* or *dholak*. The *pena* singer is traditionally dressed in a chequered *dhoti*, known as *khamenchatpa*, a velvet shirt, a white turban, bracelet and a white girdle. On the other hand the *dholak* player wears a white *dhoti*, a white or light yellow shirt, in case of a male performer. But a woman performer wears the traditional *phanek* (a long waist cloth tucked in at the waist or under the armpits) and a beautifully embroidered thin wrap, called *wangkhei phidup*. Since the woman singer's *phanek* should not touch the *dholak*, which is a taboo, a clean white cloth is wrapped around the knee.

The composition of the audience is always a mix of men, women and children. Men folk occupy the right side and women the left side from the position of the house. There are no age and sex restrictions. Young mothers go with their new born babies. People belonging to different clans, communities and religions have a free access to such gatherings. The same does not apply to all parts of the world. Lord cites one example: "The taverns are entirely male establishments, whether the district is predominantly Moslem or not. Neither Moslem nor Christian women are ever allowed in these places. This is a man's world." (Lord 1981:14)

In the villages in Manipur such singing events are a source of entertainment, and not only men, but also women from as far as three km come at night to hear the epic singer narrate his story. Women in Manipuri society have a place of their own.

Singers are highly respected in Manipuri society. The singer-audience rapport is very encouraging. The elderly village folk and even the literate people listen to the singer very attentively. They appreciate the narrative movement, rhythm, steps, high and low pitch, the beating sound of the drum and so on. When they are moved, the verbal expression, *bhalo* comes almost instinctively from their heart. They encourage the singer by giving him a cloth or currency notes of five or ten rupees. The singer also knows the sentiment and traditional customs of the audience. He respects them and sings keeping in mind the prescribed social norms. He skilfully avoids the episode of the tragic death of both Khamba and Thoibi. Nobody likes the catastrophic end of the story, and especially the family or persons who invite him feel that if the story ends tragically a spell is cast on them. So as a practice the singer chooses to end the story with the marriage of Khamba and Thoibi.

The paper has shown various aspects of origin and transmission of the Manipuri folk epic *Khamba-Thoibi*. A number of other issues concerning narrative repertoire, gender, performance based documentation, etc., may be thought of for further research.

Notes

1. *Kanglei*: the present capital of Manipur was called Kanglei in the early history of Manipur. It was the capital of the Ningthouja clan, then an independent princely state.
2. *Thangjing*: the God of Moirang. Every year in the Meitei month of *Kalen* (April/May) *Laiharaoba* festival in honour of this god is performed. This is the god behind the *Khamba-Thoibi* epic action. *Khamba-Thoibi* dance is the main feature of Thangjing *haraoba* an annual festival to please the god.
3. *Shaion* stories: the epic cycles. In all there are seven cycles each represented by an incarnation of man and woman, who serve as the hero and heroine. Khamba and Thoibi were the sixth incarnation.
4. *Moirang Kangleirol*: the chronological history of Moirang.
5. Before Manipur came under the rule of King Charairongba (1697-1709), it comprised seven independent states each representing one of the seven clans (Ningthouja, Mangang, Luwang, Khuman, Moirang, Chenglei and Khaba Nganba).
6. This fact has been recorded by T.C. Hodson in his book *The Meitheis*: "The Penakhongba accompanies the Raja and Rani on their travels, and plays the *Pena*." (Hodson 1975:69) This book was originally published in 1908. There had been a good number of *pena* singers in the king's court where there was a *Pena loishang* (Institute of *Pena*, established by King Pamheiba *alias* Garibaniwas (1709-48).

References

Brown, R., 1874, *Statistical Account of the Native State of Manipur*, Calcutta, Government Printing.

Chatterji, Sunity Kumar, 1974, *Kirata-Jana Krti*, Calcutta, The Asiatic Society, 2nd rev.edn.

Claus, Peter J., 1981, 'Indian Folk Epics' in *Indian Folklore I*, Mysore, CIIL, 6-21.

Dorson, R.M., 1978, 'Introduction', in Oinas, Felix J. (ed), *Heroic Epic and Saga: An Introduction to the World's Great Folk Epics*, Bloomington, Indiana University Press, 1-6.

Dun, E.W., 1886, *Gazetteer of Manipur*, Delhi, Vivek Publishing Company, 1981 reprint.

Hodson, T.C., 1908, *The Meitheis*, Delhi, B.R. Publishing Corporation, 1975 reprint.

Honko, Lauri, 1993, 'Studying Oral Epics' in *Nordic Frontiers*, 195-200.

Lord, Albert B., 1981, *The Singer of Tales,* Cambridge, Harvard University Press, 4th edn.

McCulloch, Major W., 1859, *Account of the Valley of Munnipore and of the Hill Tribes*, Calcutta, Bengal Printing Company Ltd.

Oinas, Felix J., (ed.), 1978, *Heroic Epic and Saga*, Bloomington, Indiana University Press.

Sanatombi, S. & M. Mani Meitei., 1996, 'A Folkloristic Study on the Manipuri Folk Epic Khamba-Thoibi' in *Eurasian Studies Yearbook*, 68: 133-42.

Singh, H. Anganghal, 1964; 1986. *Khamba-Thoibi Sheireng* (The Poetry of Khamba-Thoibi), Imphal, Chitra Press.

Singh, H. Mangoljao., 1979, 'Khamba-Thoibigi Wari Likhun Amasung Masigi Honglakliba Masak' (Origin of the story of Khamba-Thoibi and its Changes), in *Wakhal* Vol. 32-33, 14-16.

Singh, L. Ibungohal & Singh, N. Khelchandra, (eds.), 1989, *Cheitharol Kumbaba* (Court Chronicles), Imphal, Manipur Sahitya Parishad, 2nd edn.

Part II

Composition and Socio-Economic Context

6

Mopin Myth
An Ecological Epic

A.K. Das

Land: Against the backdrop of the lofty snow-clad outer ranges of the eastern Himalaya, the Siang River descends through a succession of hills to the valley to become the mighty Brahmaputra River. This rugged terrain is interspersed with numerous rivers and streams with luxuriant undergrowth. In the upper reaches there are steep gorges and narrow valleys. Massive ranges such as Pari, Bayor, Yordi Kadi and Mobuk are the landmarks of this terrain. The Donilipik is the highest peak in Central Arunachal Pradesh.

This region is conveniently divided into upper Siang district and lower Siang district for administrative purposes, having headquarters at Along and Pasighat respectively. This area is interesting from the point of view of not only topographical variations but also ecological diversity and corresponding life-style of the ethnic groups eking out their livelihood from time immemorial.

People: This region is the home of the Adis, a blanket term for a number of ethnic groups. Culturally and linguistically, these communities could be divided under two broad groups — the Galloic and Padamic. Under the first group fall the Gallong, Ramo, Bokar and Pailibo while in the second group are Padam, Miniyong, Pasi, Pangi, Shimong, Bori, Ashing and Tangam.

The Gallongs are one of the formidable and major groups of the Adis. They are concentrated in the middle hills range of the upper Siang, in and around Basar and Along river valleys. Gallongs are keen agriculturists and practice slash and burn type of cultivation locally called *jhum*. The agricultural cycle of the Gallong is intimately connected with their cosmological concepts and the world-view. The entire life-style of the Gallongs is somehow attuned to the annual agricultural cycle punctuated with rites, rituals, and celebrations at regular intervals. *Mopin* is one such celebration connected with agriculture and the cycle of seasons. The cultural dimensions of *Mopin* reveal multiple facets of creative acts of the Gallong.

The genesis of *Mopin* among the Adis is recorded in a typical myth handed down generation after generation by the word of mouth and the memory of the *miri* (traditional rhapsodists) in an ancient verbal literary expression popularly known as *abang*. *Abangs* are the Adi store-house of indigenous knowledge. *Abang*s are tribal epics, which weave their stories with the warf and weft of people's real life encounters with the mysteries of nature, as well as their interaction with the social world.

Mopin myth: The myth connected with Mopin is a myth of creation. In this myth Abo-Tani, the first man according to Gallong belief, was restored to his original form by Talo-Tenya in *doiyni-giri* (realm of sun) at the instance of Jiku-Miku, the benevolent deity, after he was killed by his brother Taki. The myth rolls through various happenings and ordeals till its culmination in the propitiation of Mopin by Abo-Tani for prosperity and good crops with the help of the first priest *doiyni-jilo*.

The entire structure of the myth could be conveniently put into five different sequences delineating the interplay of human, natural and cosmic factors.

The sequences are as follows:

Sequence One

The first man Tani and his brother Taki were born out of the union of the sky and earth (*sisi*). According to the Adi notion the sky and earth represent two facets of the known and mystic quality of nature (*prakriti*). They are animated, living and dynamic.

Sequence Two

The second sequence is build on the mundane human behaviour of love and hate. The natural jealousy of the younger brother Taki towards his elder brother Tani is well represented in this episode. As the sequence progresses the jealousy turns into a strong hatred in the mind of Taki. He hatches a plan to annihilate Tani. He persuades Tani to accompany him to the Siang River for rowing. There, Taki pushes Tani under the waterfall. Tani's body while floating down the river is caught in a *takom* (fish trap) placed there by Taki. To ensure a complete destruction of Tani's body, Taki commits the act of cannibalism at a place where the sky and earth meet. However, Taki preserves the eyes of Tani on a *rapko* (hanging platform) over the hearth. The story could have ended here with Taki becoming the 'first man'. But this was not destined. The divine intervention takes place leading to further events.

Sequence Three

The act of killing and eating the body of Tani, although done in utmost secrecy, somehow alerts Jiku-Miku, a deity who lives in the sky. He tries to find the body of Tani. He prepares a talisman (*labur*), and ties it to a bamboo segment (*jirodi-bodi*) by means of a thread (*kebo yasik*). To this he attaches the feathers from a fowl's leg. The *labur* is then thrown into the river asking it to guide the deity to Tani's body. The talisman gets entrapped in the same *takom* in which earlier Tani's body was caught. Taki is found resting at the same place. The deity's suspicion falls on Taki. Taki lies to Jiku-Miku. The deity, however, is not convinced and burns *koni koma* (bamboo shavings) and fowl's feather in a fire to detect the lie. The smoke is directed towards Taki. Taki jumps up on seeing the smoke. Having being thus caught, Taki confesses and hands over the eyes of Tani to Jiku-Miku. There is a turn of events here. The episode of Jiku-Miku does not end on the earth but culminates in heaven.

Sequence Four

The *abang* takes us to the cosmological act of re-creation of the Abo Tani from the five elements of nature in *doiyni-giri* (realm of sun). Jiku-Miku's involvement in the myth should have come to an end with the recovery of the slain Tani's eyes and handing them over to Talo Tanya, another important deity. Since Jiku-Miku is the hero of the oral epic his involvement in the re-creation of Tani continues. Jiku-Miku is asked to mould the image of Tani out of bees' wax, which is procured by Doiyni's two daughters from the forest. Jiku-Miku, as directed, prepares the image of Tani and applies *kamsi-kangi* (a kind of clay) on the mould and finally puts the eyes to the image. Jiku-Miku's role ends here. The entire event of re-creation would have passed just like any other happening. But at this stage a tension is created between the deities. The spirits and deities raise doubt about the actual period required for casting. It is felt that unless the cast is opened after the expiry of a fixed time, things may go wrong. Besides, the deities also fear that the sex of Tani may change in the process.

Sequence Five

The final episode of the oral epic culminates with a happy ending after a period of 12 days. Tani appears as a child boy. This brings happiness in *doiyni-giri*. All the deities and spirits bestow *jili bong* (boons) on Tani and give him weapons, seeds and other implements for his sustenance on earth as had been promised by them. The most important boon bestowed on Tani was by *Doiyni* (sun) who assures sunshine for the plants to grow, crops to ripen and animals to increase. Here for the first time in the epic appears Mopin, the god of wealth. His role in this myth is limited to that of a custodian of the boons that are to be given to Tani when he would, upon becoming an adult, offer sacrifice to propitiate him. This is done by Tani with the help of *nyibu* (priest). He receives all the boons from Mopin. This is the genesis of the great sacred festival of the Adis.

Mopin ritual: Propitiation of Mopin, generally at the beginning of the cropping cycle, is directly or indirectly connected with the cycle of seasons.

Omens are read and if the indications are favourable, a *kebang* (village council) is held in the *dere* (community hall). The elders sitting in the *kebang* decide the date for the ritual and select the beasts such as *mithun* (bos frontalis), pigs and chickens for the sacrifice. They also identify the donors of these beasts and consult the *nyibu* (priest) for the ritual proceedings. The *Mopin* ritual is celebrated with festivities lasting up to five days. The *Mopin* ritual is structured in the following manner:

(i) *Dipe-nam*: The rite of *dipe-nam* is performed as a prelude to the main rituals one day ahead. In this rite, the images of Mopin (the main deity) and Doli (deity connected with rain) are re-created by traditional means with bamboo sticks, bamboo shavings and leaves of sacred trees. Images are installed in the sacred site and purified by the *lore-lomen-pengam* ritual performed by *nyibu* (priest).

(ii) *Yame rutum*: This is a social function involving an active participation of the villagers in the celebration on the eve of the ritual. The village elder goes around the village meeting individual families and inviting them to the *dere* next morning for the festivities.

(iii) *Invocation of Mopin*: For five consecutive days at the place of the ritual, the *nyibu* (priest) goes on chanting and humming *mantra*s and propitiating Mopin with various acts. The villagers in the meantime stock-on piles of rice, fish, meat, *apong* (rice-beer) in the *dere* for the grand feast to be held later at night. Invocation of Mopin continues throughout the night and the priests remain busy in their religious activities. Villagers engage themselves in the organising of the feast and other such activities.

(iv) *Yudmlik-nam*: This is one of the important ceremonies in the propitiation ritual of *Mopin*. A cow, *mithun* is sacrificed on the second day of the celebration. The cow, *mithun* is carefully tied to a scaffold erected near the altar. Her head is smeared with the rice-powder soaked in *apong* (rice-beer). The priest offers the sacrifice of *mithun* with prayers seeking blessings for the people of the village. Apology is offered to the *mithun* for cutting short her life and she is asked to be happy as she is going to join her ancestors in the other world. After the sacrifice *apong* mixed with her blood is poured on the images and collected in a pit called *komar*. Along with the *mithun* a fowl is also sacrificed. After the sacrifice the women receive *rili-bong* — a kind of blessing from Mopin. The meat of the sacrificed *mithun* is taken to the *dere* for the community feast that subsequently follows.

(v) *Poper-tingum*: As soon as the sacrifice is over, the priests initiate dance performance. This dance performance is accompanied by a rhapsody called *poper-tingum* narrating an ancient myth. Subsequently, villagers start dancing in separate groups, shouting 'Hey Mopin' at regular intervals. The dancing is interrupted after some time by a girl who smears rice powder on the priests. This gives the signal to everyone for starting the act of applying rice-powder on one another's face (except relatives) ignoring the age and status. This fun and frolicking is followed by a big community feast in the afternoon. Guests are entertained later in individual houses. Priests take time off to visit the house of the person who kills the *mithun*.

During the night priests continue the prayer and ritual singing. In the meantime blood and hair of the sacrificed *mithun*, bristles of the pig slaughtered at the altar (*komi coma*), feathers of the fowl and bamboo shavings are distributed to the people, which they preserve as divine charms.

(vi) *Taboo* (*Gena*): The third day of the festival is the day of general feasting, marked by the distribution and consumption of 'Mopin cake', a kind of delicacy made of rice-powder. At mid-day a community feast is held. In this feast, the meat of the sacrified *mithun* is served. The fourth day is the special day for priests. Priests return to their homes with all the food and rice-beer received during the ritual. They serve this to all those who visit them. After this, usual chanting and other festivities continue. On this day the villagers confine themselves within the village, as it is a taboo to go outside the boundaries of the village.

Rigga: This ceremony consists of collective cleaning of the village off the litter accumulated during the festival and subsequent farewell to Mopin. The farewell to Mopin is performed by priests along with the village people at the outer boundary of the village by offering food and drink to the departing deity. The five-day festival thus comes to an end with a farewell feast. Priests take off their official robes and become ordinary villagers again.

Ponung and the Miri: In the *Mopin* festival the most significant outward expression of joy is manifested in the dance accompanied by *ponung* songs and *abang* recitation. The *ponung* dance is characterised by the presence of the *miri* — the rhapsodists who lead the girls to dance with a *yoksa* (a kind of sword) which keeps the rhythm of the dance through its typical jerking sound. The girls dance in a circle shoulder to shoulder, clapping hands, sometimes swaying their right foot with stooping body and locking their arms with each other to the accompaniment of repeated refrains of the chorus. There are several permutations and combinations of the movement of the foot, swaying of the body and the movement of hands.

Conclusion

Mopin myth in its holistic framework is not a mere literary expression but an integrated interactive 'institution', in which the sacred world and the secular world of the Gallongs coalesce. The sacred origin and nature of society and its practices are reaffirmed through the 'institution'.

The *abangs, ponung* songs, *poper-tingum*, cosmology of *Doiyni-Polo* (sun-moon God) and emergence of *Abo Tani*, the first man born of *sisi* (earth), together constitute the oral expressive tradition of the Gallong. The dance performances and the *abang* recitals during *Mopin* integrate the secular, oral and artistic traditions.

The *Mopin* ritual, which has its genesis in the creation myth, reflects the man-nature-cosmos relationship. The re-creation of the images of the deities, sacrifice of the animals, purification rites, and taboos are the sacred manifestations of these relations.

7

The Golden Vine
Chanted Narratives From the Land of the Seven Huts

Desmond L. Kharmawphlang

THE present myth under consideration was never recorded in a cohesive form before, but existed in fragments as numerous individual tales, in people's memories and books. The myth is recalled by only a few storytellers, and it would be idle to contend that it is the full version, as an exhaustive and a thorough collection has not been attempted yet.

There are two versions of the myth which I collected from two storytellers living in two different remote jungle villages in the Bhoi area of the Khasi Hills, in the State of Meghalaya, in north-east India. The first version was performed by U Di Sing Marin of Pahamsyiem village, on the evening of 22nd and 23rd December, 1991, with a few villagers and myself present.

The second version was told to me on 21st and 22nd April, 1992, by the late U Klan Lyngdoh, the lyngdoh (priest) of Iapngar village, also in the Bhoi area.

The narration of the myth by these two storytellers differ greatly in style, atmosphere, context and also dialectical nuances of the spoken language. Their social positions also differ: while U Di Sing Marin was the village chief and storyteller, the late Klan Lyngdoh was the official priest, a position that fell incumbent on him, after his maternal uncle died. He was well-versed in various rituals of the Khasi indigenous faith, and knowing the myth was part of the job (so to speak).

U Di Sing's performance was solo, but U Klan Lyngdoh's narration was interspersed with additions made by his friend, the Sohblei (lit. Fruit of God or one who clings to God), a performer of sacrifice. Thus, there are portions of joint chanting, especially near the end of the myth.

The atmosphere during the actual recording of the second version of the myth was more laid-back. There were no rituals: only a storytelling session which involved at least two highly skilled tellers. I have fully transcribed and translated the second version and I have it with me. I have transcribed and translated a part (a little bit, really) of U Di Sing's chanting but have been daunted by the formidable imperviousness of the language in which it was performed. The language is Khasi no doubt, but of the Bhoi dialect which is completely different from the dialect generally spoken. There is a boy (aged 9) of Pahamsyiem village who is attending school now and he is starting to get familiar with the dialect of Khasi that I speak, and this happens to be the commanly accepted one (it is the dialect used in schools, colleges, state assembly, etc.). In a year or two, with his help I shall be ready to begin work on the myth and I shall have to definitely rework on the rudimentary attempt I have made (only 7 pages on type-script). The other myth — the one chanted/narrated by U Klan Lyngdoh — is contained in roughly 22 pages on type-script. I had little problem working on this one because the dialect in which it was told is very similar to my own. But both the myths are similar in content because it is common in all parts of my land.

It is to be understood that U Di Sing Marin's chanting assumes a sacerdotal significance, because it is performed for a specific purpose, on a request made by a friend of his, and this required the myth to be narrated, in the course of his divination, which is only possible by chanting. This divination is called *ka shat pyrlein*. To understand this practice one must have an idea about certain aspects of Khasi mythology, which is intrinsic to the religious beliefs and practices of the people, and consequently to the egg-divination. The very act is part of a religious practice, which is conducted with the solemnity and seriousness of a ritual. It is during the performance of this ritual that the golden vine myth, narrated through chanting, emanates.

In order to understand this myth it is essential that one must accept it as basically religious and its subject-matter as the ultimate questions of human existence: Where we and the things in our world come from? Why we are here? And where we are going?

The Khasis have a very elaborate and extensive myth about all these questions and although many folk-tales have sprung up from its distended segments, the myth is in reality one single continuous whole, known to the old, albeit in their localised versions or existing in the diverse dialects spoken in Khasi and Jaintia Hills.

Here, I will briefly sketch the myth connected with man's existence, purpose, and struggle between good and evil.

> In the beginning God created the Universe, and from it, the sun, moon, nature, air, water and fire. The universe then gave birth to earth and stone, and when they emerged, water was displaced, leading to the formation of seas, oceans and rivers. God dwelt in Heaven with his sixteen children or

huts. Then God decreed that seven huts should go to the earth and inhabit its every corner, yet maintain contact with the Heavens by means of a golden ladder placed atop U Sohpetbneng (literally, navel of the skies), a peak to the north of Shillong.

The seven huts flourished on earth and ruled over all of God's creatures. One day, man thought it was time to convene a meeting of all the creatures, so as to discuss an equitable distribution of wealth and resources among all. God asked of man, 'How will you live, how will you eat and earn?' Man replied, 'We will live by earning the truth, according to your word.' *U Thlen*, the serpent, who had long nursed a grudge against man for being his overlord, replied 'My food will be of humankind and my earning will be of riches.' This shocked everyone but the serpent was unrepentant and thus his word came alive. The meeting came to a close without any fruitful discussion.

God summoned the cow who was a council elder and asked him to convey a message to man but the crow, who had already been tempted by the serpent, asked the cow to convey a wrong message. God was enraged at the cow and stripped him [sic.] of his titles, struck the side of his skull until some teeth fell, and sent him to become slave to man. As for the crow, God covered her up in a sooty black pot till she was black all over.

Slowly the serpent started sowing seeds of evil in the world, tempting and corrupting.

Through intermediaries, the serpent told man that if they do not physically cut down the *diengiei* tree, it would cover the entire world and the world would be plunged into darkness. Man, in his gullibility, cut down the tree thus forgetting or neglecting to invoke the power of the Word or Command that God gave him as a weapon to rule over all creation. To seek redress, man proclaimed a dance wherein all the animals were invited. The dance took place, but there was no peace or goodwill among the animals, as they scorned the owl as she was trying to dance, and whispered evil things as the sun and moon danced. The sun, humiliated, decided to go away. The thunder was mad with jealousy at the civet cat because all the animals were praising his swordsmanship. So he borrowed the civet cat's silver sword and after a few steps fled to the clouds and with a hard blow severed the golden bridge linking earth and sky. Meanwhile, the sun had found a cave in which to hide and in she went. The whole world was in an instant plunged into darkness. Some animals went to the cave to entreat the sun to come out but to no avail.

Finally, the cock volunteered to try and on his explicit request, was given fineries to wear, and he went inside the cave and successfully brought out the sun. A compromise was reached between God and man, but man lost his overlordship over animals, except those already in his service.

The first part of the myth is a veritable story of creation and the union of natural forces. The myth of creation is the most significant of all primitive obsessions. The shapeless or formlessness of the universe is suggested in this myth, and it, not unnaturally, reminds us of the chaos and darkness accompanying the myth of creation in the *Bible*. The Khasi myth here firmly establishes that creation can only come about by the process of birth, and the primitive philosopher is compelled to visualise a marriage of some sort. He achieves this by an anthropomorphic exercise whereby the universe (seen in a cosmic extension) is made to wed the earth, and they produce children.

It also tells of the Khasi belief that the entire world was once covered with water and the birth of earth and stones indicates the emergence of solid states and the formation of lakes, inland seas, rivers, etc. Here again we recall to mind the Biblical story of the great deluge.

Having settled and generally flourished, the question of property naturally arises between man and animals. When property is discussed discord is almost always certain to rise, and in this case, the situation is further aggravated by the consuming hate and jealousy the serpent (who now becomes identified with evil) feels for man, whom God has blessed and made ruler of all creation. The central issue of discord is the answer, the serpent gave to God: "My food will be of humankind and my earning will be of riches." Blatantly, the serpent revealed his hatred for man and made no secret that his intention was the destruction of man — and because he refused to take back his words, the words lived. The Khasis believe that once a word has been uttered and not retracted, it cannot be treated lightly; it becomes a force.

The evil slowly spreads and takes possession of the cow next, who falsely bore witness and for that he is penalised by being made slave to man and by losing some of its molar. The crow duped by the serpent's talk about riches was also a partner in the conspiracy to cheat man and for that she is penalised by being made soot-black. The crow/raven trickster-story is uncommonly in wide prevalence all over the world.

We can see that as the myth progresses, the serpent gains allies and agents and that the tiny seed of evil he planted has gradually grown into a shoot and now we can almost see the conflagration between good and evil, imminent. The last victorious temptation comes in the form of an advice through intermediaries that the *diengiei* tree ought to be cut down physically. As a consequence, man, armed with axes and other cutting implements, sets to work on bringing the tree down. This human attempt at physically cutting down the tree is the final rejection of the power of the word, a weapon by which man's authority over all creations is sanctioned.

It is in the nature of things that man, after having strayed, seeks condonation, and there, in the myth, we have him proclaiming a dance whereby all creatures would congregate and in unison, pray for God's forgiveness. The attempt is noteworthy, and the animals heartily participate but the evil had seeped in so deeply that a peaceful dance could not take place. First, the animals scorned and ridiculed the owl who was ungainly on her feet, something they would never have done before. Next, they talked ill of the sun and her brother the moon, and accused them of having incestuous relationship. Next, the thunder, envious of the civet cat and his nimble feet, stole his sword and severed the golden ladder. This last step is the final show of complete repudiation of divine authority. The flight of the sun and moon to a cave to hide is natural to persons wronged against and for this, the whole world suffered as darkness enveloped it. It was only when the cock, adorned with fineries of red and gold and a plumage, entered the cave and beseeched the sun to come out, did light slowly fill the earth again. This is interesting in the sense that the cock's crow always precedes the break of day.

U Di Sing Marin's storytelling fame in his area is rivalled only by another aspect of his power — that of being a tigerman. He is reputed to transform into a tiger once in three years, during a sacred ceremony. He is also an expert in egg divination — the reading of signs by breaking an egg. This is the most common and frequently used augury of the Khasis. The present myth was performed in accompaniment to an egg divination ceremony, which was done for a friend of his. Before getting to the performance, U Di Sing Marin went into an elaborate preparation, mentally and physically. The evening started with casual conversation, while we warmed ourselves by the fire in his hut. There were a few of his friends and liquor (*ka kiad um* — rice beer) was brought in. After an hour of drinking, he asked a young friend of his to prepare a pipe and they all smoked what I suspected to be opium. Then U Di Sing stripped off his loincloth, tied a colourful headband around his head, squatted on his haunches and proceeded.

The things which he used while performing the egg divination were (i) *ka jongkhan* or an egg used for divination, (ii) *ka diplin*, a rectangular wooden slab with a small hollowed projection for keeping soil, (iii) a fistful of red mud, and (iv) rice grains.

He first took the egg in his left palm and rice grains in his right palm, and after blowing on the egg he engaged in a dialogue with the egg, which brought out the myth I recorded. The way in which the story element in the myth was presented was not in a style popular with ordinary hearth-side audiences, because the performance was too intense, too powerful in a totally involved and absorbed way. The listeners were not very much in tune with the performance, because my friend, U Di Sing did not mean it to be entertaining.

All the while he was occupied with the egg, smearing it with red mud, rolling it in his palm and placing it on the *diplin*. He urged the egg to show him the signs which would manifest themselves in *ka lar* and *ka kem*, broken egg shells lying respectively on their convex and concave sides.

U Di Sing Marin's narration is fraught with terms and usages, sounds and exclamations, which are impervious to direct translation and I have reasons to believe that many are esoteric. I have also rendered some 'sense' translation, which is opposed to 'meaning' translation. The point I am trying to make is that one has to be there to even begin to absorb the telling power.

The atmosphere of the performance is charged, with meaning, (not necessarily word meanings) coming to surface, and all the elements — viz., word power, songs, action, gestures, looks, prayers — inter-locking into a total experience.

I have named the myth, 'The Golden Vine' myself because of the dominance of this particular object, throughout the myth, in its pictorial and symbolic aspects. I have left Khasi onomatopoeia untranslated; otherwise a sense infringement might be effected. The translation of the text is far from being perfect due to some very obvious reasons. I find it impossible to match the interest of the original, as extending meanings into different language necessitates the throttling of the poet's/storyteller's voice. The translated text is also bereft of some very elemental supports such as actual vocal rendering with all its accompanying pitches, pauses, gestures, body language, etc. — indeed, the drama that the performance veritably is.

The recording of the performance was possible, not because I was able to impress upon U Di Sing Marin the necessity of performing for me for whatever use I may have of his powers. No, I approached him as a learner, and after a long time, was accepted as a friend of Pahamsyiem village.

8

The Dayak Epics of Second Burial

KMA M. Usop

Historical background

1. The Dayaks or the Proto-Malays of Borneo (Kalimantan as termed by Indonesia) are considered to be among the early (around 4000 BC) Mongoloid Austronesians who migrated from East Asia to Southeast Asian archipelago and some of whom settled in the most inland parts of the island which is the biggest in the archipelago. The later East Asian migrants (in AD 1000) were the Malays or the Deutro-Malays who settled themselves in most parts of the coastal areas. The present position is that the Dayaks are encircled by the Malays.

Biological, lingual and cultural changes took place in the western parts of Indonesia since those Austronesians mixed with the existing Austroloids resulting in the dark brown skin of most Indonesians and the widespread Malay language and culture. With their cultural, religious and ethnical differences, they formed a nation of 'unity and diversity' (*bhinneka tunggal ika*) which has been undergoing a dynamic process of integration.

Contact with India has been recorded to have taken place in Kalimantan, especially at the gold-deposited coastal regions, even before AD 400. Indian cultural elements of Brahmanism were introduced to the small coastal kingdoms as well as to some dominant inland tribal chiefs. The Taruma Kingdom of Java, established around AD 400 or 500, had absorbed Hindu influences. So did the kingdoms of Brunei of North Borneo and Kutai (AD 400) of East Kalimantan leaving the oldest inscriptions in Indonesia. Some archaeological artifacts like *lingam* and *yoni, Nandi and Hindu gods* were found in Kalimantan: Buddha and Brahma statues of AD 1000 in West Kalimantan and at Kombeng caves of Mahakam River (East Kalimantan) and also those of AD 1200 at Santubong and Limbang (Sarawak).

Most of the coastal kingdoms, including Brunei, came under the great Hindu Kingdom of Majapahit in the fourteenth century. The existence of Hindu kingdoms of Berau in East Kalimantan, Sambas and Sukadana of West Kalimantan, Banjarmasin of South Kalimantan and Kotawaringin of Central Kalimantan has been recorded. At that time, China was still dominant in trade: a Chinese colony of Ming dynasty was established in AD 1375 by the Kinabatangan River of Sabah (North Borneo). Majapahit influences declined after it fell under the Demak Sultanate in sixteenth century.

More than 3 million people now live in North Borneo (Brunei Darussalam and Malaysian Sabah and Sarawak) and more than 10 million in Indonesian Kalimantan. Most people of Kalimantan are Muslims : in Central Kalimantan, for example, about 66 per cent of its 1.5 million people are Muslims (about half of them are Dayaks), 15 per cent Christians (mostly Dayaks) and 17 per cent (Dayaks) Kaharingans (registered and integrated under Hindu Religion since 1980 by the name of Hindu Kaharingan Religion).

The Dayak epics

1. It is some fragments of the *Kaharingans' sacred epics or oral literature* that I describe in this paper. It is certainly a form of tribal dynamism believing in spirits and gods. However, it is not within my present power to determine to what extent it is Hindu or whether it is a pre-Hindu religion, since no special studies have so far established it.

   Some interesting characteristics of the epics are:

The creation

1. The Kaharingans' myth of creation consists in a consistent *double-aspect God and Nature*: God and his shadow (*maya*?): *Ranying* and *Jata*; male and female; golden mountain and diamond mountain; the *batang haring/batang garing* tree of life, having the elements of eternal water, fauna and flora, the disintegration of which brought to life the first man and woman who gave birth to three sons (Maharaja Sangiang, Maharaja Sangen and Maharaja Bunu), of whom the third was brought down to earth to become the ancestor of man.
2. That characteristic is also found in the form of the so-called *semantic-parallelistic* or *semantic-integralistic nature* of its four lines of poems: the first with the second and then the first and second ones with the third and the fourth ones. It is different from the Malay *pantuns* with its similar ending sounds in every line.

This double-aspect nature is meant to describe a certain concrete or abstract object.

Methods of transmission

1. It is orally transmitted: the *topic-comment* form of the language is very dominant and intonative.
2. It is patterned in form and accompanied by monotoned musical beats of the seven long slender and cylinder-like percussions played simultaneously by seven priests sitting on one specially made long bench, facing the ritual materials.
3. It is chanted first by the head priest, the *upo*, sitting in the middle and then followed by three chanters sitting on his right side and another three on his left. This way of communication has been passed on from generation to generation. When the *upo*, the senior one, retires due to incapability or old age, the best among his chanters takes over and another new chanter is recruited. Thus, the oral tradition continues.
4. The head priest is called *basir* which literally means a hermaphrodite. Though, nowadays the head chanter and chanters are males, the word *basir* significantly indicates the existence of the 'double-aspect' human being, who was considered as the ideal spiritual medium. The Proto-Macasarese of South Celebes, for example, also term the traditional priest of such nature as *bissu*.

Aspects of chanting

1. The recitation is always followed by the beats of percussions in accordance with the number of words recited, not with that of syllables. The beating speed can be slow, medium or fast in harmony with or corresponding to the meanings and styles of recitation.
2. The male and female lines or the *mantra*s are primarily recited by the head priest and then simultaneously re-recited by his followers, with all of them continuously and rhythmically beating the percussions.

   Samples

   [Male] Iii...*Nyaho hai mamparuguh tungkupah Iii*...The great thunder opens its power

   [Female] *Kilat panjang mamparinjet ruang* . . . The long lightning blazes the space

   [Male] ...*Lewu tataw habras bulaw* ...The rich country with sands of gold

   [Female] *Rundung raja habusung hintan* The kingly place with piles of diamonds

[Male] *Lewu tataw dia rumparmg tulang* The rich country in no necessity of hard working

[Female] *Rundung raja isen kamalu uhat* . . .The royal place not needing of toiling

3. The sessions start in the evening and continue till late hours of the night, allowing sufficient time to rest and sleep in order to continue the recitation the next night. Each session consists of one recital part describing a certain phase. The ceremonial and ritual matrials are prepared during the day.

4. The ceremonial opening of the recitation consists of *mantra*s conditioning the priests to be in a certain state to be possessed by spirits or gods. In the same way, the closing part allows the priest to release himself from the spirit. In this spiritual condition, we can say that the spirits or gods join the priests in presenting the rituals.

The ritual context

1. The chants are usually recited by the seven chanters on the occasion of the second burial rituals of *tiwah*: when gods possess the mediums for bringing the souls of the dead to their eternal abode in accord with the will of God, *Ranying Mahatala Langit* (literally: the great *maha* of the sky).

2. The chanting sessions are held in the house of the chief organiser of the *tiwah* (*bakas tiwah*) in his village. On this occasion, a considerable number of families from other surrounding villages join the ritual which may take seven days and seven nights in bringing the souls of their deceased to their abode. [The bones or the remains of the dead bodies are taken out from the grave and then cleaned by water and fire to be put into a specially built construction called *sandong*.]

3. The organisation of the second burial is based on reciprocity: the members of *tiwah* have the right to receive contributions from other persons or families in the form of money or in natura (e.g., buffalo) and also have the duty to similarly give contribution of the same kind or value at another burial fiesta. The ritual related to this is called *lalohan* (contribution).

4. Normally the *tiwah* is attended not only by the family members and relatives, but also by the general public from other villages or cities. The guests of various religious beliefs (including Muslims), who may turn out to be about a hundred daily, are served properly with permissible (*halal*) foods.

5. Whoever makes disturbances or engages in activities, which are categorised

as violating the traditional (*adat*) law during the ceremony, are sanctioned accordingly in form of fines.

6. The Hindu Kaharingans also believe in the 'seven-layers of the sky': (1) underworld of man (*pantai danum kalunen/panungkup*), (2) the world of spirits and gods (*pantai danum jalayan/lewu tataw panungkup*), (3) the world of higher gods (*lewu tataw tungkop/sangiang*), (4) the abode of the three maharajas, (5) the abode of the first created godly man and woman, (6) the abode of the seven kingly and godly men and their seven wives, (7) the abode of God; and the existence of Satanic beings. They believe that the living man's soul, *jiwa* called *hambaruan*, and the dead one's *liaw* consists of (1) *liaw karahang tulang* (spirit of the material bones), (2) *liaw balawang panjang* (spirit of the body), and (3) *liaw haring kaharingan* (the sacred spirit). It is the journey of the *liaw* which is chanted by the priests as the mediums of gods to bring the souls or the three *liaws* into a reunion in heaven by the power of the '*Ranying*' God. Without *tiwah* rituals, the souls would remain in the waiting abode and would never enter the world of eternity.

Conclusion

1. The consistency of the double-aspect philosophy of the epics is astonishing: the double-aspect conception of God, nature, the priest and the form of the epic itself is semantic integralism.
2. The concept of religio-cultural-artistic integration of such epics inherent in such rituals is very clear. It is quite natural and rational for us to conclude that such integration has been a natural human development. Its values are relevant even to the present era of declining scienticism/modernism and ever-rising morally-oriented post-modernism.
3. It appears that it is not sufficient for us to describe an aspect of something without refering to its other aspect as well and to live only physically/rationally and not spiritually as well. It is worthy to live rationally, beautifully and spiritually.

9

The Tamil Epic: Mathurai Veeraswami Kathai

Sheila Asirvatham

Introduction

THIS paper deals with the Tamil oral epic *Mathurai Veeraswami Kathai*. Before taking up the epic for a detailed discussion, it is essential to provide a general background to the Tamil oral epic tradition.

Tamil oral epics have a distinct place in Tamil folklore as a prominent and popular genre and are closely related with the religious life of the people and can be called the 'sacred Vedas' of the rural folk. The Tamilians perform them with the belief that they are harbingers of prosperity and wealth. The Tamil epic narratives have a definite origin at the beginning of the sixteenth century. They gained popularity in the eighteenth century and began to be used in different arts forms. Among them the bow song and shadow puppetry gained importance, since these were being performed as rituals. Shadow puppetry was at its peak in the eighteenth century, during the rule of the Maratha Kings in Tamil Nadu. These kings brought shadow puppetry performers from their lands and supported them financially. These performers who came from Maharashtra, learnt Tamil and started practising their art in Tamil in Tamil Nadu. They narrated the *Ramayana* and thereby gained the support of the Tamilians who believed that such a performance in their villages or places would bring prosperity and wealth to them. These performers who used this art form as a means of livelihood, performed for about three to five days and made a decent living out of this. Now their condition is very pitiable and their livelihood is at stake. The present generation of these performers is in a very pathetic condition in Tamil Nadu because they do not know any other work except this art, which has lost its attraction for the public owing to several factors.

The Tamil oral epics may be sub-categorised themetically as follows:

1) Historical narratives

2) Sociological narratives

3) Narratives containing fragments from classical texts.

4) Mythical ballads

5) Religious ballads

Historical narratives deal with historical characters and incidents with common narrative formulas. *Kattabomman Kathai, Sivakangai Ammanai, Ramappaiyan Ammanai* are some of the examples of historical narratives.

Sociological narratives deal with social problems such as caste hierarchy, gender bias, marriage institution and conflict with in-laws. Stories about local heroes and chieftains also fall under this category. *Nallathankal Kathai, Mathurai Veeraswami kathai, Kathavarayan kathaipadal* are some of the examples.

Narratives based on classical epics contain fragments or characters from the *Ramayana, Mahabharata* and *Cilappathikaram*. Oral versions of written epics may also be included under this category. Characters here are depicted as ordinary human beings with natural emotions and desires. *Pavalakodi-Malai, Alli-arasani Malai, Aravalli-Suravalli Kathai, Eni-ettam, Seethapuranam, Ram Charithram, Kannaki Varalaru, Kannaki Ammanai* come under this category.

Mythical narratives deal with deities, their supernatural acts and heroic feats against evil. *Sudalai Madan Kathai, Ayyan Kathai, Sastha Padal, Amman Kathai Padal* can be cited as mythical narratives.

Religious narratives borrow their characters from Christianity, Islam, Jainism and Buddhism. *Gnanasoundari Kathai Padal, Mary Matha Ammanai, Nabikal Thuthi* are examples of such narratives.

All these sub-categories of Tamil oral epics share a common feature (with the exception of narratives based on classical texts), that of deification of the protagonist at the end of the story as a mark of respect. This is most common in sociological narratives. This sub-category deals with local heroes and chieftains who die for the sake of their caste or community. They are later deified and worshipped by the group.

Mathurai Veeraswami Kathai

This epic comes under the sub-category of sociological narratives, because it deals with caste hierarchy. The narrative runs like this:

> Mathurai Veeran, son of a cobbler, grows into a man of valour and bravery. His father Mathika Chinnan, even though a cobbler, works under Bommanna Naikkan, the ruler of the town, quite faithfully. In the meanwhile Bommanna

> Naikkan's daughter Bommiammal attains puberty. She is made to stay in a hut made of raw coconut leaves away from the town.[1]
>
> While Bommiammal is living in the hut Mathika Chinnan is appointed as a guard to look after her. Once, when it is raining heavily Mathika Chinnan is not able to go to the hut and sends his son instead. Veeran goes to guard the girl. He sees the girl, falls in love with her and asks her to marry him. Attracted by his handsome looks she accepts his love and both of them get married secretly.[2]
>
> Bommiammal is taken back to her house after thirty days, where a grand feast is held for her along with rituals and ceremonial rites.
>
> Both she and Mathurai Veeran feel the pains of separation. Mathurai Veeran is not able to live without his wife. So he meets her secretly and asks her to run away with him. She obeys her husband and they go to live in Trichy. There Mathurai Veeran joins the king's army and serves him faithfully.
>
> Veeran is sent to King Thirumalai Naicker on his request to control thieves in Madurai. There he fights against thieves and captures them. Thirumalai Naicker is very pleased with his victory and honours him. There Mathurai Veeran meets Vellaiammal and falls in love with her. He carries her away to his place but is caught by the soldiers of Thirumalai Naicker and ultimately hanged to death. Bommiammal and Vellaiammal, on hearing this news, rush to the funeral pyre of Mathurai Veeran and jump into it. Mathurai Veeran, Bommiammal and Vellaiammal are later deified.

The hero of this epic belongs to a lower caste, while the two girls belong to a higher caste and hence he cannot marry them openly. He elopes with them and for this he has to pay with his life. Hero Mathurai Veeran, though a man of lower caste, in his bravery and valour is at par with high caste soldiers. Since he fights against the thieves of Madurai and defeats them, his valour is honoured and he is made the guardian deity. He is worshipped as the community deity by the scheduled caste communities of Chakkiliya and Paraya, whereas others worship him as guardian deity. Mathurai Veeran worship is in prevalence in the southern districts of Tamil Nadu even now.

The word power

The text uses many poetical devices to create powerful images of the events, characters and their attributes. While narrating the wrath and anger of Mathurai Veeran when he fights the thieves in Madurai, the performer uses apt words in Tamil to depict the ferocity of his sword:

> Veeran sees the thieves and is full of anger
> Mustache shivers with wrath

Jumps on the horse with a big sword
Like a lion surfing through
Like a leopard leaping through
Plunges into the crowd of thieves.
They die in thousands to the swords' swing forward
And another thousand to the swing backward.

The above depiction is an example of word power. A visual imagery conveyed through words helps the fight scene become alive for the listeners. Here is an example of a monologue used by the performer to convey Veeran's state of mind when he falls in love with Bommiammal:

O, dear, can I sit in this rain alone
Getting drenched all the time.
Bad it is to keep men like this don't you understand

Is it good to remain alone in this darkness
Crores of goodness it would be to invite me inside
Evil it will be to keep men outside
And make them shiver in the rains

A dialogue that takes place between Veeran and Bommaimmal is another example of word power:

Lady are you not moved by my request
My request will melt stones and harden sea
Don't be afraid of anything
I am the lad who is meant for you
When Veeran asks like this
Bommi hears this like pea-hen
And cries thinking many things
Then she looks at him and says
A handsome man like you can't be seen in three Worlds
Beauty of your chest will bring crores of women

Dramatisation in the narrative is seen at every step in the story, in the actions of Veeran, and the kings, Bommi and Vellai. Descriptions of Kasi town and its prosperity, the throne of the king, the king's qualities, reveal the depth of imagination and the word power of the performer.

Pool of tradition

The pool of tradition consists of plot structure, necessary and optional episodes, stock descriptions of key events, repeatable images, formulas and phrases. The plot structure in this narrative consists of the actions of Veeran such as his love fcr his master's daughter, eloping with her and kidnapping of Vellaiammal. It is a gradually ascending plot which culminates with the kidnapping of Vellaiammal. This type of ascending plot structure, optional episodes, such as the birth of Veeran, stories related to Bommiammal, stories of Thirumalai Naicker, stories of other chieftains who wanted to marry Bommiammal are the important features of the epic. The performer uses stock descriptions to depict key events such as bravery of Veeran, love between Veeran and Bommiammal, secret marriage, puberty feast for Bommi and valour of Veeran.

Pool of tradition helps the performer prepare a mental text on the basis of which he creates a fresh performance everytime.

Performance context and audience

When this narrative is sung in the temples of the deity Mathurai Veeran by his caste group people, he is depicted as the son of a cobbler who is killed due to intercaste conflicts, which helps strengthen caste solidarity among these people. When it is sung by other caste people who worship Veeran as the guardian deity, a different story of Veeran's birth is narrated. He is depicted as the son of a king who is thrown into the jungle by his parents because they are warned by a fortune teller that the child's birth will bring destruction to the king and the country. In the jungle he is found by the wife of a cobbler who does not have a child. She brings Veeran home.

Similarly when the epic is being performed in front of an audience that consists of females only, the performer depicts that it is Veeran who pleads for Bommi's love and later for that of Vellai. In the case of male audience, it is Bommi and Vellai who pine for Veeran: Bommi and Vellai see the valour and strength of Veeran and fall in love with him and plead with him to marry them.

This narrative is mostly sung for two days during the worship of Mathurai Veeran as a family deity. On the first day the performer sings about Veeran's birth, his education, his valour and strength and his love for Bommi and his fighting ability. Each of these details is described very vividly for several hours. However, the narrative is condensed into a three hour performance when Veeran is worshipped as the guardian deity. During the ritual called *puravi eduthal* (taking of a horse) it is the valour of Veeran alone which is sung.

The epic of Mathurai Veeran is mostly performed in shrines as *Villupattu* (bow song). At a few places it is performed in *Kummi* and *Oyilattam* dance forms. As a bow song it is sung for days together. But in the dance form, it is sung for an hour or two only. This epic is performed both in prose and verse as part of the dance tradition. Verses from this narrative are also sung by the people who make mud statues of horses for the ritual horse taking. Making of horse statues itself is performed as a ritual to invoke the blessings of Mathurai Veeran. Apart from this, it is sung during the ritual ceremonies performed in the shrine of this deity and also during the festival of 'Puravi eduthal'. When performed in the shrine, it is accompanied by possession among the audience, who get possessed at certain specific points during the performance. In Ramanathapuram District of Tamil Nadu, this narrative is performed by women. When these women get into a trance, they are replaced by male subordinates.

The narrative and the performative competence of the performer play a considerable role in the shaping of the performance. The performative competence varies from performer to performer. Modern performers use cinema tunes to sing the narrative, in order to attract the audience. Some performers have a wide range of jokes and witty expressions, which enhances their performative competence. Others include social themes and yet others compete with the help of assistant singers, and traditional tunes which attract the elders. Narrative competence includes both verbal and non-verbal expressions to develop a narrative totality.

Method of transmission

Tamil epic narratives are transmitted through manuscripts (palm leaves) and also printed form. Narratives of deities are written on palm leaves and are kept in the shrine of the deity. These manuscripts are taken out once a year during the festival of the deity, and the narrative is recited from the manuscript. Even when the performer recites it from his memory without seeing the manuscript, it is taken out from the shrine and is kept open in front of the performer. After the performance is over it is put back inside again. Only the priest of the shrine is allowed to handle the manuscript.

Many narratives are available in print form nowadays. Srimagal Company and Rathina Nayakar & Sons are among the well-known publishers. They print these narratives in big bold letters and call them 'big lettered narratives'. The text is printed along with pictures. Of late, some folklore scholars and universities have also published these narratives. Modern mass media also plays an important role in the transmission of these narratives.

Notes

1. Among the Tamilians it is customary for girls to live in a thatched hut made of raw coconut palm leaves away from home at the onset of menarche for fifteen days or three weeks or a month. This thatched hut should be made either by the maternal uncle or his son who are prospective grooms of the girl. By doing so they exhibit their rights over the girl. If two or more persons have the right to marry her, there may be clashes among them. The person who succeeds in making the hut becomes the groom ultimately.
2. Another version of this epic has the girl making the first move.

10

Oral Epics in Kalahandi

Mahendra Kumar Mishra

KALAHANDI is a rich treasure of traditional knowledge. Folklore in Kalahandi plays an important role in retaining and regenerating the traditional values. The folk songs, tales, legends, tribal myths, oral epics, proverbs, riddles, and folk performing arts are to be found among the different classes of people irrespective of their caste or tribe.

The literacy rate of the district is 34 per cent. In fact about 95 per cent people live in rural areas and out of them 30 per cent belong to tribal communities. Major tribes like the Gonds, Kondhs, Sabars, Bhatars, Banjaras, Parajas, Bhunjias, Binjhals and Paharias are prominent in this district for their distinct ethnic culture. The Gaurs (milkmen), the Keutas (fishermen), the Kumhars (potters), the Sundhies and the Kalars (liquor sellers), the Lohars (blacksmiths) are the major castes constituting the peasant society. All these tribes and castes share a common folklore repertoirc. In addition to this, the tribal communities have their own folklore in their own languages.

Oral epic is a comparatively new area of study in folkloristics. Generally, a poetic rendering of a story performed by the professional singers and the ethnic bards accompanied by musical instruments and owing allegiance to a particular religion or performed on a specific social occasion is called an oral epic. In a high society, the bardic tradition was in existence. The Suta, Charana, Bhata and Magadha were the royal singers representing the glorious history and caste genealogies of Hindu kings in India.

The royal dynasties of Rajput lineage in Kalahandi were the Nagas and the Chauhans. Prior to the Naga and Chauhan rule in ancient Kalahandi and Khariar kingdom respectively, the Gonds, the Kondhs and the Bhunjias were the tribal rulers of this region. The glorious history of the origins of the Nagas and Chauhans are found in the written form, whereas the tribal rulers had their own clan-bards to keep the records of their caste history and genealogies. These caste-bards or clan-bards were patronised by the clan-master.

As mentioned earlier, the occupation based castes in villages and tribal communities have formed the agricultural society. The Kondh tribe in eastern Kalahandi and the Gonds in western Kalahandi were the real landowners, administrative heads and the religious heads till independence. This structure of village administration is still continuing in tribal villages of Kalahandi in spite of the modern *panchayati raj* system. The village head-man was called *gauntia*. The religious head was *jhankar* for the Gonds and the *jani* for the Kondhs. These heads continue to operate till date.

The Gonds and the Kondhs also have their own clan-bards or professional singers. The caste genealogies and the origin myth of these tribes including the local history recited by the caste-bards clearly indicates the predominance of the Gonds and the Kondhs as traditional administrative heads exercising their power over the society. Besides these dominant tribal rulers, other tribes and castes also have their own caste or clan-bards. Those who do not have caste-bards have other specialists to preserve their ethnic history and legends through oral narratives.

The bards have their own clan-masters from whom they are believed to have originated. They are sub-divided into various clans according to their own clan-master. The bards earn their livelihood by singing epic songs, making handicrafts and tattooing. Most of them are nomads, who wander from one place to another for at least six to seven months in a year. They own land and houses separate from their clan master's.

The epic singers of Kalahandi may broadly be categorised as:

1. Ethnic singer or professional caste-bard.
2. Castes and tribes that have no bardic tradition but sing the epics.
3. Male and female priests in tribal communities.
4. Singers not owing allegience to any specific caste or tribe.

Ethnic singers or professional caste-bard

The table (no.1) shows castes and tribes in Kalahandi that have ethnic bards.

TABLE I

Tribe		Sub-caste/ bard/ ethic singer	Musical instruments	Name of epic songs/ caste genealogy
Gond & Bhatara	-	Parghania	*kikri* (fiddle) *bana*	Purja caste geneology, *Chitalsing chhatri*
Kondh	-	Marals	*dhundhunia*	*Janamkhena* – creation myth, *Bhima sidi* (Rain God Bhima)
		Boguas	(one string instrument)	Nangmati *Rajphulia* – epic
Binjhal	-	Birthia	*mandal*, *jhanj* (cymbal)	*Jati janam*-creation myth, origin of *Binjhal Karma* (festival associated with epic song), Bariha king of Borasambar
Banjara	-	Bhat	*dhap*	*Meramma*-creation of Goddesses, *Lakha Banjara*-cultural hero, *Mithu Bhukhia Sewa Bhaya*
Gaurs (milk man,	-	Ghogia Jachak	*brahmaveena* local harp *bans*-wind instrument.	*Kharatmal*, *Barakhena bansgeet*
Dom (schedule caste)	-	Birthia	*muhuri*, *tasa*, *dhol*	*Jati Janam* – How they became a musician community. *Madhab* king *katha-geet*, *Salaban raja katha-geet*

Castes/tribes, that do not have bardic tradition, but sing the epics

The majority castes like Mali, Teli, Keutas and Kumhars and tribes like the Bhunjias, Paharias (Kamars) and Sabars have no caste-bard. But they have origin myths, epics about their cultural heroes and ancestors. The singers emerge from the community itself. They can neither be compared to the caste-bard nor are they patronised by the community for whom they sing. Anyone who is keen to master the epic songs can be a singer in his own community. It is said that they had their epic singers or clan-bards, but in course of time the bardic custom was abolished because of the huge payments demanded by the bard for his sevices. The Paharias say that as their clan-bard demanded high price/alms for his singing, they shot the bard with an arrow out of disgust and got rid of him.

The Table (no.II) lists castes/tribes that have no caste-genealogists but there are singers in the community who preserve tradition, knowledge and culture.

TABLE II

Caste	Tribe	Epic songs / cultural hero and narratives about supreme gods
	Bhunjia	Origin of Bhunjia, *Kachra Dhurua*, a cultural hero of the Bhunjias
	Paharia (Kamar)	*Baddevtar khena* (Origin myth), *Gandhu Paradhiya* (cultural hero)
	Sabar	Dance, the song of tatooing, romance epic of Oriya literature, *Sashisena*, *Jarasabar*
Teli	Bhat-	Caste origin from Lord Shiva and Parvati, Caste occupation; ritual song 'marriage of gods and goddesses (Shiva and Parvati)'
Keut (fisher folk)		*Kaivarta geeta* – Origin of Kaivarta caste from Brahma and Vishnu.
Kumhar (potter)		Origin myth, epic story of king Chandradhvaja *Kurala Purana* by Poet Deena Krishna Das.
Mali		Origin myth, rituals.

Priests/priestesses attached to caste and tribe

In this category priests and priestesses of different castes and tribes perform the ritual and play the role of sacred singers. They sing mythical epics of gods and the goddesses and transmit them only to persons who are nominated as priests by the deities in dreams. The priests also recite the local legends of migration or supremacy of one god/ goddess over the others. Similarly the myths and legends of ethnic heroes and heroines associated with gods and goddesses are also sung by the priests on different occasions. For instance, during *Dasahara* and *Navanna*, the mythical songs are narrated while the ritual is being performed. During the worship of ancestors – *duma* – the priest narrates the glorious deeds and heritage of the *duma*. The *jhankar* and the *dihari* are the priests and the shamans respectively in the Gond community. The Kondh priest and shaman are called *jani* and *dishari* respectively. While the *dihari* or *dishari* represents the deities or *duma*, the priest mediates between the supernatural and the human. He establishes communication between the spirit and the man. Though the first progenitor is mythologised, the *duma* of the recent past are all ancestral spirits and cultural heroes.

The epic songs are considered sacred. They make the caste/tribe aware of its glorious heritage. The status and functions of the priests are given in Table III.

TABLE III

Tribe	Priest	Shaman	Myths & sacred Epics	Function
Gond	*jhankar*	*dihari*	*Budharaja* *Lingadeo* *Jungadeo*	Ancestor worship
Kondh	1. *govajani* 2. *khutjani* 3. *jogjani*	*dishari*	*Janamkhena Purana*, origin of caste settlement, buffalo sacrifice	Good harvest, ancestor worship, appeasement of the earth-mother
Kondh Bhunjia Parja	*gurumai* female priest *ghogein*	*gurumai* female shaman	*Bhima sidi* *Bhima biha* (7 days ritual)	Marriage of the rain god Bhima
Bhunjia	*jankar*	*dihari*	Origin of Goddess and origin of Bhunjia, *Kachra-dhurua*.	Annual ritual and ancestor worship

There are some singer communities independent of caste and tribe affiliation. They are known as Devgunia and Basudevia Brahmans and are found in the adjoining Gariabandh district of Madhya Pradesh.

The Devgunias are the professional singers who depend on singing for their livelihood. They move from door to door singing the glory of Goddess Laxmi, selling the paddy craft and begging alms. Especially in the month of *Marghasheersh* (December to January) they move from village to village. They are a local non-tribal caste.

Women purchase images of gods and goddesses made of paddy from the Devgunias and worship them throughout the year. They also hear the epic of Goddess Laxmi and offer alms to the Devgunias. Sometimes the villagers arrange the *Purana* performance programme especially in the month of *Marghasheersh*. Besides, the Devgunias are the scribes who use palm leaf manuscripts and are popular as *natguru* — Drama Director in rural areas. They write and organise folk dramas based on episodes taken from the *Ramayana* and the *Mahabharata*.

The Basudevia Brahmans are also a local caste. Their ethnic origin is not known. It is uncertain whether they are of tribal origin. However, their culture and customs are similar to Gonds. Like the Parghania-bard of the Gonds, they use *kikri* and sing the local version of the *Ramayana*.

The *geet kudias* (male singer) and the *geet kudien* (female singer) are talented performers popular for their spontaneous recitation of songs, especially when a dance or a song competition between *dhangra* and *dhangri* (young boys and girls) is organised in the village. They also sing the epics, though they are not professional epic singers. Their repertoires are full of legends, songs, riddles, and myths.

The Harijans living in the village together with the tribal communities also possess wide knowledge of tribal language and culture. Details of the singers are given in the table (no. IV).

TABLE IV

Category	Singer	Epics	Musical Instrument	Function
Professionals	Debgunia or Debguru (Male)	*Laxmi Purana* Legendary Epics Folktales	*brahmaveena* (a local harp)	1. Worship of Goddess Laxmi 2. Prepare paddy craft 3. Public performance 4. Folk Drama-Guru 5. Prepare palmleaf manuscript (notes) 6. Sing legendary epics about local heroes.
	Basudevia Brahmans (Male)	The *Ramayana* & the *Mahabharata* in local version	*kikri* (a local	1. Recite sacred narratives. 2. Sing legendary epic stories 3. Folk tales about cultural heroes (prose verse)
Amateur	*geet kudia* (Male)	Love song Folk tale		Dance, sing, compose songs in performance context.
	geet kudien (female)	Love song folk tale	*ramkathi*	Compose song in performance context, tell folk tales, narrative songs

The content

The epic songs in different performance context are of various kinds. These can broadly be divided into sacred narratives and secular narratives:

SACRED NARRATIVES

Sacred narratives are specific to place and time. When performed in a ritual context, they are governed by certain rules to be followed by the priest. In rites and rituals, fairs and festivals, during the invocation of *duma* — the ancestral spirit, the *jani* or *gurumai* sing to glorify gods, goddesses and ancestral spirits. These narratives are held to be true and are performed during certain rituals. They also spell the rules of performing these rituals.

The content of sacred narratives is mainly based on the origin of the universe, origin of the earth and nature, evolution of animals and human beings, procreation of mankind, struggle for survival, family and social bonds, kinship, migration and settlement, ethnic occupation, origin of gods and goddesses of each ethnic group, clanwise distribution of land and jungle, distribution of gods and goddesses on clan basis, history of fight against other tribes for land and jungle, settlement of villages, sharing of land with their supporter caste-group, spread of caste/tribe to other areas, invention of farming technology, invention of iron instruments, cultivation of paddy and pulses, village administration and religious organisation, friendship and hostility with other ethnic groups, worship of gods and goddesses for victory and security, worship of the first progenitor, first priest and the first ancestor.

The Parghania-Gond bard recites the caste genealogy. *Purja* is a long sacred narrative. The Gond priest *jhankar* recites the invocation song to Chaturbhuj Budhadeo, Lingadeo and Janghadeo representing the ancient glory of the Gonds.

The Bogua and the Marals, two distinct ethnic bards of the Kondhs, recite *Janamkhena* — creation of the Kondhs, and *Bhima sidi* — the ladder of Bhima. Bhima is the rain god and cultural hero of the Kondhs.

Similarly, the Birthias for Binjhal tribe and Doms recite the *Jati janam* and *Purthi-janam* during the *Dasahara* festival and other community rituals. The Kamars recite *Baddevtar khena* as their creation myth.

The Ghogias for Gaur caste sing *Barakhena bansgeet* representing their clan gods and goddess. These narratives are recited during post harvest festivals and marriage ceremonies.

The *gurumai* and the *ghogien* in Gond, Kondh and Bhunjia community sing *duma utra*, songs about family history or caste genealogy of respective tribes. *Bhima biha* is another ritual found among these tribes. It is performed when scarcity of rain or drought occurs in Kalahandi. People organise the marriage ceremony of the Rain God, Bhima with a young girl of the tribe named Kondhen. This ritual marriage is believed to bring ample rain for their harvest.

The sacred narratives are known as *Janamkhand Purana*, *Baddevtar khena*, *Janam khena*, *Jati janam*, *Purthi-janam*, *Purja*, *Bhima sidi* and *Bhima biha*, and are commonly termed as *geet*, *purana* or *khena*, *janam khand* and also *jati purana*. Their content varies from tribe to tribe, depending on its socio-economic status. The Gonds have their *Purja* which contains the history of the Raj Gonds who are shown as land-owners and administrative heads. The Kondhs have already adopted cultivation as their major occupation. In their *pod puja* – buffalo sacrifice festival – the main priest (*govajani*) worships *Dharnimata*, the Mother Earth along with goddesses Laxmi and Durga. He offers milk to Laxmi and sacrifices buffalo to Durga.

The buffalo-sacrifice ritual reflects the origin, migration, settlement, transition from food gathering to food producing technologies, patterns of land ownership and local administration of their *chak* – habitat. The Kamars, a minority tribe, in their *Baddevtar khena* – a long narrative song – invoke their supreme god to help them in hunting, collecting forest products and keeping the jungle intact from external attacks by other communities.

The main function of sacred narratives is to invoke gods for ample harvest, security and prosperity. They are performed to appease ancestral spirits and gods to keep the habitat free from disease and external attack, and the jungle evergreen. They are worshipped in order to obtain food and rain. People believe that if their ancestral spirits are not satisfied with their actions, they will curse them. So they promise their gods and ancestors that they will be righteous and will follow the moral and ethical codes established by them. The possibility of gaining worldly objects is symbolically examined in ritual performance. Rituals establish their link with the past and regulate the present.

Secular epics or epics about cultural heroes

The narrative songs which can be performed in front of an audience irrespective of caste, sex and age may be termed as secular epics. Though they have emerged out of the sacred narratives, they have a strong ethnic background and are less religious and more legendary in character. They are called *akhyana* – commonly termed as *khena* or *geet* or *katha*. These epic stories, held to be true, sing about ethnic heroes of the recent past. These narratives are attached to a specific place, time and events.

The professional epic singers have a big repertoir of *geet* and *katha* related to their ethno-historical background.

Each ethnic group has its own epic narrative. The Gond tribe of Kalahandi has epic songs like *Chittal Singh Chhatri*, *Lohagundi Raja*, *Kadel Kachhar katha* and *Kachra Dhurua geet*. The Gonds of Kalahandi have a rich cultural heritage associating them with the Gonds of Central India. They have a number of local heroic legends sung by the Parghanias.

The Boguas and the Marals sing the narratives of *Madhab Raja*, *Nangmati Rajphulia* and *Maradeo Raja*. *Nangmati Rajphulia* is a tragic song recited by the *Bogua*s about a woman who commits suicide on discovering that the man she has chosen as her husband is her own brother. *Maradeo Raja katha* is a secularised form of the mythic song of the Kondhs. The Banjaras have their clan bards, who sing the epics of *Lakha Banjara* and *Sobhanaik Banjara* which represent their ethnic occupation and depict the bravery of their heroes. The Kamars or the Paharias have a number of epic narratives, and *Gandhu Paradhiya*, *Koko Bhaini*, *Luhagundi Raja*, *Kamul Surua Raja* are some of the popular epic songs representing their ethnic culture. Similarly the Binjhals have the epic, *Karma* and a long narrative song depicting the establishment of Binjhal kingdom in Bora Sambar. The Bhunjias have their *Allah Uddal* and *Khalnia Veer katha* reflecting their culture.

Each narrative is named after the main dramatic personae of the epic. The Gaur epic songs have been named after the hero and the heroine. There are twelve *khena* or twelve episodes. Each episode represents the story of a hero and the heroine, e.g., *Rupadhar-Hirandri khena*, *Sunadhar Ramela khena*, *Kotrabina-Ramela khena* and *Hadukurria-Nilendri khena*. Some epics are named after the hero only, e.g., *Lakha Banjara* and *Gandhu Paradhiya*.

Secular epics depict themes of love, war, victory, gaining or regaining of kingdom and supremacy over other tribes. The content and motifs of these epics have a striking resemblance with martial romances of Europe. The epic story represents the fantastic world of demi-gods and goddesses belonging to the spiritual world of traditional culture. Magic, witchcraft and sorcery are some of the elements that help heroes and villains to become powerful. Supernatural powers help the heroes and heroines to win. In ethnically-based epics, innovations in agriculture, invention of equipment and tools for agricultural work, for getting water from Indra and the demi-god Bhima and a bumper harvest are some of the key motifs that charecterise the hero. These epics are charter of traditional customs and occupation. In most of the heroic epics the hero is neglected by elderly parents resulting in his absence. On the way he faces many obstacles and overcomes them with supernatural help from saints, friends, gods and goddesses. Frame-repetitions are recurrent in such epics and ultimately the hero wins the race, punishing or killing the villains/enemies. He is also rewarded with regaining of power, as well as marriage to beautiful girls.

Visual epic or *drusya kavya*

Some of the local epic-stories found among the tribes exist in drama form, which clearly indicates the multi-generic form of folk epics. The Kondh-Paraja tribes and the Dom caste perform the epic-drama called *desianat* which means regional drama. *Desia* is the link language in Kalahandi and Koraput district used by more than 51 tribes and other non-tribals. This epic story in drama form reminds us of the *kavya-natya* form and the *chhanda-natya* form, as the dialogues in *desianat* are in verse form composed by the local folk dramatist. Sometimes professional singers also compose these epic-dramas.

While the sacred narratives fulfill religious aims, the secular narratives have a socio-cultural role. Their heroes are legendary characters taken from the recent past. Through a chronological arrangement of life-events of these heroes people associate their caste history and genealogy with a specific place and time. These epics represent the racial memory and ethnic identity of tribes and help promote their group consciousness and ethnic solidarity.

Transmission of oral epics

Sacred narratives are transmitted from one generation to another by professional ethnic singers. The Parghanias recite *Purja* — the caste genealogy of the Gonds, which is considered secret and is transmitted to male family members only in ritual context. Similarly the *govajani*, the priest singer of the Kondhs, sings the *govautra geet* only in the ritual place of goddess *Dharnimata* during buffalo sacrifice festival (*pod puja*). The recitation starts in the evening and it continues for the whole night till next morning. The new singers assist the *govajani* and the learning of the narrative is achieved by rote memory. Similarly the Boguas and the Marals — the Kond bards — also transmit their oral epic song to family members only. The clan bard, priest and the *gurumai* recite the song without the ritual performance. Some rituals take place once in every twelve years, e.g., *pod puja* or buffalo sacrifice of the Kondhs. In case the *govajani* fails to present the narrative in proper order, the elderly persons from the community help him in rearranging the events.

The epic songs named after cultural and legendary heroes are open to all. There is no fixed time and place for them, but they are mostly performed at night.

The main singer of sacred narratives is accompanied by three to four young singers with musical instruments. The junior singers master the narratives by repeating the mainline of the main singer and this also helps the audience to comprehend the narrative. However the heroic epic songs are recited without the repetition. To remember the lines the singer uses nonsense syllables till he gets them fixed in his memory. Further, his refrain helps him in taking a pause to jump from one event to another. Whereas the method of transmission of sacred narratives is vertical within the family and clan group, it is horizontal in respect of secular epics.

Epic composition

Each ethnic group has its own epic cycle. It consists of two, five and twelve cycles.

Each cycle is known as *khena*, *khand*, *katha* or *geet*. The local meaning of *khena* means the branch of a tree. Probably the nomenclature has been derived from the Sanskrit word *akhyana*. *Khand* means one part of the *purana* or epic cycle. In Sanskrit, epics like *Koshala khand*, and *Utkala khand* are available. Similarly the *Bhima sidi* sung by priests and *gurumai* are (1) *Janamkhand Purana* and (2) *Nangarkhand Purana*. In the first part the birth of the hero and in the second part his heroic deeds are described. *Katha* and *geet* refer to tales and songs. The epic song represents a narrative performed in poetic form. Hence the use of these terms for the epic are justified.

The most important aspect of epic study is the textualization of epic performance into epic composition formulae. The process of composing the mental text in the mind of the poet and its verbal expression are some of the the important aspects in epic studies. Epic composition is performance oriented. The nature of composition varies from one performance to another according to the context, time, mood of the singer and audience's response. However content of the epic is revealed through culture specific language and phrases which are highly proverbial in nature. It is found that the epic composition has some stock language and metaphorical phrases, which help the traditional singer to express the text in a given framework. Therefore, the language of the epic text is different from the day-to-day spoken language of the same singer or audience. It has a literary and cultural flavour. However the structure of the epic remains intact; it means they compose the epic without breaking the story.

In the course of performance epic narratives make use of multigenres of folklore: proverbs, folk metaphors, images, similes, phrases, songs, lullabies and lamentations make the epic language lively. The mental text of the singer composed of episodes is expressed through the poetic language and cultural symbols. Each episode in an oral epic or a myth is like a tree with various branches (*khena*). The singer has to link one *khena* with the other and arrange the episodes in such a manner that the events have a logical sequence leading to the total epic text in a systematic order, so that the epic tree is complete with all the *khena*s.

During the epic performance, if the singer fails to correlate one episode with the other thereby distorting the text, elderly persons from the audience guide him. They tell the singer, "You must water the plants in such a manner that it saturates from starting point to the end point without breaking its flow." According to them epic is like a tree and the singer is a gardener. He must know how to make the epic tree blossom.

Most of the epics and caste genealogies are long narratives. Each epic performance takes nights together to complete the total cycle. Even the *Bhima sidi* is recited for seven nights. *Barakhena bansgeet* is recited for twelve nights. It is learnt by the youngsters through the process of rote memory. While performing they repeat the mainline sung by the singer. This is the essence of the song. So it is called *gova*. Till the second line is uttered by the main singer, the youngsters keep repeating the first line. The age-old proverbs, sayings, and experience form the essence of the song which is related to customs, rituals and tradition.

Transition in epic narrative

Due to the influence of Puranic tradition the bards infuse their text with mythic characters and events. The episodes or events or characters of Puranas that are found to be similar to the ethnic hero of their traditional epics, are assimilated into the mental text of the bard. The assimilation into ethnic culture of Puranic lore gives a new force to epic singers and the ethnic groups to enrich and identify their glorious heritage with the Puranic tradition of India. For instance, the Debgunias claim their ancestry from *Devaguru* Vrihaspati and the Basudevia Brahmanas from the Brahmans of Gaya of the *Ramayana* age. The Parghanias are said to have their origin from Lord Shiva or Mahadev. The fishing community (Keut) associates itself with sage Parashar and the potters (Kumhar) with the Pandavas. Through this process the local epic heroes get identified with the Puranic heroes and vice versa.

Glossary

Parghania: Gond bards in Madhya Pradesh and Maharashtra are called Pradhans whereas they are known as Parghania in Kalahandi. Each Gond clan occupies a cluster of villages identified as *Parghana*. The clan bard assigned to the Gond clan in a particular *parghana* is Parghania. Each Parghania considers his *kikri* as his *vana* – caste symbol.

Boguas & Marals: The Boguas and the Marals are Kondh bards. They are minority sub-tribes of the Kondhs. Both of them play *dhundhunia* – a one-stringed musical instrument.

Gogia or Ghogia: Clan bard of Kondhs/Gond castes. They use *brahmaveena* – a local harp.

Jachak: Those who come to give something. Here the bards give ethnic knowledge to their main caste.

Birthia: The bards who sing the heroic songs. *Bir* means warrior, the man who sings the glory of the *Birs* are *Birthia*.

Govajani: *Gova* means essence and *jani* means Kondh priest. The essence of the sacred myth is always recited by the *govajani*. The co-singers of *govajani* use *sadki* – a wooden musical instrument with twinkling bell played with both the hands to keep the rhythm of the narrative.

Devgunia: A man who praises the valour of the gods and goddesses. *Deva guna* means the valour of the gods and *Devgunia* means the singer of it. They use *brahmaveena* especially dedicated to Goddess Laxmi. They show their ancestry from *Devaguru* Vrihaspati.

Basudevia Brahmana: A minority nomadic caste found in Gariabandh district of Madhya Pradesh adjacent to Kalahandi district of Orissa.

References

Thapar, Romila, 1978, *Ancient Indian Social History*, New Delhi, Orient Longman.

Sing Deo, J.P., 1987, *Cultural Profile of South Kosala*, New Delhi, Gian Publishing.

11

Scroll Narratives of Andhra Pradesh

Bittu Venkateswarlu

Introduction

THE scroll means a cloth or a paper of 20 to 40 meters in length and 2 meters in width with a legend or a story on it, in the shape of pictures or scripts. These scrolls are used for narrating mythology and are called scroll narratives.

These scrolls are used to exhibit pictures without narration also. Similar pictures can be seen on the ceilings of palaces and temples, on the *gopuras* of temples, and on the walls of palaces and temple *mandapas*. In some cases dolls of wood or clay are also used to narrate the stories. In some art forms they perform in front of the curtains and in some others, like leather puppet shows, at the backside of the curtains.

These scrolls are available either in the shape of a single map containing a picture, or collective maps or groups of maps containing many pictures. These scrolls can on be divided into three types, i.e., *sanchara patams*, *sthira patams* and *chalana patams*, based on the style of performance. Legends, epics, ballads, histories of great warriors and other historical figures, religious matters, social events and caste legends are propagated through these performances.

Historical background

Like so many art forms, scroll narrative performances also have sufficient historical evidences. Buddhism had used art forms from all quarters to propagate the religion and to educate and entertain people. It also used the scroll narratives. Jainism also used the scroll narratives to propagate itself. Ancient Buddhist, Jaina and Brahmanical literature refer to scroll narratives as *pata chitras*. Classical Sanskrit texts mention these as *yama patas*.[1]

Here, Byzantium's words are worth mentioning:

> One specific aspect of Tibetan Lamaistic art, namely the Tibetan painted scrolls, generally known as *TANKAS*, deserve special mention. These paintings, usually on cloth, seldom on silk or embroidered, are typical of Tibet and Himalayan countries, to serve magical purposes, to induce meditation and also to illustrate the lives of the Buddha and of Saints.[2]

In 'Encyclopaedia Americana', we find the following reference to Dead Sea Scrolls:

> [It is] a collection of ancient manuscripts retrieved since 1947, from a series of caves on the West Bank of the Dead Sea and in the neighbouring area of Jordan. The bulk of the Scrolls are Biblical and religious texts written in Hebrew and Aramaic. The manuscripts are not homogeneous. They represent deposits made at different times between the first and eighth centuries AD and vary in language, content and date. Some of them have been preserved as fairly extensive rolls, while the vast majority have survived only in the form of pitiful fragments (often no longer than a postage stamp), which have to be carefully pieced together and even then leave unfortunate gaps.
>
> The Dead Sea Scrolls include the oldest known copies of the Old Testament scriptures as well as the long-lost originals of several books of the Apocrypha and of such celebrated pseudoepigraphic or non-Biblical, Jewish religious works as the books of Enoch, Jubilees, and the Testaments of the twelve patriarchs.
>
> Besides the Biblical and religious texts there are also secular documents (including military despatches and legal writs) in Greek, Latin, Nabalaean and Arabic.[3]

Thus, there is evidence that, many religions used the scrolls for religious propagation throughout the world. Mittal (1987) writes:

> The scrolls of Bengal, Bihar and Orissa illustrate the local variations of Hindu Mythology while Rajasthani and Gujarathi scrolls illustrate the Jaina Tantric themes, Jaina *tirtha*s, or *holy places* and brave deeds of local heroes. *Yama Pata*s depict the journey to heaven and punishment sinners suffer in hell.[4]

Other States of India also have the tradition of propagating culture through scroll narratives. These scrolls are called *paja chitra* in Bihar and Bengal, in Maharashtra as *Pat*, in Rajasthan as *par*, and in Orissa and Karnataka as *pata*.[5]

In Andhra Pradesh these are called *kaki padagalu* and *patam kathalu*. Several castes from Andhra Pradesh propagate caste legends (*kula puranam*s) through performances of various kinds. Scroll narrative performances play a significant role in the propagation of these caste legends. Scrolls are in the possession of some dependent castes, for whom they provide a means of livelihood. These castes comprise seven sub-castes in Andhra. These sub-castes are dependent on seven related castes called host castes. The sub-castes have a right to tell these legends and enjoy the property donated to their ancestors by the host castes. Mittal (1987) observes:

> Scrolls narrate the origin of a particular caste and eulogise the daring exploits of their legendary heroes. Occasionally they incorporate episodes from Hindu Mythology and the Puranas but the traditional characters predominate, woven into the narrative. They were painted by local artists and used by minstrel picture showmen who travelled to the different villages, performing the appropriate stories when invited by people of a particular caste. This caste element was very strong and prevailed not only in the theme, but also with the audience, even though other villagers were sometimes allowed to witness the show.[6]

The system of caste dependence is operational even today. For example, the Madiga and Mala castes have more than 14 sub-castes. These sub-castes occupy different positions. Some work from the top position, i.e., from *gurusthana*, while others beg. Some sub-castes are totally dependent on the host caste for survival. The main caste is responsibile for providing livelihood to these sub-castes. Sub-castes earn by telling caste legends to their host castes.

Gowda Chetties tell the *Gowda Puranam* for Gowda caste people, Machaiahs tell the *Madelu Puranam* for Rajaka caste people, Kakipadagalavaru tell the *Mahabharata* to the Mudiraj caste people, Kunapulivaru narrate the *Padma Puranam* for Padmasale caste people, Addapuvaru narrate the caste legend to the Mangali caste people (barbers), Gurrapuvaru tell the caste story of Malas to Mala caste people and Dakkalivaru tell the caste story to Madiga caste people through scroll narratives.

These sub-castes are paid by their host castes through a system of payment called *mirasi*. *Mirasi* can mean: a permanently donated land; a recognition of the right of sub-castes to ask for money or grain from the host caste; and/or financial assistance to the performers. Some sub-castes have to beg for a living. Begging is also considered to be a type of *mirasi* or *vatanu*. However the top sub-caste people are honoured as priests and they tell the legends through scrolls.

Almost all the castes of Andhra have sub-castes with whom they are linked through the *mirasi* system. Some castes may have more than three dependent castes whereas others may have one or two dependent castes. The host castes and their dependent castes follow the same traditional mode of performing the life-cycle rituals. Each caste has its own identity on traditional lines, relevant within the group of dependent and host castes.

Those dependent castes that work as priests, perform life cycle rituals for their host and co-dependent castes. They have a stronghold on the temples of their caste gods and play an important role in caste rituals.

Rajakas consider the Machaiahlu as their priests.[7] Gowdas consider the Gowda Chetties as their priests. However Madigas and Malas do not consider Dakkala and Gurramvaru as their priests and treat them at a lower level. These performers have to beg for food, clothes and money. Madiga caste people treat the Dakkali caste people as untouchables. The other scroll narrating castes enjoy respectable social status.

There is no marriage relationship between the sub and the host castes, though they do exchange food. The scroll narrators have an independent and separate social identity.

Performative strategies

After completion of stage arrangements, the troupe starts the performance with a prayer song.

The stage is set for the performance by hanging the scroll on the wall or on two sticks. The audience sits facing the scroll. The narrator stands by the side of the scroll with a hand stick and other performers sit on the side with their instruments. A supporting singer stands beside the narrator and follows the movements and narration of the main performer as a *venta* (chorus). The instrumentalists operate the instruments such as *maddela*, cymbals and harmonium. The eldest man in the troupe sings the prayer song. This man may or may not be the troupe leader.

The narrator offers prayers to Ganapati, Sarasvati and caste goddesses. Then he introduces himself and his troupe, and explains the purpose behind giving the performance.

After this the main performer starts the story. Assistants role out the scroll according to the story. At the end of the story, an animal is sacrificed to the gods. The performers through their narration make the audience identify themselves with the legend. The performance ends with the prayer, i.e., *mangala harathi*. Some troupes collect the money in the middle of the performance and some troupes collect it at the end of the performance.

Thus, the performance begins with the prayer song and ends with the concluding prayer, *mangala harathi*. Differences in behaviour can be observed among the artistes during different events, e.g., during and after the prayer song.

Relationship and interaction between the performers and the audience

Every performance has its qualities and limitations. Scrolls are also no exception to this. Here the performers and the audience share an inseparable social relationship.

As already mentioned the narrators come from dependent castes, who perform caste legends for their host castes through scroll narratives. The dependant castes are performers, and the people of the host castes are the audience. The performance is a ritual and is not performed for entertainment alone. The performers are not just entertainers but also preachers. Similarly, the audience are not just observers and listeners but also participants in the ritual. The host people who arrange the programme protect the sanctity of the ritual by behaving in an appropriate manner.

As pointed out earlier, some of the narrators enjoy the high status of a priest, while others are treated at the low level of beggers. However, at the time of the performance both are given the same amount of respect.

The host castes gather and arrange the performance. The performers are not unnecessarily anxious about the audience' reaction to their performance. They just narrate the legend and complete the performance. There is no necessity for them to focus on the quality of their performance. Since the performance is arranged in a ritual context, the audience also do not care about the entertaining quality of the performance. They see the performance as a devotional process. They seek mental purity and peace and not entertainment. There is no interaction between the performers and the audience in the form of jokes, or humourous exchange. However, the audience may ask the narrator during the performance to explain the sanctity of the legend and he obliges accordingly.

Contexts of the scroll narrative performance

Generally the host castes request the performers for a performance. The community organises the performance collectively. The people of the host castes gather to arrange the performance of scroll narrative generally once in a year. Somebody from the community takes the initiative to organise and collect money for the performence. In some contexts, the people of the host castes from four to five villages arrange a common performance in order to share the financial burden. The performances are arranged in spacious temples so as to accommodate people from other villages. People of the same caste from nearby villages also participate.

Generally at the time of the annual ceremonies of caste rites, the host castes organise the scroll narrative performance. These rites belong to the category of *mylatudupulu* which sanctifies or purifies the community of all the *myla* by conducting the *puja*. These rites are also conducted during the festival days and at the time of marriages. When a birth or a death takes place the community becomes *myla*, i.e., impure and no sacrificial activity can take place without *mylatudupulu*. Madiga and

Kuruma communities arrange performances of scroll narratives of their caste story at the time of marriage in their homes. The communities of Gowda, Mala, Madiga, Padmasale, Mudiraju arrange the scroll narrative performances as a mass festival of the community. During such festivals relatives of the community come and join them in celebrating and preparing the meat of sacrificial animals.

Rich people of the community arrange performances at the time of some major celebration in the family. The owner of the house invites both the performers and the members of his community to celebrate the ritual.[8] Though the audience has no role in the organisation of the performance they participate as devotees enhancing the ritual atmosphere.

The performance takes place during general caste festivals. The community people together collect the money for the expenses and arrange the performance.

The hosts organise these performances at their convenience and create a suitable occasion for it. This type of celebration reflects their devotion to community gods. It also contains an element of entertainment.

The performers also create contexts. The performers, who need to earn their bread, create an appropriate climate and encash the sentiments of the people of the host caste. If a performer wants to create a context for the performance, he plans for it and moves according to his plans. He searches for the suitable place and persons, who may encourage his performance. He never goes with a plan which may not be acceptable or without sufficient information about the host. So, there is no scope for failure. He evokes the sentiment of devotion towards the caste gods in his caste people. Such contexts are purely of performer's creation. Sometimes people forget to perform their rituals. The performer reminds them of this lapse and takes the initiative to arrange the ritual. Then the performance takes place. He also draws their attention to the rituals that must be performed during the caste festival, general celebrations, marriage celebrations and certain traditionally fixed days. He thus persuades them for the performances.

Recently these performers have crossed the caste barriers and are giving performances for other castes also. In such contexts the emphasis is on entertainment.

Nowadays the Government bodies are also using folk art forms including scroll narratives for propagating their policies like family planning, adult education, illiteracy, AIDS, and health and childcare. The performers insert the policy item in-between the caste stories when giving the performance. The people react to these items with same devotional feelings as towards the legends. Private organisations on their general celebration days and political parties at the time of elections are also utilising these forms. The researchers and research organisations also ask for performances. These contexts may be new for the performers, but they perform with enthusiasm. The context plays an important role in the scroll narrative performance.

Central idealogy behind the scroll narratives

In olden days people of all castes lived as interdependent units without any hierarchical organisation. Later the discrimination started between castes and hierarchy appeared.

The society respected the upper castes and their professions and neglected the lower castes and their professions. This continued for generations. Sufi movement in the medieval age tried to generate self-confidence in the lower classes and inculcate a sense of pride in their professions. It rejected discrimination based on caste, creed and gender and spread the message that all are equal and everybody can attain *moksha*. Self-respect and confidence increased among the lower castes through this movement.

Veera Shaiva movement in Andhra Pradesh and Karnataka in the medieval age also encouraged the feeling of self-respect and self-confidence in the lower class people.

The Veera Shaiva movement used the biographies of the devotees from different castes. These biographies and histories served as caste legends and were called *kula puranams*. The upper class utilised the written literature and the lower class utilised the oral literature as their vehicles. These caste legends are narrated among the community people as caste legends in different ways, i.e., in the shape of dramas, dances, story-telling with or without the scroll. Such performances bring the people of all castes together and emphasise values of equality, fraternity and integrity which strengthens the society from the grassroot level.

Notes

1. Jagadish Mittal, *The India Magazine*, April 1987, 'Scrolls', Vol. 7, p. 74.
2. Byzantium, 'The Great Ages of Man' (Time life Books), *Illustrated Weekly of India*, 20 May 1973.
3. 'Dead Sea Scrolls', *Encyclopaedia Americana*, Vol. 8, p. 553.
4. Jagadish Mittal, 'Scrolls', *The India Magazine*, April 1987, Vol. 7, p. 74.
5. *Ibid*.
6. *Ibid*, p. 75.
7. The writer visited *Madelu Puranam* performance of Siddiah Troupe at Siricilla of Karimnagar Dist., of Andhra Pradesh on 1-11-1992.
8. The writer collected the data from Gowda Chettilu about the *Gowda Puranam* performance from Aler of Nalgonda Dist. of Andhra Pradesh on 4-10-94.

12

Burrakatha
A Telugu Folk Narrative of Andhra Pradesh in History and Performance

Daniel Negers

BURRAKATHA is a folk narrative and theatrical form in the Telugu language which has been exceedingly popular in the whole Andhra region (the North Coastal Districts or North Coromandel area) of Andhra Pradesh for the last fifty years, since it developed as a specific form in the early 1940s. In fact, we should rather say that it used to be popular, as its attraction has slowly declined all along in the 1980s with the ever increasing influence of radio, cinema and T.V.

Since its coming into existence, *Burrakatha* has been considered as a means to promote learning (*prabodham*), entertainment (*kalakshepam*), and propagate a message (*pracharam*), though it has been used in such a large variety of circumstances as weddings, religious festivals and social or political happenings (electoral canvassing and publicising government developmental schemes).

This paper aims at offering a general outline of this highly codified folk performing art form both in terms of historical origin and performance. It briefly describes the cultural and political background in which it constituted itself, taking into account the changes that occurred in the related field of literature, theatre and folk forms. It also hints at the ways a new political or ideological context promotes the emergence of cultural change in a seemingly fixed traditional heritage to serve new objectives.

Consequently, this also means that *Burrakatha* has assimilated various literary and religious aspects predominant in the society at large in this process. These aspects seem at odds with the original political purposes that first gave its *raison d-être*, and continue to mould it to some extent, but show that religious values can never be kept aside for long in any cultural achievement in India.

Kapila Vatsyayan (1980) has shown the interconnections that constantly occur between Indian theatrical and narrative art forms, not only within but outside regional areas as well. It also appears to me that mutual influences (not to speak of real interdependence) between various art forms are at play at the local level. This is very true for *Burrakatha*. It cannot be properly understood, if separated from the larger folk performing art context of which it is a part. This seems sufficient reason to succinctly present other art forms which are to be seen performed along with *Burrakatha*s in similar festival circumstances, and which altogether form a complementary coexistence in shaping folk cultural representations.

I also hope to demonstrate that the highly popular success of the *Burrakatha* narrative and theatrical art form all over Andhra in the nearly five decades since coming into existence has made it develop into an artistic medium of regional significance in terms of (cultural and linguistic) group identity. This was done by gradually assimilating a large spectrum of story-telling and singing/acting traditions embedded in various specific art-forms, borrowing either particular aspects in the mode of production/ transmission or in inspiring new stories out of the repertoire of these forms. In so doing, *Burrakatha* seems to illustrate the tradition of *Yakshagana*(m) in "utilising all the literary styles and modes which poets and authors had evolved in the preceding centuries," continuing it in the modern time, in its own specific way.

Then, to come to the articulation of this paper:

I first present the three geographical regions which divide the twenty-three districts of the Andhra Pradesh State along traditionally distinct cultural/linguistic/political (sub-) areas, keeping in mind that the Andhra region is the area of prevalence of *Burrakatha*.

I then turn to a historical perspective, describing the cultural and political conditions that brought *Burrakatha* into existence, and also account for its specificity.

I describe other observable narrative and theatrical forms in the local and regional background, contending that altogether with *Burrakatha* they represent a unique and complementary way in which local society and culture sustain, elaborate, transmit and, in a way, control a vast body of cultural and ideological representations.

I will finally turn towards the description of *Burrakatha* as such, showing the two main structural dimensions of *Burrakatha* in performance: on the one hand, the three-member *Burrakatha* troupe's dynamic narrativeness, whereby each member displays one specific narrative aspect (*katha, rajakiyam, hasyam*) and is functionally identified with it, being respectively called *kathakudu, rajakiya, hasyagadu*; on the other hand, the structure of the performance, which may be divided in three unequal parts — 'prologue', 'story', and 'closing' of the performance.

I shall not reflect here on the ways in which these two structural levels of performance (distribution of narrative functions between the three members and articulation of the performance phases) are to be seen in relation to a structuration of scenic space and time. I shall content myself by describing the bi-dimensional organisation through which an epic narrative of heroic quality (that may be puranical, 'historical', or 'social-political') is included in a larger narrative structure which allows comic and social/political discourses and messages.

The Andhra Region of Andhra Pradesh

Notwithstanding its major importance in regard to its contribution and influences in south Indian literature, theatre, vocal music and dance very little is known about the history and levels of achievement of the Telugu language. There is also but a relatively small amount of research concerning the state of Andhra Pradesh in the various fields of Indian research (be it society, culture or literature), in comparison with Tamil Nadu for instance.

The modern state of Andhra Pradesh is a merging of three main cultural and linguistic sub-entities: Andhra, Telangana and Rayalasima. *Burrakatha* is mostly to be found in the Andhra region. This coastal region (the former Northern Circars) centres on the two Godavari districts (east and west) and on the Krishna and Guntur districts. Its influence extends to the three northern districts of Vishakhapatnam, Vizianagaram and Srikakulam, which are considered as eastern in local parlance, and to a part of Khammam district formerly belonging to the Godavari district in the Madras Presidency of the British Raj. (In terms of cultural regional identity, Prakasham and Nellore districts, though coastal, are considered outside Andhra). Andhra is considered far back in history as the birthplace of the Telugu language, and has till today a unique status in regard to the alleged purity of the Telugu which is spoken there.

Antecedents to the birth of *Burrakatha*: Changes in the cultural field

The immediate origins of the *Burrakatha* form are to be understood in the political context of the struggle for Independence. They relate to the changes that affected several cultural fields (written literature, theatre, folk narrative forms) which were clearly distinct until then (culturally as well as sociologically), but which were to find a common synthetical path under the influence of political militancy. As such, one should remember that the *Burrakatha* structure of performance relates expressively to the ideological aim (to bring a new political consciousness) for which it was considered particularly a fitting medium or 'vehicle' of expression.

The evolution in the fields of (written) poetry, literature and theatre (mainly dominated by Brahmanic culture) which was to be seen in Andhra since the 1880s with the advent of prose, social reform ideology and the influence of Shakespeare's plays (and Ibsen to a lesser extent) through Poona and Dharwar Marathi theatre took a new, more radical turn with the nationalist credo which came to the fore at the time of and after the *svadesi* and *vande mataram* movements.

This 'socially and politically motivated' evolution in the artistic field had a strong influence on the 'democratisation' of the literary and written language which gave rise to the modern Telugu Movement (*vyavaharika bhashodyamam*), that was later to indirectly favour the popular writing of *Burrakatha* by numerous uneducated authors and in simplifying access to written literature. Let me just state here the names of Kandukuri Viresalingam Pantulu (1848-1919) and Gurajada Appa Rao (1861-1915), two great writers and social reformers. They are the foremost innovators in the evolution of literature and theatre for the period 1880 to 1910. Apart from a play in prose on contemporary 'social evils' in society Gurajada Rao is particularly renowned for patriotic songs and a new metre in prosody that later found their way into the structure of *Burrakatha* alongside the inescapable reference to his name.

From the early 1910s Telugu theatre plays (*natakalu*) were a discrete means to convey new social or political ideas, often in a traditional garb. They again took an even more radical turn in the 1920s with plays being directly inspired by political events, while incorporating songs written by folk writers as well. At the same time, erudite writers took inspiration from oral folk literature (*janapada sahityam*; *janapada sangitam*) in writing folk songs themselves to convey the nationalist message to the people at large. So much so that:

> There were during 1930-1947 hundreds of such songs relating to the fight for independence, and the movement against untouchability and the uplift of the down-trodden Harijans. . . . During those days, bands of patriots were awake at early dawn, and marched along the streets, singing the 'songs of awakening'.[2]

This cultural and ideological evolution led to the formation of a Progressive Writers Association Movement (*abhyudaya sahityodyamam*) which was to have a strong theoretical influence on the cultural strategy of the Communist Party of India (CPI) in the late 1930s and early 1940s, when it created a cultural branch (the *praja natya mandali*) to help define and implement slogans and changes in the traditional folk domain. In fact, it organised militant camps (*sibiram*) in which the formation of artists and troupes (*dalalu*) was one of its leading preoccupations. From then on, newcomers outside the scope of hitherto traditional occupation (*vrith*) would come into the field of 'folk performing arts' particularly through *Burrakatha* writing and acting.

The *Jangam katha*

Until then *Jangam katha* was very popular in Andhra. *Jangam katha* is a traditional folk narrative that specialises in the expression of heroic ballads (*viragadhalu*) expressed by *Jangamas*. These itinerant mendicants of the *veera Shaiva* faith have a priestly-caste status, mostly in funeral rites, with Shaivite groups of the shudra *varna* such as weavers (*devanga*), potters (*kummari*), washermen (*cakali*) among others. *Bobbili yuddham, Palnati yuddham* and *Mugguru Marathilu* (the three Marathis) represent the three main stories of their repertory. *Bobbili yuddham* (the war of Bobbili) and *Palnati yuddham* (the war of Palnadu) are also to be found as the most important stories in the present repertory of the *Burrakatha*.

These are stories of local wars between small kingdoms (*zamindaris*; *samasthanalu*) which show the intrusion of a foreign invader. Roghair (1982) has presented a good study and translation of the epic of Palnadu in a specific tradition, while giving its otherwise general context of production, including medieval literature as well as *Burrakatha*. Whereas *Palnati yuddham burrakatha* is more popular in and around Guntur District, *Bobbili yuddham burrakatha* is largely the main favourite story in the North Coastal Districts. The action, historically asserted, takes place in the mid-eighteenth century.

It tells how the prosperity of a kingdom is brought to ruin when a rival kingdom brings in French colonial power to help destroy its local enemy. Alongside the theme of the king's death on the battlefield and the king's self-sacrificial offering, the alternate allied theme of the queen's chastity (in the larger conceptual frame of *pativratyam*) offers an exemplification of what is to be found in *Burrakatha* at large in terms of the main thematic content inherited from traditional heroic ballads (*viragadhalu*).

Alluri Sitarama Raju is the third main story in the *Burrakatha* repertoire. It tells of a local armed struggle in 1822-24 led by hill-tribals organised against the British by a patriot of kshatriya origin. Playing in a more hidden way on the similar theme of the heroic death of the king, it shows clearly how traditional stories like *Bobbili yuddham*, focusing on the evils brought about by a foreign power, were put in the service of a new type of message directed toward a mass of non-literate people — a message said to lead to political consciousness, and centered on the modern idea of the strength of organised resistance by people in face of oppression by the rulers.

From *Jangam katha* to *Burrakatha*

In Andhra, many authors and the 'authorised' public at large (*Burrakatha* authors, interpreters, erudite locals and scholars on the subject) see the *Jangam katha* as the main source of influence in the constitution of *Burrakatha* as a specific form. They sometimes specify that *Burrakatha* came to existence as it is because *Jangam katha*, already having a structure of performance well-fitted to pass on a propagandist message, had begun to be used to express political ideas. I shall not deal in detail with this subject but wish to point out a few facts in the evolution of the *Jangam katha* which confirm this viewpoint, and show that *Burrakatha* did not come into existence before the 1940s.

Interviews that I conducted in the field with old-age *Burrakatha* artists point to a strong metamorphosis of *Jangam katha* in the 1930s. They say that traditional interpreters transformed their mode of narration in response to the political context of the period which was seeing educated militants using the narrative structure of the *Jangam katha* in their own, non-sophisticated way (they had no musical training). It seems that, prior to this, the first political *Jangam katha* (a manuscript never published) had been written in 1919 by Abburi Ramakrishna Rau, a Brahman and a poet, on the tragedy of Jalianwalabagh at Amritsar. On the other hand, the first *Burrakatha* booklets which were printed in the mid-1940s were still adjoining the term *Jangam katha* to titles of stories written in the form of *Burrakatha*, whereas the term *Burrakatha* itself did not come into printed existence before 1946 or 1948.

Sheik Nazer, a Muslim and a communist, is recognised today as the founder — the 'grandfather' — of *Burrakatha* (*Burrakatha pitamahudu*). His biographical details show that he was trained in *Burrakatha* with *Jangam*s, when he successively joined several communist-oriented troupes in or around 1942. At that time, these troupes were mostly narrating modern militant adaptations of *Bobbili yuddham* or stories with an economic or social content written by communist writers, such as 'The Bengal Famine' (Bengal *karuvu*) and 'Life Difficult' (*kashtajivi*). After having learnt the mode of rendering these stories, in performance and oral training, Sheik Nazer formed his own troupe. Influenced by a communist writer, Sunkara Satyanarayana, a celebrated composer of *Burrakatha natakam*s among other folk and literary forms, he began to write *Burrakatha*s along the same lines. He was instrumental in bringing a variety of structural changes both in the mode of composition as well as in the mode of performance of former *Jangam katha* stories. Nazer's first *Burrakatha, Palnati yuddham burrakatha*, was written through the 1940s while he performed it, gradually taking in new poetical or theatrical aspects from *Natakam*, and incorporating other metric and singing patterns from diverse traditional narrative forms. These modifications were to remain as the basis for *Burrakatha* codification still to be seen in writing and performance several decades later.

We can understand this process of gradual evolution and transformation of one form into another (that is *Jangam katha* into *Burrakatha*) still better, if we keep in mind the way the *praja natya mandali* (the cultural branch of the CPI) patronised a systematic training of militants in various folk forms under their traditional specialists, while communist writers were engaged in devising slogans and stories to be told in these new evaluative styles. When it noticed the popular appeal of the new-born form in the mid-1940s, the Congress Party soon joined in training and using *Burrakatha* troupes for its own political propaganda. This was even truer when the Communist Party of India organised a revolutionary movement in Telengana in the late 1940s-early 1950s. Social and political themes and stories were written or composed in the *Burrakatha* style by the two political parties.

All along an assertion of the nationalist and independence movements, the political struggle that developed in the Andhra region of the Madras Presidency during the first half of the century also had very strong regionalist overtones, often linked with linguistic re-vindication with respect to the Telugu language. These first played on an opposition between Andhra and Rayalasima. This was to lead to Andhra/Telugu militancy of the 1950s for a separate Andhra State organised on linguistic basis. It culminated in the fast unto death of Potti Shriramulu in 1952, the violent riots that followed his death, and the subsequent formation of the Andhra State and Andhra Pradesh State in 1953 and 1956 respectively, with the merging of the Rayalasima and Telengana areas. Again, the political struggle took violent linguistic and cultural overtones in the early 1970s with the *Jai Andhra* Movement which saw a regionalistic opposition between Telengana and Andhra. Each time *Burrakatha*s were used by the political parties as a most efficient means of communication and propaganda in the guise of a traditional popular entertainment.

The other local performing arts forms

Taking a clue from my own field experience in Andhra, I believe that when talking about 'folk performing arts' in India we are confronted with a deficit of knowledge both in terms of a repertory of the variety of their forms (which though large is by no means indefinite) and in terms of accurate descriptions concerning their artistic content (literary value — written and oral aspects — structure of performance) as well as the whole sociological context of the modes and circumstances of 'production'.

Therefore, prior to describing *Burrakatha* as it stands concretely today, I wish to give an idea of the main 'folk performing arts' usually seen in Andhra. This general background will help us understand better the specificity of the *Burrakatha*. Let me also point out that, due to scholarly re-assessment and prevalent democratic ideas, the modern generic appellation 'folk performing arts' is now very much present in local society and includes them in a general and common artistic category, notwithstanding the strong diversity of their sociological determinants. Expressions such as *janapada kala rupalu, janapada sangitam, janapada sahityam* cover all these forms.

Today most people concerned with these folk arts are preoccupied with the public disaffection towards them, even in rural areas, more particularly so with the younger generations. This is mostly due to the spread of modern means of communication and entertainment, formerly cinema and increasingly T.V. now. One should also mention the fascination of youngsters for western culture and music.

During performances, artists themselves include commentaries or humorous sketches which call on the public to be aware of this decline. In Andhra, they usually cite *Harikatha, Tolu bommalata, Jamukulakatha* alongside *Burrakatha* while addressing their plea to the audience. We must also mention the existence of *Natakam* and *Venkanna babu pata*, a popular denomination for a type of *Golla bhagavatam*, in order to give a good general idea of the variety of the folk 'performing arts' scene (*kala rangam*) in Andhra. However, we have excluded here other narrative and theatrical forms found within 'processional bodies' of the *jatra* type (and which are not yet recognised as 'folk performing arts').

HARIKATHA, TOLU BOMMALATA, GOLLA BHAGAVATAM AND NATAKAM: PRESENT-DAY YAKSHAGANAMS?

Telugu scholars point out the relation of *Harikatha, Tolu bommalata, Golla bhagavatam* and *Natakam* to the former *Yakshaganam*. This is also indirectly true for *Burrakatha* that evolved from *Jangam katha*, the traditional heroic ballad form (*sampradayaka viragadhalu*) which is rightly considered to be the main source of influence in the constitution of the *Burrakatha*. To me, this is a subject of open debate. What is known as *Yakshaganam* appears to be very diversified in terms of sociology, geography and history.

In fact, *Yakshaganam* seems to be a generic term for various narrative and theatrical forms which have existed in Andhra, Karnataka and Tamil Nadu, and were possibly born of a common Telugu/Kannada stem far back in history. Nineteenth-century historical information on oral forms of literature tend to show that *Jangam katha* was, at any rate, distinct from *Yakshaganam* in that period. *Yakshaganam* always seems to have had a higher degree of theatricality, whereas *Jangam katha* is related more to the narrative function (here, one could also mention the existence of *Bhattrajukatha* — another heroic ballad form, the scholarly knowledge of the history and description of which is quite deficient).

HARIKATHA

Said to be born, or at least re-defined, in the late nineteenth century, the Telugu *Harikatha* (the story of Hari, i.e., Visnu) definitely shows strong acquaintances with Brahman or Brahmanistic culture. Mostly taken from the *Purana*s the stories are told by a single 'stand-up' interpreter (man or woman) usually wearing a red *dhoti*. He is accompanied by two sitting musicians: one is playing fiddle, the other plays on the *mridangam*. The narrative told in the form of a typical half-sung recitative[3], sometimes inclusive of *shlokas*, appears like a rhythmed prose of uniform metre and is followed by narrated commentaries. One may find short humorous intervals, whose contents or themes though shorter are common with *Burrakathas*. *Harikatha* exponents belong to the Brahman community, with a majority of them coming from the often Sanskritised Vishva Brahman caste. Though there is no bar on anyone performing the *Harikatha*, one does not generally find performers from untouchable communities.

TOLU BOMMALATA, VENKANNA BABU PATA AND JAMUKULAKATHA

I will not say much about the *Tolu bommalata* (literally 'leather images' play), a variety of shadow-theatre. It is strictly associated with a single community of remote Marathi origin called *Telugu Bondilis* having a status bordering on untouchability. Four or five vocal interpreters (belonging to the same lineage from children to old people), in accompaniment with instruments, render *Ramayana* stories. The pattern of the metre and (consequently) their way of singing show a definite affinity with *Venkanna babu pata* and *Jamukulakatha*, two other traditional forms of story-telling closely associated with vocational specificity of the (sub-) caste — the Pune Golla (a shepherd caste of low status engaged in the priestly function) in the first case; the untouchable Mala community in the second.[4]

NATAKAM

It can be described as a type of lyrical theatre form which evolved from the Andhra tradition of *Yakshaganam* in the late nineteenth century under the influence of the British-oriented Dharwar and Poona theatres. Brown (1991:19) shows that *Yakshaganam* was a musical literary genre in its own right in the first half of the nineteenth century, belonging or identified with the larger class of 'musical compositions' (*sangitamulu*). It was distinct from the other two written literature forms (*samanya kavyamulu, maha kavyam*), being the only form to mingle 'couplets' with 'stanzas'.

Stories such as *Sita kalyanam, Rukmini kalyanam* which were typically seen in this theatre form are still prominent in today's *Natakam* repertoire. They have found their way into the *Harikatha* repertoire, and are also found in *Burrakathas*, usually with troupes that are more oriented towards Brahmanic culture or are less politically motivated. Compared to other 'theatrical-narrative' forms mentioned above, *Natakam* is definitely closer to 'theatre' by Indian as well as western standards. Compared to *Burrakatha*, performers here act and identify with the character. They sing and tell their part, but have no musical role, which is taken care of by the instrumentalists who are there in front of the stage. A few characters may dance sometimes, but this is rare.

In the local context *Burrakatha, Harikatha* and *Natakam* are at the same level of performance. These three forms compete for patronage as a source of entertainment during religious festival nights. The pattern of selection depends on the cost of the performance. Usually though, all these three forms will find their way once or several times on the same local stage during the many nights of festival celebrations. Yet they usually follow a certain time-structure in the performance hours.[5]

Let us now proceed towards a closer look at the artistic specificity of the *Burrakatha*, beginning with the meaning of the term.

The term *Burrakatha*

The term *Burrakatha* can be understood in a variety of ways. Some say it displays a relation to the percussion instrument called by various names (*dakki, gummeta*), among which *burra* is one. It could then mean something like a story (*katha*) told while playing the instrument *burra*. Others look for a seemingly far-fetched etymological relation to the word *tambura* that designates the (three or four) cord instrument which is played by the central performer. In both ways, the name given to the form shows a relation to one of the instruments played as a musical accompaniment to story-telling. This is one of the common modes of denomination for folkforms to be found elsewhere in Andhra with *Tamburrakatha, Jamukulakatha, Kanjirakatha* and others.

Many informants point out that the name *Burrakatha* is given to the folk form which gives pre-eminence to wit and humour. *Burra* is indeed a slang term for the top, the back of the head. By extension, it metaphorically designates 'intelligence' and 'wit'. At another level of signification, the term *Burrakatha* refers:

(a) to a certain type of story pertaining to a general repertory (to so and so story written and told in a certain typical style, e.g., *Bobbili yuddham burrakatha*).

(b) to a definite mode of performance in which a story is interpreted, or 'shown' (*Burrakatha pradarshanam). Burrakatha* is most commonly said to be 'told' (*Burrakatha ceppadam*), although the term *Burrakatha a datam* ('played') may also be used, when solicited. *Burrakatha* is never said to be 'sung', even if it is sometimes considered under the category of *janapada ge yalu* (folksongs).

(c) to a troupe specialised in interpreting these performances.

The term *dalam*

The term *dalam* is usually applied to designate the *Burrakatha* troupe, though the troupes may also be called *vrindam* or 'party'. The term '*dalam*' has several connotations. It means a 'group of men', a 'multitude', an 'army'. This connotation no doubt explains that the term was used by the communists who first trained and organised many *Burrakatha dalalu* in the 1940s. In local parlance the word *dalam* also means a 'closely tied stem and two leaves'. The term emphasises the coherence and homogeneity of the three members within the troupe, among whom are deposited three complementary aspects of an implicit single narrative aim of a higher order.

> The story (*katha*), humour (*hasyam*), and 'politics' (*rajakiyam*) together constitute the inseparable triple dimension of *Burrakatha* on the model of the Ganges with the (triple) *tresse triveni*. The *Burrakatha dalam* is serving the country (*desa sevaku*) as the *tulasi dalam* is serving god (*daivasevaku*).[6]

The *Burrakatha* troupe

The *Burrakatha* troupe always has three members. Men or women belonging to various castes may mingle, usually without caste-status considerations. Most *Burrakatha* interpreters belong to a shudra caste of 'middle-range' status, though Brahmans are also to be found in good numbers, more often than not in mixed troupes. Family troupes (husband/wife/daughter or son; husband/wife/ husband's brother) are not rare either.

Each interpreter composing the *Burrakatha* troupe has a distinct role or function which is never associated with any single or particular character of the story being told. Though some specific situations or episodes of the stories can theatrically be 'played'/enacted at times: for instance, the main story-teller will dramatise the pregnancy pains of the heroine; the two side-members will vividly parody a cock-fight with their percussion instruments. Rather, each 'character' of the *Burrakatha* troupe identifies with one narrative function (i.e., *katha, rajakiyam, hasyam ceppadam*) that he embodies individually; the three of them being respectively called *kathakudu* ('the one [who tells the] story', or 'story-teller'), *rajakiya* ('politics', understanding *rajakiya ceppevadu*: 'the one [who tells] politics', or 'social/political commentator'), and *hasyagadu* ('the one [who makes] humour', or 'jester').

The *kathakudu* wears a kingly attire. He is also called the *Burrakatha* 'king-emperor' (*Burrakatha chakravarti*). The *rajakiya* is sometimes called *mantri or mantrigaru*, and the *hasyagadu* is jokingly referred to as *pantulugaru* ([Brahman] teacher) in a mock-reference to his ignorance. This three-dimensional set-up appears then as a kind of metaphorical prolongation of the three moral/religious divisions of *dharmam*, *artha* and *kama*, but the complexity in analysing this relation is outside the scope of this general presentation. Let us only say here that two distinct hierarchical levels are noticeable in the system of appellation of the division of roles in the *Burrakatha* performance.

The story-teller *kathakudu* is singled out, as the central and main performer, whereas his two acolytes or companions are subsumed together under the same vocable of *vantalu*. This plural term means something like 'those that support or accompany', those 'that are on the sides'. (The *vantalu* are also frequently called with a Telugu anglicism 'side-artists' (*saidu, said artistu*); concurrently, the *kathakudu* is also called *sentaru* (centre) as he stands in the middle of the stage. He is also the one who plays a stringed instrument whereas his acolytes play drums.

Let us now turn to the concrete division of roles in the *Burrakatha* performance. It may happen that another instrumentalist plays *mridangam*. He generally sits against a wooden pole of the *pandal*, does not participate in the telling of the story, but accompanies *bhogam* dance intervals or other intervals that are interspersed in the performance, which usually lasts for some two hours on average (between one-and-a-half hours to three-and-a-half hours at the very most).

The narrative structure in the *Burrakatha* performance

THE DIVISION OF FUNCTIONS

Kathakudu

The prime narrator (*pradhana* or *mukhya kathakudu*) or main character or artist (*mukhya kalakarudu*), often simply called story-teller (*kathakudu*), stands in the centre of the stage (He keeps moving back and forth on the stage all through the performance). He tells the main, central story, which displays an epic character, even when narrating contemporary social or political events turned into a story (of heroic type). In fact, this 'epic story' may be drawn from or created out of the puranic lore, past historical events with a high legendary value or more recent events. They are always centred around the heroic deeds of a single character, thereby continuing the tradition of 'heroic stories' or *viragadhalu*. They are also linked with the *Yakshagana* tradition.

The *kathakudu* mostly narrates the story through songs, in accompaniment with *tambura* for tonality (*shruti*) and *andelu* for rhythm (*talamu*).[7] He is also known as *gayakudu* for that reason. This succession of short songs (some 20 of them in a two-hour performance) shows a very large variety of pattern in the metre and melodies (much larger than the more monotonous and purely oral traditional narrative heroic stories). They are generally not recognised as poetry and are considered quite imperfect in regard to poetical rules they tend to follow. The aesthetical unity of these songs is brought out through similar recurrent refrains of varying metre patterns (such as *tandana tandani tandana* and *bhalabhali*). Appropriately conforming with the songs and in alternation with a few more refrains, these are sung in chorus by the side-interpreters throughout the performance.

His *vantalu* (acolytes) may themselves sing various songs during the performance. These do not pertain to the narration of the central story. Hence, only the *kathakudu* is recognised as *gayakudu*. This relates no doubt to the fact that 'oral literature' or story-telling' can never be dissociated from sung aspects in Andhra tradition. This also points to the particular relation between prosody and singing. Yet, at times, between songs, the *kathakudu* himself also narrates the story in a spoken but literary or Sanskritised way. In fact, commentaries on these songs for introducing, explaining or developing them are told either by the *kathakudu* or by the *rajakiya*.

The presence of dance in *Burrakatha* theatricality is noticeable in the dance-bells (*gajjelu*) that the *kathakudu* will always wear as part of his dress. He stresses the *rasas* (mostly heroic, pathetic, 'erotic' and furious) presented in the rhythmic/metre pattern of the songs through a code of gestures (gestural and facial expression) and dance patterns, in part common to various forms, in part specific to this form. All of these are simple in form: eyes and mouth widenings, body extensions, quick jumps and repeated rotating movements. He uses his *tambura* to give aesthetic emphasis to his postures, holding it in various positions — changing the inclinations on the vertical and horizontal planes — according to the rhythmic and emotional content of the story. Whereas the dance-steps and movements of the *kathakadu* are executed on a straight line central to the stage, dance (or bodily movements) of the *vantalu* are done in an oblique way on each side of the *kathakadu*, from a close position to him at the front of the stage to a more distant one at the back of the stage.

Rajakiyabushana

The right-hand side stage character plays a dual role: he develops and explains (this is called *vachakam*) the events narrated mainly through songs by the *kathakudu*; he also comments on these through a 'commentary' (*vachanam*), in comparing them with present, contemporary (social or political) events or situations. He is often helped in doing this by interruptions brought in by the *hasyagadu*.

Hasyagadu (*hasyakalanidhi*)

The left-hand side character has the main, explicit function of making the audience laugh. His dress and make-up should already predispose the audience to laughing (he may paint false glasses around his eyes or wear funny dresses)[8] and enhance the constant comic effects he is always willing to bring to the foreground through his wit, parodical stances, change of voice-tone and exaggerated bodily movements.

He is the one who usually enables the *rajakiya* to make detailed comments on the social and political situation, on the difficulties or evils of the day, by first interrupting him when he goes on to explain some point in the story, pretending he doesn't understand either a word, a name, or a situation in the central story. Taking stock of the events in the main story, he will also develop long jokes, the thematic content of which compares comically with what happens in the story.

Apart from the stylistics at work, the opposition between the levels of the central story and that of humour in terms of content is quite significant. It implicitly displays the discrepancy between the ideal, noble model of the epic story and the difficult and practical reality or situation which is being displayed in the joke or humorous comment.

THREE NARRATIVE PHASES IN THE PERFORMANCE

The *Burrakatha* performance begins with a very similar introductory part for every troupe. It includes salutations to the relevant gods, to the kings and poets of old and recent past — very regionally and linguistically determined, to the patrons of the night performance, and to the assembly of people, the *sabha*.

Its remarks are directed toward the public which gives the impression of a dialogue with the audience. Here, the *hasyagadu* has a particular duty to make the audience sit, to pacify them and to attract their attention through humour. He begins by expressing a false fear of performing badly; the *rajakiya* answers with didactic explanations why the gods were first celebrated and what an assembly is and why it should be revered.

The freedom struggle's political heritage in the *Burrakatha* folkform is still clearly present in the way India is revered as 'Mother India' (*Bharat Mata*). The regional and linguistic Andhra/Telugu identity is also strongly expressed in a similar way. The Telugu land (*Telugu bhumi*) is Mother Andhra (*Andhra Mata*), the Telugu Mother (*Telugu Talli*): She is celebrated as having given birth to so many great kings and heros, who fought for the independence of the Andhra/Indian land. The greatness of the heros of Andhra is brought to light in refrains also: sometimes with a colouring of communist ideology.[9] The context of the freedom struggle is again present in the concluding 'taking leave' song of the performance, with the evocation of the freedom fighters' sacrifice.

The three narrative dimensions of *katha, rajakiyam* and *hasyam* start as soon as the salutations to the gods (mostly the Goddesses under the names of Vijayalaksmi, Amba, Vani-Sarasvati) and the introductory *shlokam* (usually to Vighneshvara) are over. This is common and remains similar from one troupe/performance to the next, but differs from other local folkforms. Contrary to comic remarks, jokes, or social/ political satirical comments in the main performance, the initial humorous repartee is often provided, alternatively through *kathakudu* songs and *rajakiya* didactic comments in printed booklets. This 'prologue' ends with the presentation of the story chosen for the night-performance.

The main part of the performance lies in the delivering of the story which gives its title-name to the particular *Burrakatha* being interpreted (say: *Krishna Arjuna yuddham, Rama Anjaneya yuddham, Kashta jivi*, and so on). The practical codification of *Burrakatha* as a folkform is also at play in the way dynamic interruptions are provided for in this central part of the performance: the 'epic story' is subject to humorous parallels and social/political comments. These may supplement the implicit ironical or satirical message contained in jokes. Usually initiated by the *hasyagadu*, the interruptions in the main story open the dialogue between the *hasyagadu* and the *rajakiya* in a narrative mode that gives much pre-eminence to an oral system of punctuation of short *énoncés* and repetition of sentences.

The performance ends with a salutation song to the audience, bidding people a good-bye, with a wish to come back and see them the following year.

Conclusion

I hope to have shown that *Burrakatha* today strongly appears as a unique and specific codified artistic folkform. Emerging out of a specific, much older folkform, in a new, modern, and political context, it helps us to understand how tradition finds its way in redefining culture when the time comes to carry on a different message.

The thematic orientation of heroism (*vira rasa*) initially given by the ballads still remains predominant in all *Burrakatha* stories. It echoes narrative traditions embedded in Andhra 'heroic stories' (*viragadhalu*). A few *Burrakatha* stylistic aspects (among which the impact of refrains is not to be disregarded) also emphasise the influence and permanence of a cultural level formerly associated with purely oral literature. Yet, *Burrakatha* can be considered as a king of synthesis of various Andhra literary, narrative and theatre traditions previously belonging to distinct or divergent cultural and sociological 'milieux', and now brought together in a single popular form.

What is the logic behind such an assimilation? It is quite in line, indeed, with what is to be often observed in the Indian context. The Telugu language itself is a perfect case in point: the frequency of synonymous words coming from Sanskrit, Telugu, Persian or English and imbibed by the living language reveals an astonishing richness and vitality. The process of assimilation and adaptation at work in the formation of *Burrakatha* also seems related to former shifts of similar nature in Andhra/Telugu literature and theatre, which *Yakshaganam* probably exemplifies at several moments in history.

Therefore, one can legitimately wonder if the large assimilation process to be seen in *Burrakatha* shows a continuation of the tradition of *Yakshaganam* in modern times. Is it linked with the necessity of folk/local culture to recreate new forms out of the older ones in order to retain its appeal and attraction? Is this triggered by the obsolescence of these forms, which somehow compels changes in order to survive, albeit in a new clothing, or is it mostly linked with external, political factors?

With *Burrakatha*, both traditional symbols and modern values testify and affirm the strong, perennial, regional identity based on language and culture. The way these two idioms combine in written composition and performance to give *Burrakatha* part of its specificity and attain a large popular appeal also confirms the idea that literature and theatre forms are never so active and attractive as in a period of strong political struggle or change. Today, in face of the dangers of deadly change that modern artificial modes and systems of communications bring with them for local, 'life-organic' culture and society, folkforms may appear doomed. Let's hope they will manifest enough adaptability and strength to retain their full local creative significance, breathing fresh life into living literature, humour and poetry.

Notes

1. Vatsyayan, 1980:41.
2. Sitapati, 1968:192.
3. The *Harikatha* recitative mode of narrating is often parodied in one way or another during *Burrakatha* performances.
4. The Pune Golla have definite ritual functions in Brahmanical temples such as Tirupati's Sri Venkateshvara. The second fulfils a priestly function in rituals of the local goddess (*grama devata*). Mala instrument players along with the vocal interpreter, who is a caste fellow tell the story of the goddess and predict oracles in her temple for the shudra patrons during her festival.
5. Similar to Brahmanistic lectures, such as *Sundara kanda upanyasalu*, *Harikatha*s sometimes begin around 6.00 pm, mostly when they are performed in a Brahman locality or in a context dominated by Brahman culture, such as a college festival or conference for instance. Elsewhere and more generally, they are performed around 8 or 8.30 p.m. They last for two hours or so. *Burrakatha*s are rarely ever performed before 8.30 p.m.; they usually begin any time between 8.30 and 9 p.m. They tend to begin earlier (starting around 8 p.m.) in a Brahman area. Though totally different in content, form, audience and destination *Tolu bommalatas* are usually performed at the same time and for the same duration as *Burrakatha*s though they tend to begin a little earlier. *Natakam*s usually begin around 9.30 pm and last until late in the night, close to day-break.
6. Nadira, 1977:31. *My translation from Telugu.*
7. Subba Rao, 1977: 34-5.
8. In the long interview he gave me Sheik Nazer explained that the *hasyagadu's* funny dress was originally born out of the political will to ridicule the religious function of the *Jangam*s through a parody of the religious paraphernalia.
9. 'Listen O heroic Brother Andhra the old heroic story'.

References

English

Ashton, B.M., & Christie B., 1977, *Yaksgana*, New Delhi, Abhinav Publications.

Brown, C.P., 1840, *Essay on the Language and Literature of the Telugus*, Madras, 1991 reprint, AES.

Gargi Balwant, 1962, *Folk Theater of India*, Washington, University of Washington.

———, 1966, *Theatre in India*, New York, H. Wolf.

Mudiraj, G.N.R., 1971, 'Minstrels Beggars of Telengana: Custodians of Oral Literary Tradition', *Folklore*, 12: 223-7.

Ramaraju, B., 1978, *Folklore of Andhra Pradesh*, New Delhi, National Book Trust.

Rao, B.V., 1973, *History of the Eastern Chalukyas of Vengi* (AD 610-1210), Hyderabad, Andhra Pradesh Sahitya Akademi.

Rangacharya, Adya, 1969, *The Indian Theatre*, New Delhi, National Book Trust, 77-90.

Roghair, Gene H., 1982, *The Epic of Palnadu*, Oxford, Clarendon Press.

Sarma, Mallampalli Somasekhara, 1948, *History of the Reddi Kingdoms, Circa* AD 1325 *to Circa* AD 1448, Rajahmandry, Andhra University.

Sitapati, G.V., 1968, *History of Telugu Literature*, New Delhi, Sahitya Akademi.

Subbha Rao T.V., 1980, 'Telugu folk additions to Mahabharata', *Asian Folklore Studies* 39: 137-44.

Varadpande, M.L., 1979, *Traditions of Indian Theatre*, New Delhi, Abhinav Publications.

Vatsyayan Kapila, 1980, *Traditional Indian Theatre*, New Delhi, National Book Trust.

Telugu

Bittu Venkatesvarlu, 1990, 'janapadakalalu: o paricayam', in *Rashtristhay janapada kalotsavalu*, Hyderabad, Telugu Visvavidyalayam, 47-53.

Donappa, T., 1978, *Telugu Harikadha Sarvasvam*, Nagarjuna University.

Joga Rao, S.V., 1961, *Andhra Yaksagana Vangmaya Caritra*, Andhra University Publications.

———, 1975, *'Yaksagana'*, in *Telugu vani*, Hyderabad, Prapanca Telugu Mahasabhala Pratyeka Sancika, 189-92.

———, 1977, 'Yaksagana', in *Natyakala*, Janapada Kalala Pratyeka Sancika, Hyderabad, 3-15.

Kongati, Gopalakrishnayya, 1990, "Janapadakalarupalu - Prajanatyamandali Patra", in *Rashtristhay Janapada Kalotsavalu*, Hyderabad, Telugu Visvavidyalayam, 43-46,

Kolhatkar, Inak, 1975, 'Natika', in *Telugu vani*, Hyderabad, Prapanca Telugu Mahasabhala Pratyeka Sancika, Hyderabad, pp. 265-8.

Mikkilineni, Radhakrishnamurti, 1975, 'Janapada Kalarupalu', in *Telugu vani*, Prapanca Telugu Mahasabhala Pratyeka Sancika, 382-86

Nadira, 1977, *'Burrakathalu'*, in *Prapanca Telugu Mahasabhalasandar Bhamuna Pracuritamu*, Hyderabad, Andhra Pradesh Sangita Natak Akademy, 1-47.

Natyakala, juin 1977, *Janapada Kalala Pratyeka Sancika*, Hyderabad, Vol, 11, section 6.

Ramaraju, B., 1958, *Telugu Janapadageya Sahityamy*, Hyderabad, Andhra Racayitala Sangham.

Subba Rao T.V., 1977, *'Burrakathalu'* in *Natyakala*, Hyderabad, Janapada Kalala Pratyeka Sancika, June, Vol. 11, section 6., 24-58.

Tirumalarayu, Jayadhiir, 1987, *Prajakalarupalu*, Hyderabad, Master Art Printers.

Vijaya Kumar, P., 1990, *Burrakatha Samajika Paristhitulu*, Ph.D. thesis, Nagarjuna University.

13

The Hero and His Context
The Oral Narrative of Kaba and Baji

Ajay Dandekar

THE last two decades have witnessed an increased interest in oral narratives of South Asia (Blackburn 1985; Sontheimer 1989, 1991; Bruckner *et al.* 1993). In this paper we have discussed the oral narrative of Kaba and Baji, nomadic and the sedentary antagonists of the Gavli Dhangar milieu of the semi-arid tract of the Deccan plateau.

For the sake of clarity and continuity of the argument, this paper is divided into four sections. The first section discusses the Gavli Dhangar milieu in the ecological context. The next section then outlines the historical background against which the oral narrative unfolds itself, and also argues for more 'space' to cattle pastoralists and highlights the role they once played on the Deccan plateau. In the subsequent two sections we have taken up the oral narrative of Kaba and Baji, the contextual change it reflects and the concept of a 'hero' as it understands.

I

> Well, as we stay at Javali, the day we start (on our migration/transhumance) our first stop is at Naikobawadi. Since Naikobawadi is near to our place it is convenient for us to do so. Next day we start, as usual, grazing our sheep along the way. Availability of water is not a problem at all as in the month of *Deepawali* there is plenty of water. If there have been recent rains, then we get good grazing areas throughout our migration tracks. At times though it may happen that the sheep may not get any fodder. But we have no choice; we must continue with our transhumance. Now our next day's halt is at Phaltan. There are seasonal streams on the way, hence water and fodder are not a major problem in this area. Our next halt is at Kalaj. Then we start from there and halt at Lonand. After Lonand we come straight to the grazing grounds of Bhade. After that, due to afforestation (our grazing fields are lost to us) we do not stop and come straight to the

bridge at Mandi. From there we start and our next halt is at the grazing grounds in Bhor. This is our traditional market place. We do our marketing there and the next day we start and reach Hurdushi. Now what happens is (traditional experience) our sheep may not get sufficient grazing, or fodder, but of water there is no major problem. Since it is the month of *Deepawali* (i.e., just after the monsoons) water is not a major problem though green and good fodder is a problem.

Our next halt is at Manjari (through the Bhor ghat). We reach Manjari in the evening. Next day we start from there and reach Birawadi. Now here the paddy has just been harvested, and thus there is plenty for the sheep to graze. There is thus plenty of water and plenty of fodder. At Birawadi we 'perform' a *jatra* of gods. Here we sacrifice some sheep. We offer the meat to Gods, and later it is distributed to the people. After Birawadi, we come to Kamble. Here the people (from my clan) who have to go to Mahad stay there and we come ahead to Mahad and the next day to Dasgaon. I come straight to this place (at Pale). Next day I reach 'my' village at Devali-Moor. Now, my brother goes to Devali, I to Moor, my cousin Rama and my uncle Gaju go to Pain. Farmers await us egerly We normally do not ask anyone's permission to pen our sheep in their field; we inform them after they have been penned. In fact, our experience is that the farmers are extremely happy, if thus informed. Now, we then turn by turn pen our sheep in everyone's fields. This decision about penning the sheep in someone's field entirely remains with us. We try to accommodate everyone in our cycle of penning. Our sheep also get to eat the remains of the paddy (once the harvesting is over). Later the fodder gets scarce as fields are prepared for the new season. In-between (after the month of *Magh*), pulses and other related crops are sown. This is ready for harvest with two/two-and-a-half months of sowing. Once this is harvested, we again let our sheep in for grazing.

Now our dealings with the village is fixed. Normally we get six *paali* of rice (1995 information) per 100-125 sheep penned. Some give it immediately, and others take a while and give it from the next crop. We also give them sheep (for sacrifice) during festivals. Thus, we spend almost six months there (on the west coast). The moment we get to the seventh of June which is also the era of the *Mriga nakshatra*, we start back for our *desa*. Once the rains begin there is no chance of us staying on. Thus, we start back immediately (before the seventh of June). Now the question is how do we decide on this date of seventh of June? Because the rains of the *Mriga nakshatra* start on that day. So we start back a little early.

Who decides as to who will go to which village? Our tradition is that my grandfather and my great grandfather used to come here (in this region). My father too came here and thus I also come to Moor. Now at Moor for instance there is enough 'work' for only one Dhangar; hence, the rest are

> not required. One can easily survive and sustain himself here. Similarly at Devali and other places too, at Naigaon, at Pale, where my grandfather used to go and now my uncle and my cousins go. Suppose somebody else also comes, for instance, to Moor, then how is this problem solved?
>
> It is like this. I now identify myself with the people of Moor. I give them sheep, pens. The people of the village also see to it that no other Dhangar comes here. He can come only if I 'allow' him to. They cannot claim hereditary rights over the grazing fields of this village. In case people violate this basic norm, then there are severe sanctions, which might lead to ex-communication also. This decision is taken by caste *panchayat*.

The above description by an informant details the migration of one Dhangar *wada* from the region of Phaltan towards the west coast. In order to understand the context of the narrative, it is imperative on our part to understand the changing nature of the context, especially the ecology, before we move on to the next section.

The area of study falls within the present state of Maharashtra. The two primary relief divisions in the area are the plateau and the coastal strip immediately to the west of the plateau. Major parts of the plateau are underlain by the rocks of volcanic lava. This area can be further divided on the basis of the relief. The suggested subdivisions, following in a sequence from west to east, are the coast land, Western Ghats, plateau tracts and the river valleys.

The western coast is a narrow strip of land, 75 km at its widest. This narrow coastal strip is sandwiched between the Arabian sea to its west and the massive wall of the Western Ghats to its east and offers a pleasing contrast to the rugged landscape in the plateau.

The uneven topography of the coast consists of transverse ridges of the *ghats*, isolated hills, low lying plateau and narrow river valleys. Physiographically the coast land can be divided into three zones. The eastern zone is bounded by the massive wall of the Western Ghats. This landscape widens into gently undulating plateau to the west of the eastern zone towards Ratnagiri. The western zone is demarcated by the formation of the tidal waves.

Vaiterna, Ulhas, Amba, Savitri and Vasisthi are the major rivers of the area. All these rivers are seasonal in character and are unfit for navigation except at the river mouths.

The importance of this narrow strip of land lies in its ports. The main ports on the western coast are Revas, Mora, Dabhol, Ratnagiri, Vijaydurga, Malvan, Vengurla, Thane and Sopara. Though the coast stands in seemingly splendid isolation from the mainland it nevertheless is an important integral part of the same. For centuries overseas trade has been carried on through these ports, which has had an important bearing on the mainland. One aspect of this trade is of some importance. The coast experiences heavy rainfall in the four months of monsoon. This heavy rainfall entails the termination of the movement of goods across the passes and on the ports, which in turn reduces the effective trading time that is available. This is an important factor having some bearing on the 'regions'.

Thus, the western coast, though physiographically isolated, nevertheless constitutes an extremely important component of the area under study.

The mountains present a different picture. The Western Ghats that run in a continuous line from north to south form the western edge of the plateau. The coastal line proper is a succession of high plateaus and occasional rounded peaks connected with low saddles. These chains of hills take a width of 30-40 km and rise to a height of 915 to 1220 meters. Erosion and local faulting give them an appearance of 'chains of plateau tops'. Local weakness breaks these plateau tops in passes. Heavy precipitation restricts agriculture to only a limited area.

Western Ghats play an important role in the totality of the landscape. The *ghat*s decisively influence the rainfall pattern in the area which in turn sets other variables in motion.

A narrow strip of land mass, not more than 25 km at its widest divide, forms the transitional zone from the wetter west to the drier east. The sheep-keeping Dhangars are primarily located in this semi-arid tract which is bounded to its east by the transitional strip of the Maval and to its west by the rice-growing areas. The core of this vast semi-arid zone is formed by the eastern parts of Pune, Satara, Kolhapur and Sangli districts and the entire Nagar district.

The fall of rain follows the topography. It has been noticed that the precipitation decreases to the leeward side of the Western Ghats due to the rain shadow of the *ghat*s (Deshpande, 1971 : 30-1: Ray 1986 : 200; NCAR, 1976). The semi-arid zone thus receives less than 750 mm rain per annum and in some pockets it is even as low as 450 mm. The semi-arid zone is thus characterised by uncertain and lower rainfall, millet cultivation and dry deciduous thorny forest cover today. Agriculture as a system is an extremely late phenomenon here as one really cannot 'undo' a desert or a semi-arid zone (Amiran, 1977 :7). Today this vast semi-arid belt is occupied by the sheep-keepers, the Dhangars of Maharashtra.

II

Enthoven has listed twenty-two endogamous and one hundred and eight exogamous groups of Dhangars, the sheep-keeping pastoralists of western Maharashtra. He enumerated the early twentieth-century Dhangar population at 467,622 and they were found all over the Deccan, the Konkan and the southern Maratha country. Four decades later, Karve recorded that the Dhangars were to be found in what is today known as Madhya Maharashtra. Malhotra (Malhotra and Gadgil, 1984), in his most recent findings, notes that the estimated population of Dhangars is nearly three million, and these people are spread over all the twenty-six districts of Maharashtra. Malhotra further notes that sheep-rearing Hatkars, and blanket weaving Kannade, Sangars, buffalo-rearing Dange, and the meat-selling Khatiks occupy a predominant position over others within the Dhangar caste cluster. Compared to these communities, the Nikhar, Ladshe, Hande, Kurma, Kannade, Telangi and others number only a few thousand and obviously are a minor component of the Dhangar caste cluster. Almost all these scholars agree that the largest concentration of the Dhangars is to be found in Madhya Maharastra, i.e., the semi-arid tracts of Maharashtra.

The Dhangars divide themselves into a group of three-and-a-half. These three-and-a-half divisions include the Hatkars, Mhaske or Gavlis and Khutekars, and the Khatiks as a 'half caste'. The Hatkars also call themselves Khillari Dhangars. We shall discuss the significance of this particular association later.

We are also of the opinion that the number three-and-a-half is not a random selection. This number has cosmological and religious significance. We find that such numbers as seven, three hundred and fifty, are entities with significance. '350' happens to be an ideal number of sheep for a unit (*vadi*) of 5.7 Dhangar families. In Dhangar mythology the Lord Biroba outplayed 350 shepherd boys. According to an account of the famous Khandoba temple at Jejuri the temple has eighteen arches, 350 lamp pillars (*deepmala*) and 900,000 steps.

Though the number of steps cited for the temple at Jejuri is definitely fictitious, the number of arches and pillars is correct. The auspicious character of the number three-and-a-half is also reflected in the three-and-a-half auspicious periods (*sadetin muhurta*). The Dhangars, it seems, are aware of the significance of this particular entity, and wish to associate with its auspicious nature.

The Khillari Hatkars have been described as "landholders, potters, messengers, house servants, shepherds and a few money chargers". It is also recorded that they raise Khillari breed of cattle, and it should be noted that till today, the home of Khillari breed of cattle is western Sholapur, eastern Satara and Sangli districts.

Etymologically, the term Hatkar can be reduced to *hatti*. Captain Fitzgerald, as quoted by Syde Hussain, states,

> The general idea is that originally there were twelve tribes of Bargi dhangars, who came from Hindustan and the country about Hingoli was called Bara

> Hatti, which the Hatkars say is a corruption of the words Bara Hatkars, or the country of twelve Hatkars.

Thus, the *Bara Hattikar* would mean country of Dhangars of twelve *hatti*s. According to the Dravidian etymological dictionary h (~ p) *atti* has the following meanings: pen or fold (Kannada); hamlet (Malayalam); Cows fall, sheep fold (Tamil). A *hatti* therefore would mean a sheep pen, or a camp or a settlement of pastoralists. In old Kannada lexicon *hattikara* occurs as a synonym for *gavali* or cow herd. It is, therefore, clear that a relationship is straight away established between the pastoral group and its occupation. The Dhangars do not use the term *hatti* for settlement any more (the term in use is *vadi*) but, as their oral tradition indicates, they are aware of it. This term occurs in one of the tales in which Lord Shiva is searching for Yelu Gavlan: "He came to the third forest. There he came upon a *vada* of Gavdas. He approached the *vada*, called to the Gavdas. A *vada* of twelve *hatti*s." Thus, the 'memory' of *hatti* and its original meaning is preserved in the Dhangar traditions.

III

"But before the Dhangars there were Gavlis" – (Sontheimer, 1989). We must contextualise the Gavlis in the habitat they find themselves in today.

Malhotra and Gadgil estimate the Gavli population at 85,000 in 1977 (Malhotra and Gadgil 1984:443). Today they are primarily located along the Western Ghats 'from 19°N to 13°N latitudes' covering the crescent of Maharashtra, Goa and Karnataka (*ibid.*). It is interesting to note that though the Gavlis share the habitat with the mouse, deer, barking deer, sambar, wild pig, porcupine, black napped hare, jungle fowl, and others they curiously lack any tradition of hunting. Perhaps they did not belong to that habitat earlier.

Ethnographic studies reveal that the Gavli eco-niche does not clash with the Kunbis' though they share the same habitat today.

The traditional pattern of subsistence of the Gavlis can be analysed in terms of the butter economy. The Gavli settlements are located away from any markets, and hence fluid milk has no takers. The clarified butter is sold to the nearby markets. In this economy the clarified butter is exchanged for *ragi* (*Eleusine Coracerna*) or *jowar*. The ethnographic study by Gadgil and Malhotra indicates that apart from cereal the other requirements of the Gavlis are few. These include edible oil, lentils, jaggery, oil and a few miscellaneous items such as salt, condiments, tobacco and dried fish.

The Gavlis, confined as they are in the Western Ghats, are relegated to the margins today, with sheep-keepers emerging as the dominant pastoral group in the semi-arid zone. But was that always the case?

We have sufficient evidence to definitely suggest that the Gavlis once occupied the strategic position of sheep-keepers, before a part of them were forced to migrate to their new habitat.

It is stated that after the disintegration of the Satvahana empire in the middle of the third century AD the Abhiras founded a kingdom in Khandes (Suryavanshi, 1962). The Abhiras are the classic cattle-breeders of the Sanskrit literature. One of the Abhira kings has left an inscription dated AD 250 in the Nasik caves.

One of the earliest towns in the 'scarcity zone', Mhasvad is referred to as *Mahisa-vada* in some sources (Khare, 1961: p. 202). According to an oral tradition of the temple there, there was a settlement of Gavlis, i.e., cattle-keepers in Mhasvad. This list can be increased. We have Vir on the Nira, which has a strong pastoral tradition, a devastated Gavli *wada* and Mhasoba temple at the outskirts of the village. The oral tradition says that the Dhangars "came with his cattle and sheep" to the village. (Arole, 1982: p. 4) In fact, wherever we turn in the scarcity zone, the oral tradition of the sheep-keepers suggests that they were preceded by the Gavlis. Almost all the major Dhangar *vadi*s have a ruined Gavli *wada* in the near vicinity. If we pull back in the Bhima river in the east, i.e., almost at the edge of the existing 'pastoral region', we come across Dhangars who still maintain a multispecialised herd. In the scarcity zone, actually at the other end, near its western edge near the town of Baramati, lies the village of Mhasobavadi, a typical example of a village based entirely on cattle herding. The village sustains 1500 head of cattle and 4000 sheep. The god of the village is of course Mhasoba.

Gavli — Dhangars

We had earlier noted that Dhangars call themselves also Khillari Dhangars. On the basis of the available evidence it becomes clear that the entire area encompassing the river valley and stretching up to Maval once sustained a multispecialised herd, and gradually it moved towards mono-specialisation. Archaeological evidence suggests that pastoralism with multispecialised herds was in vogue from 1500 BC onwards. (Dhavlikar, 1988)

We have also suggested that the Gavlis once occupied the plateau tracts. The Gavlis, Hatkars and the Mendhke (shepherds) claim that they all were originally one. This is, amongst other things, borne out by the strong memory retained in the oral traditions. (Sontheimer 1989: p. 122). Genetic studies have revealed that these three groups are amongst the closest in the entire caste cluster of 23 endogamous castes of Dhangars. (Malhotra and Gadgil, 1984) All the three groups have a number of clan names in common; their deities also suggest their composite nature.

So far, no conclusive argument has been put forward to explain the bifurcation of the two.

IV

Text

It is against this historical possibility that the cattle-keepers were once the dominant force on the plateau, that we must turn to the oral narrative of Kaba and Baji.

> Kaba was the head of Dwantada clan. His *wada* was at Dohldarya. Now when the *wada* was at Dohldarya, at that time there were no sheep but cattle. Now when Kaba had cattle and when the *wada* was at Dohldarya there was a famine. Nowadays, people call it famine, but during those days they use to call it *burg*. *Burg* meant famine in those days. Now so there was no water to drink, no grass to eat (for the cattle). Then what Kaba did? He appointed pairs to locate water, pastures, among other things.
>
> First pair was appointed, it was sent to Khandesh. Second pair was appointed, it was sent to Mandesa. Third pair was appointed, it was sent to Mudhi Moglai. Fourth pair was appointed, it was sent to the Konkan area. Then the fifth pair was appointed. They were asked to go to Phaltan Gujari. The pairs thus were asked to find out about the availability of grass and water. Now the pairs started coming back from the areas they had been sent to. First to come back was the Khandesh pair. They reported that they could not identify enough water and pastures. They said there was no point in going there. Now that pair met with a failure. Next to come back was the pair from Mandesa. They said there was not enough pasture there: 'There is some near the mountains but not enough. We do not want to go there.' Now the pair sent to Mudhi Moglai came back. Now they also said that they could not find water or pastures there. Then to return was the pair sent to the Konkan area. They also reported similar failure. Thus the first four pairs were a failure. They said, let us see what happens with the pair sent to the Phaltan area. The fifth pair in the meanwhile had arrived in the Phaltan Gujari area. They were in the area of Asu Songaon. The rains had been excellent there, the wheat crop was blooming in the field, the pasture land was green, and there was plenty of grass and water for the cows. They picked up five bundles of grass, tied them up and started on their way back.
>
> Back home Kaba, the *mirdha* of the *wada*, was waiting. He told his wife Pemabai that four pairs were already back without any success. Now the fifth was the pair from Phaltan Gujari area. They seemed to be happy, hence they should welcome them with an *arati*. Pemabai prepared the *arati*, but when she was performing the *arati*, the *vat* went out. Why this bad omen, she thought! She asked, 'what is the matter!' They said, 'Pastures

are there, water is there, everything is adequate.' 'Where is it?' (she asked). The crop is blooming, the grass is in plenty. But where? They said at Asu Songaon. 'These are the five bundles of grass. But there has been a bad omen,' says Pema, 'Let us not go there.' Kaba said, 'These women!' He said, 'We will go.' Pema said there has been a bad omen. The *arati* could not be performed. He said, 'No, I'll go'. He took only the cows along with him. His first stop was at Raidandav. It was now midnight. It was the *amavasya*. He said, that the tiger might come to take cattle. Let me take a nap. Asked everyone to be vigilant. Then he got up. Asked others to sleep. The tiger came. The tiger came to steal his cattle. Kaba said, 'You....,' Kaba ran and got hold of the jaws of the tiger. He then tore the tiger into two pieces. He then came back and slept. He said, 'Now that I've killed the tiger, he won't come again.' Pemabai got up at dawn. She looked for fuel wood, finishing morning chores. As she came out, she saw that fearsome animal lying there. Pemabai was terrified. She ran towards Kaba and fell on him. She could not speak. Kaba said, 'Why did you fall on me. As it is I've had little sleep in the night.' She told him about the tiger. Kaba said, 'I already killed him in the night.' Then she came out and completed her morning chores.

Now they have come up to Ridanda. Now they are near the Asu Songaon. They have camped at Raidand. Kaba is sitting there. He has taken his *batwa* out. He is not chewing his tobacco. The cattle has started browsing in the green pasture land of Asu Sangaon. They grazed today in the forest and the next day in the fields of Asu Songaon.

Baji Sonalkar is the head of the village. He is informed. He asked, 'Who is this enemy.' 'Not a crop is standing now, in our fields,' said Baji. 'I must meet him.' Baji got up in the morning. Had his ritual bath, performed *puja*, girdled his sword and went to meet Kaba at his *wada*. Who, Baji Sonalkar. He went to meet Kaba. Kaba welcomed him. 'Come Bhavji, (Baji happened to be Kaba's brother-in-law), eat with me.' Baji thought, 'I must somehow kill Kaba. I can inherit his wealth.' That is how Baji thought. Thinking thus, Baji said, 'Come, let us go and eat the red vegetable in the forest...' Come for a hunt, he said. Kaba agreed and started off with Baji on a hunt. Kaba on foot and Baji on the horse. In the forest they came across deer first. Kaba said, 'Bhavji, come on, kill them.' Baji said there is no manliness in killing a deer. He repeated a similar refrain when they came across wild bear, rabbits and other animals. Finally they reached a denser area and a groove. Those days there was a thick forest here. Now it has all gone. The Nira ran across with forest on both sides. Baji urged Kaba to get into the grooves. Baji said that the real *shikar* was inside that groove. Kaba went inside the groove. Kaba was confronted with the tiger. Kaba was a man. He killed the tiger inside the groove and came out. 'Bhavji,' he said, 'why did you run away like a shore!' Baji said, "Bhavji, one tiger was not for two of us, hence I stayed behind." Kaba said, 'Allright Bhavji, let us drink water. I am thirsty.' They went to the river Nira. Kaba was tired after his exertions.

> Kaba bent down and saw the reflection of Baji's sword in the water. Kaba felt Baji was joking. As soon as Kaba drank water, Baji beheaded Kaba. Kaba cursed Baji in his dying moment. He said, 'My wife is pregnant. If a son is born, he will kill you in front of the entire *chavdi*. If a daughter is born, she will serve you.'
>
> Now Pemabai had nobody to turn to. She therefore had to stay with Baji (her brother). Pemabai gave birth to a son. As the son grew up, Baji realised that Kaba's curse may come true. Kaba's son understood what fate had befallen on his father. He vowed that he will take revenge. Baji heard this. Baji ordered that Kaba's son should be killed. The entire village went to Pemabai's house to kill Kaba's son. Pemabai started crying and requested her son to eat his last meal. She knew that Baji had sent these men to kill her son. Kaba's son told her to collect herself. They charged him with the encroachment of their fields and said he will be killed for this. Kaba's son got angry. He killed all of them and went straight to Baji's house. Pulled him out of the *chavdi* and beheaded him. He took the beheaded head to his mother and asked her to sit on Baji's head and have a ritual bath. Even now we can see the memorials and temples of Baji, Kaba and Kaba's son at Ratandi.

Certain factors clearly emerge from the story. It can be suggested that the cattle-keepers hold an upper hand over the sedentary agriculturists, as is clear in the manner in which Kaba is treacherously murdered by Baji. Secondly, the story provides the necessary 'textual' background to the silent hero-stones that depict death, and are found in abundance in this part of the semi-arid belt. We must examine the historical context suggested by the hero-stones before drawing any conclusions.

Sati and hero-stones are largely found in Western, Central and Southern India. We come across basically two types of hero-stones from Rajasthan. They are the *paliyas* (single-panelled stones) and the *govardhan* pillars that have a sculpted top. The *govardhan* pillars are memorials for those who died in the cattle raid, but battle scenes are also depicted at times. A Sati would normally be shown by a depiction of a couple facing each other. Chronologically, these stones would fall between the sixth to the thirteenth and fourteenth centuries AD. The Saurashtra series is of a relatively recent period, belonging to the last three to four hundred years. Here the most frequent occurrence is of *paliyas*. The *paliyas* are normally linked to cattle raids, skirmishes and village disputes. South India and Maharashtra can be easily termed as the heartland of hero-stones. The hero-stones from Tamil Nadu fall roughly between the sixth and the twelfth century AD. A majority of these are related to the cattle raids. The study of the Tamil Nadu series is still in its formative stage. The *chayastambhas* of Andhra Pradesh are not strictly speaking hero-stones. Karnataka and Maharashtra contain a large number of Sati and hero-stones. This series falls in the 'early medieval period' (fifth, sixth century A.D. onwards) and have been dated from fifth to fourteenth-fifteenth century AD. The series from Maharashtra does not contain any inscriptions and hence the dating has to be done on stylistic grounds. Apart from these areas we come across memorials in Madhya Pradesh, Bihar, Kashmir and Orissa on the east coast. The Madhya Pradesh series is largely attributed to the local tribal context though some influence from Rajasthan is noticeable there. Generally though, the western and southern series surpass the central, northern and the eastern one in variety and numbers.

Form and content

Normally the Sati is represented on a slab of stone by a symbol of hand and arms covered with bangles on a pillar. The arm is bent at a right angle at the elbow. Sometimes the couple is depicted along with the *lingam*, *yoni*, and the sun and moon symbols. According to Sontheimer the significance of the pillar still awaits satisfactory explanation. (Sontheimer, 1976). Another way of depicting the Sati is by merging the pillar with these symbols in a hero-stone. Such Sati-hero-stone combines are to be found in central and western India. In such cases the wife is either lying down with her husband or both of them are depicted in a sitting posture. Sometimes the hand and arm symbol is carried on the corner of the hero-stone itself. In Rajasthan, at times, only the real hand-print on walls indicate a Sati. There are interesting variations in this normal form where in one peculiar depiction we find a pillar which is cubical in shape and has four faces. A simpler form of Sati memorial in western India is from Maharashtra where there is a small rectangular stone with a pair of foot-prints.

The hero-stone is usually divided into three panels. The lowest panel depicts the event in which the hero has died. There is a tremendous variety in this panel. If the hero died in a battle than a battle scene would be depicted; if the occasion was a cattle raid then herds of cattle would be depicted. On the Western sea coast there are some stones where naval battle scenes have been depicted on the lowest panel of the stone. The middle panel depicts *apsara* carrying the hero towards heaven. Sometimes, the hero is seated in a palanquin, or in a shrine-like structure. The topmost panel depicts the hero worshipping the deity which is usually a Shiva-*lingam*. Here also the deity may change according to the local influence. The sun and the moon symbols accompany the stone. In this standard form there occur tremendous variations, depending upon a particular context of the stone. Often there are stones that have four or five panels. This increase in panels is necessitated by the need to give more details of the event in which death has occurred. Also in the depiction of panels there are interesting solutions of accommodation of two or more than two persons who have died. In such cases the two events are merged. If more than two persons have died and have to be depicted on the stone, then they are accommodated in a quadrilaterally carved stone with four faces of its attendant panels. Generally, it has been observed that the central, northern and eastern series represent the earlier version of a hero-stone. They have less number of panels than the western series. The earliest of the multipanelled stone has been approximately dated to the sixth century AD. The *govardhan kirti stambha* of Rajasthan in western India is also representative of the earlier forms of hero-stones. Unlike the northern, central and eastern series, the *govardhan stambha* is a structure resembling a shrine. Deities are carved on all the four faces of the shrine. Though by and large the hero stones belong to the 'early medieval period', in some instances their exact dating is not possible. This is so because those stones do not carry any inscriptions on them. The series from Maharashtra is one such example. In such cases dating is attempted on stylistic grounds.

Sati and hero-stone are an important but relatively less studied field. The hero-stones from central India have emerged from a tribal context and concern tribal chiefs. As such they are invaluable in understanding attitudes to death and belief patterns of tribes from Central India. The hero-stones from western Indian reflect the physical and social ecology of the area in their pictographical context. Those that depict cattle raids in their lowest panel are understood as indicators of a dominant pastoral economy of the past. These hero-stones that depict cattle raid are found only in a specific area of the semi-arid tract of western India. In this area even today we come across pastoral communities like Kurubas in Karnataka, Dhangars in Maharashtra, Abhiras of Gujarat and Rabaris of Rajasthan engaged in sheep-rearing activities. Here historically speaking, plough cultivation was introduced only after the 'Pax Britannica'. Those hero-stones that depict cattle raids are thus of paramount importance as they are an important source of the existence of pastoral economy. They are also an important indicator of nobility, for hero-stones were not erected for everyone. A classic case in this instance would be Rajasthan, where we can in fact study the emerging Rajput nobility through the hero stones as they were an important status symbol which were perhaps not accessible to everyone. Evolution of certain cults has also been linked to the tradition of hero-stones; in this case the famous *bhakti* movement cult of Viththal in Maharashtra can be cited as an example. A detailed research of this aspect is expected to throw more light on the history of cults and their development in the early medieval context.

Thus, the field of Sati and hero-stone research is of tremendous importance to historians, art historians, anthropologists, archaeologists and sociologists.

The story of Kaba and Baji fills an important gap in the studies. It provides for a more local, immediate and rooted context within which the analysis of the story as well as of the cattle raid-depicting hero-stones becomes possible.

The story also raises the entire issue of Gavlis. As can be surmised, if the pastoralists were indeed dominant, then what were their reasons for a shift? When did it occur? Do we get any more evidence from the oral traditions? It is important that such questions be raised as they provide an important insight into the history of pastoral societies of the yesteryears.

References

Amiran D.,1977, 'Arid Zone Development : A Case of Limited Choice', in Yair Mundlak and Singer, S., eds., *Arid Zone Development*, American Academy of Sciences.

Arole, 1962, *Srinath Mhaskoba Devacem Caritra Vir.*

Blackburn, S.H., 1985, 'Death and Deification: Folk Cults in Hinduism', in *History of Religions*, 24 : 255-74.

Bruckner H., Lutze L. and Malik A., 1993, *Flags of Fame: Studies in South Asian Folk Culture*, Delhi, Manohar.

Deshpande C.D., 1971, *Geography of Maharashtra*, New Delhi: National Book Trust.

Dhavalikar M.K., 1988, *First Farmers of Deccan*, Pune.

Khare G.H., 1961, *Persian Sources of Indian History*, Vol. V., Pune.

Malhotra K.C. and Gadgil M., 1984, 'Subsistence Strategies amongst the Pastoralists of Maharashtra', in J.R. Luckas, ed., *People of South Asia*, New York, Plenum Press, 441-57.

National Council of Agricultural Research (NCAR), Vol IV., 1976.

Ray H.P., 1986, *Monasteries and Guilds*, Delhi, OUP.

Settar S. and Sontheimer, G.D., 1982, *Memorial Stones*, Dharwad.

Settar S. & Kalaburgi, M.M., 1982, 'The Hero Cult: A study of Kannada literature from 9th to 13th Century', Settar S. and Sontheimer, G.D., *Memorial Stones*, Dharwad, 17-36

Sontheimer, G.D., 1989, *Pastoral Deities in Western India*, Trans. Anne Feldhaus, New York, OUP.

Sontheimer, G.D., 1991, *Ramayana in Contemporary Folk Traditions of Maharashtra*, in Horstmann, M. Thief ed., *Ramayana and Ramayanas*, Wiesbaden, 115-37.

Sontheimer G.D., 1976, *Some Memorial Monuments of Western India, German Scholars on India*, Vol. II, New Delhi, 264-75.

Suryavanshi B., 1962, The Abhiras, *Their History and Culture*, Baroda.

Thapar R., 1981, 'Death and the Hero', S.C. Humprys and King, ed., *Archaeology and Anthropology of Death,* London.

14

The Ambivalence of Power
Representations of Women in the Oral Epic of Devnarayan

Aditya Malik

THE epic of Devnarayan is first and foremost a 'religious' narrative, i.e., it embodies and constructs a discourse concerning items of religious significance: 'divine testimony', 'worship', 'sacred territory', 'devotion', 'sacred power', and others. Issues of religious importance for the community of worshippers are thus articulated in the narrative. However, the narrative is more than a religious text in the sense that it thematises interrelationships between different social groups that are encompassed by the community of worshippers, as well as such groups that might fall outside the community of devotees. In addition the narrative is also a statement about the 'history' of the devotees of Devnarayan as a community connected to the 'history' of the deity.

Thus, at least three discourses of meaning emerge in the narrative; a discourse on (a) religious sacred power, (b) interrelationships within the community of devotees (sociality) and, (c) historicity by which an 'imagined' history of the community is implied. Each of these discourses is related to and dependant on the other. Thus, the discourse on interrelationships within the community of worshippers is intimately connected to the discourse on community history. The discourse on community history is again related to the discourse on religious power, sacred territory, worship, and so on. Within the domain of these three discourses there are various 'sub-discourses'. Thus, for example, within the discourse on sociality (i.e., interrelationships within the community of devotees) there is the discourse concerning relationships between men and women. Crucial to this 'sub-discourse' and to the larger discourses on sacrality and intergroup relationships is a notion of power. However, given the understanding of the narrative as being a 'martial' epic there is a tendency to assume that the epic is dominated by a set of values and ideas sustained and generated by men who also define and wield power. From this perspective women would feature in subordinate or 'passive' roles. Although this observation is partially true, it is still worthwhile to examine the question of how power is and can be defined, and whether there are different sources and forms of power each with a capacity to influence and dictate events. It is in this context that I will be dealing with images of women in the epic. The questions I intend to pose are: How are women represented in this martial epic? Do women's voices express a 'counter' system? Are women simple passive objects? Are they covert players or overt actors? What are the different contexts in which power issues from women? How is power defined in these different contexts? What kinds of tensions surface in the narrative when it is observed from 'gender specific' perspective?

Women feature in a series of different contexts in the narrative. In some contexts they appear anonymous and passive. In others they emerge as immensely powerful, deciding over issues of life and death. In still other cases they seem to work as catalysers and 'hidden' integrators in situations which have a potential for conflict. Moreover, women are represented in terms of a number of social and religious 'identities': as mothers, daughters, wives, sisters, widows, devotees, and goddesses. Some women feature more prominently in the narrative than do others, for example, Devnarayan's mother Sadu Mata plays a central role throughout the narrative not only as the wife of Savai Bhoj and the mother of Devnarayan, but also as a paramount devotee of Bhagavan. Conversely, one does hear of the other 23 brothers' wives, but not all of them recur in the narrative. And, while we are told that Devnarayan marries on three different occasions, it is only his third wife, Queen Pipalde whom we encounter in a number of episodes in the narrative, and who occupies a central position in the cult as well. Queen Jaimati, who is perhaps the most powerful person in the epic, draws her power from being the incarnation of the goddess Bhavani, who is ultimately responsible for the slaying of the 24 Bagaravats. Images of women and the power accorded to them thus expresses itself in three main contexts: (a) marriage, (b) devotion, (c) divinity.

Marriage

Although there are a number of marriages throughout the epic, marriage as a theme is predominant in the first part of the epic. At the outset it needs to be re-emphasised that the discourse on intergroup relationships and that on gender overlap significantly. Thus, marriage is also a metaphor for intergroup relationships. But I will be paying attention here to images of women rather than representations of sociality expressed through intergroup marriage.

The very first series of marriages occur in the so-called 'preamble' to the narrative. This section of the narrative is narrated in prose. The events described in it prefigure later events in the epic. There are three successive incidents in which marriages take place. In each case the context in which the marriages are to take place is problematic, and marriage itself shows up as a thorny issue which requires ingenuity and initiative in order to arrive at a satisfactory conclusion. And, in all three cases it is the social identities of the persons involved that creates a problem. The marriages narrated in the 'preamble' all relate to Devnarayan's ancestors, who are, as will become apparent, of a decidedly 'mixed' social background.

EPISODE I

The narrative begins at a time when Brahma is performing a sacrifice (*jug*) in Pushkar — the famous pilgrim town in the district of Ajmer. Brahma invites all the gods and *rishi*s to his sacrifice. Among them is a group of 24 *rishi*s living in the Nag Pahad, a mountain chain running parallel to Pushkar. The *rishi*s are disciples of Shankar. Shankar forbids them from attending the sacrifice, but they insist on going because they have received invitations from Brahma. All of a sudden Shankar grows ravenously hungry. The *rishi*s suggest he eat the fruits growing in the forest in which they live. But Shankar says this will not satisfy him. He wants more than plain fruit. But what else is available in the forest? There is no cereal or grain either. So what does Shankar do? He turns to his disciples and begins consuming them one after another. After he has eaten them and satiated his hunger, he then visits Brahma's sacrifice himself. The sacrifice comes to a halt because of the sin Shankar has committed. He asks Brahma how he should atone for his sin, whereupon Brahma informs him that the only means would be to offer the *rishi*s his own body in a future existence, in which the *rishi*s are to be born as the 24 sons of a single father.

The narrative shifts now to a more historical time. It is the reign of King Bisaldev of Ajmer. The populace is being terrorised by a lion that feeds on one individual every night. On one particular night, a Rajput called Hari Ram offers to take the place of a boy whose turn it is to be eaten by the lion. He sets up a trap for the lion and beheads it. Then in order to wash the blood off his sword and to cleanse himself of the sin of slaughter, he goes to the holy lake of Pushkar carrying the lion's head on his shoulder. It is a full moon night (*purnima*). Exactly at the same time on the opposite bank a Brahman girl, Lila Sevri, who has taken a vow never to see the face of a man is performing ablutions and bathing in the lake. While bathing, she sees the reflection of a man's body with the head of a lion on the surface of the lake, and conceives. She insists that Hari Ram marry her now, but he vacillates saying that such a marriage is not possible because she is a Brahman and he a Kshatriya. Finally, however, King Bisaldev allows him to marry the Brahman girl. After nine months their son is born. He has the head of a lion and the body of a man, and is named Bagh Simh. Later because of his unusual and fearsome appearance, no one is willing to marry his daughter to him. He lives alone in a garden attended by a Brahman cook. One day on the festival of swings (*akha tij*), a number of young girls of various castes come to the garden attracted by Bagh Simh's silken swing.

> The Brahman allows them to use the swing on the condition that each of them circumambulate Bagh Simh. While they are doing this, the Brahman performs the necessary engagement rites. Unknowingly they are engaged to Bagh Simh. Later Bagh Simh marries twelve of them. Each of his wives gives birth to two sons who are collectively called the Bagaravats.
>
> The Bagaravats, whose mothers belong to different castes, are all married to Gujar women. Of the 24 Bagaravats, Savai Bhoj is the most valorous. Each day Savai Bhoj takes the Bagaravats' cattle herds to graze on the slopes of Nag Pahad. One of the cows regularly leaves the herd and returns on its own in the evening. One day Savai Bhoj follows the cow and discovers that it is being milked by the ascetic Rupnath. As compensation for milking their cow, Rupnath gives Savai Bhoj a sack full of grain. But the brothers have no use for the small quantity of grain, so they feed it to birds. The next morning, however, they discover that the few grains left sticking to the seam of the sack have turned into gems. They realise their folly and Savai Bhoj returns to the ascetic to become his disciple. One day Rupnath has Savai Bhoj heat a cauldron of oil and circle it, while he himself follows. While they are circling the cauldron, the ascetic tries pushing Savai Bhoj into the boiling oil, but Savai Bhoj leaps over with the help of his cowherd's staff. In the next round Savai Bhoj follows the ascetic and pushes him into the cauldron. Not so agile, the ascetic falls into the boiling oil. Instantly his body turns into solid gold. While Savai Bhoj stands there repenting his crime, the ascetic reappears in the hermitage as though nothing had taken place. He explains that the golden image is a gift that will grant the Bagaravats unending wealth for a period of twelve years after which both wealth and life (*maya-kaya*) shall come to an end. He also gives Savai Bhoj the gifts of a mare, a cow, and an elephant, all of which have special powers. Savai Bhoj returns to his home. The brothers ask Tejaji, the eldest amongst them, what they should do with their newly acquired wealth. Tejaji, whose mother is a Banya, advises them to bury the money in the ground and hoard it. Nevaji, one of the youngest brothers, suggests, however, that they do good deeds with the money, i.e. build wells and temples, distribute the wealth and make a name for themselves since both the wealth and their lives will end after twelve years. The brothers choose the latter alternative. Soon their fame spreads far and wide.

In all three cases narrated above, marriages are between unequal partners. Unequal either in social terms or in purely 'physical' terms. Whereas in the first case Hari Ram and Lila Sevri belong to different castes, in the second case Bagh Simh himself is half-human, half-animal and his wives are human. The 24 Bagaravats who are born of the liaisons of Bagh Simh and his multi-caste wives, do not have a perceptably clear social or caste identity. They in turn are married to women who belong to a single well-defined social group. In the case of Hari Ram and Lila Sevri it appears that Lila Sevri is the more powerful of the two since it is she who has taken a vow not to look at a man's face, and it is she who insists that Hari Ram now marry her, although from a conventional point of view this would seem impossible. It is the king who then overrides societal conventions and allows the two to marry. However, Lila Sevri's curse comes to fruition and their son Bagh Simh is born half-man, half-lion. Regardless of his potential divinity Bagh Simh is 'exiled' to a garden distant from the main settlement, where he lives alone except for his Brahman caretaker. Whereas the marriage between Hari Ram and Lila Sevri could be seen as resulting from 'accident', the bond between Bagh Simh and his wives is clearly the result of deceit and trickery. The innocent young girls are manipulated into circumambulating Bagh Simh on the promise of being able to use his silken swing. Here too there is a relationship of social unequals or at any rate of socially distinct individuals. Bagh Simh, a child born of an unconventional marriage, marries women from different *jati*s. The women enter into a bond with Bagh Simh unknowingly and therefore also passively. Once the marriages are consummated, the strengths of the children born thereof are determined by the character and strengths of the caste identity of Bagh Simh's wives, for example, Bagh Simh's son born from his Banya wife has the personality of a 'typical' Banya, the son born of a Rajput wife has the 'typical' qualities of a Rajput and so on. Thus, the character and qualities of the 24 Bagaravats is not so much fixed by their father Bagh Simh, but by their respective mothers. This in turn results in the heterogeneous nature of the Bagaravats. The point in this example is that although Bagh Simh's wives are represented in an anonymous, passive, and non-volitional manner, they do play a central role in an underlying causality that determines who the Bagaravats will be as heroes. Thus, it appears that difference and heterogeneity are at least in the textualised discourse of the narrative more valued than the clear-cut boundaries of homogeneity.

The 'passive' role of Bagh Simh's wives is in the last example reversed: it is the Gujar women who take on an 'active' role in marrying the Bagaravats before they remain unmarried forever. Whereas Bagh Simh is successful in assimilating many different groups through his marriages, the Gujar women are successful in assimilating the heroes and as a consequence also the cult into the fold of a single group, which then becomes a point of reference for the cult in general, and for intergroup relationships within the community of worshippers. If Bagh Simh's wives are about heterogeneity, the Gujar women are about homogeneity. For the first time here there is no trickery or deceit involved in the process of marriage: the Gujar women 'choose' to marry the Bagaravats. By doing so they also lay the foundations for Devnarayan's birth in their community. And, in terms of a chronicle of births, the Gujar women, especially Sadu Mata, tie up to Lila Sevri and Bagh Simh's wives, who in each case determine the nature of their offspring. It is Lila Sevri who curses Hari Ram that their son will have the body of a man and the head of a lion; the social background of Bagh Simh's wives determines the personal qualities of each Bagaravat; Sadu Mata's devotion draws Bhagavan into incarnating himself as Devnarayan.

In terms of the representations of women in the context of marriage we can perceive both an underlying consensus as well as an underlying shift. The underlying consensus relates to the notion that women prevail over the domain of birth, not only in an obviously physical sense, but also in a substantial sense by providing their children with essential qualities that will mark their journey as heroes in the narrative. The underlying shift relates to the movement from women representing different groups to women representing a single group. Both aspects are important for the cult as a whole, which simultaneously has a relatively well-defined social reference point, and a relatively open access for other social groups. In context of marriage images of women, therefore, also relate to both control and assimilation.

Devotion

Let us now turn to the second context mentioned earlier, namely devotion: How does devotion or *bhakti* figure as a source of power? What kind of power issues from devotion? To what extent is the role of Devnarayan's mother, Sadu Mata defined and outlined by *bhakti* ? How far is Bhagavan's incarnation as Devnarayan explainable in terms of his mother's devotion? If we examine various episodes featuring Sadu Mata we find that they are characterised by devotion and ascetism. The first episode narrates the circumstances of her birth and the meaning of her name.

EPISODE II

> Duloji Khatano had two wives. But both of them were childless. A Mahatma used to practise *tap* in front of their home. They looked after the Mahatma and served him for twelve years. After twelve years were over, in the evening (the Mahatma called out:) 'Dula baba, come over here!' 'Yes, Maharaj!' 'I'm leaving the *dhuni* today.' 'What for, Maharaj?' '(I'm leaving) because my *tapasya* is complete after twelve years. That's the reason!' 'Why, Maharaj, aren't you happy?' Well, anyway Duloji went back to tending his cows and buffaloes. And, Babaji prepared to leave. Before he left, he said: 'Look, (Dula) baba, take care of my *dhuni* (when I'm gone).' It was some time before Duloji (went home). He went home and ate his food. He asked his wives: 'Did either of you say something to the Mahatma yesterday? Did you not give him his food or milk at the proper time?' 'No we didn't do anything (wrong)!' 'Well, Babaji's left today! He's left the *dhuni*.' (The wives said:) '. . . we served Babaji. And, because of him we're childless. (Should) we ask for something? Is there nothing we could ask for? So what did Babaji say?' 'All he told me was to take care of his *dhuni* in the morning.' (Duloji's wives decided:) 'Let's do the following. Let's go (down the road). If we find Babaji, then we'll stop him, we won't let him go any further. If we don't catch up with him, we'll tend his *dhuni*.' So Duloji's wives got ready, they washed their hands, and went towards the *dhuni*. (But) they

> didn't find Babaji. So they tended the *dhuni*. From the *dhuni* there came out a ball. And, out of it a baby girl appeared. (I'm telling you about Devnarayan's mother's birth). So Dulaji said: 'Baba didn't give us a baby boy. He gave us a baby girl. And, that's fine.' Duloji's eldest wife pressed Sadu to her chest. She gave her her breast. Milk began flowing out of Duloji's wife's breast. (Later) two boys were born — Amo (and) Nimo. And, one girl by the name of Salun was born. She was Bhunaji's mother, and was married to Bagaravats.

Sadu Mata is thus born out of an ascetic's fire-place. Her name is said to derive from Sadhu (ascetic/mendicant). The ascetic component visible in the story of her birth is strengthened in the scene in which she practises *tap* on the Malasari Hill while awaiting the manifestation of Bhagavan. The devotional component is well displayed in a prior encounter between Sadu Mata and Bhagavan, who approaches her disguised as a wandering mendicant.

EPISODE III

> Bhagavan assumed the form of a leper. Well, sir, blood and pus were oozing out of his body. Nevaji said: 'The old man himself is coming to test us. He's taken on such a form. What should we do? We should fill up jugs with milk and *ghi*. Cows milk. Some of us should pour milk over him, and some others should drink the *charnamrit'*. They came and stood in front of Bhagavan in the forest. 'Why are you doing this to me? I'm a leper — why are you touching me?' (The brothers said:) 'It's a leper that we want. We've been looking for you, but were not able to find you so long. We've been looking for you for so many days. Today we've found you!' Some of the brothers poured milk over his head, and some drank *charnamrit*. Savai Bhoj drank one handful of *charnamrit*. He took a second handful. When he was about to take a third handful, Bhagavan caught hold of his hand (and said:) 'Daughter's father, one becomes the Lord of the triple world by taking three handfuls. . . .' Yes, that's why Savai Bhoj is known as a great *bhagat*. Bhagavan reflected to himself: 'They are such *surgyanis* (wise) these Bagaravats, there's no pair of men or women who are like that (?). But the women won't be that *surgyani*. Let me go to them!' He abandoned that form (of a leper) at that place. That was in a forest. Quickly he took on the form of a *jogi* (in) ochre robes. (He) went there and sat down in front of the door. At that time Sadu Mata had prepared to bathe. (She) had taken off her clothes and all, and was bathing. At that time (the *jogi*) said: 'Alakh!' (Sadu Mata) said: 'Maidservant go — Jogeshwar is calling. . .' The maidservant went and said: 'Maharaj, what do you want?' 'No, no, I won't take anything from you!' 'Well, then?' 'I want it like — the mistress of this house — the mistress — I'll take it from her hand. You're a maidservant.' 'Well, Maharaj, should I fetch my mistress?' 'Yes!' 'On your guru's name promise you won't leave these steps!' Then Bhagavan said: 'Go to your mistress. If she dresses up and all, I won't accept anything (from her). She

should appear in front of me in the way she's sitting outside. Then I'll accept (her offering).' The maidservant went to Sadu Mata: 'Well, maidservant, what have you come for?' 'What for, Maharaj? Today the Sadhu won't receive anything from me. He's calling you. And, he's summoning you – the way you're sitting here – he says to come that way.' Sadu Mata said: 'Go, don't worry!' She quickly – like one does when she bathes – tied her hair together into a knot, and took a plate (of offerings). So, when Sadu Mata showed up, Bhagavan turned his back to her. 'Why, Maharaj, why did you turn away?' (Bhagavan said:) 'Mother, put on some clothes!' 'Now, you sent for me, did you send for clothes? (No,) you sent for me to come like this! There's no shame for sons and daughters in front of parents. What's there to be afraid of in front of one's parents. I've come to you in exactly the way you'd sent for me.' So, he said: 'Mother, open the knot in your hair.' Maji Sadu opened the knot of hair. Now when her hair hung down long, Bhagavan cast a look of mercy, and created a dress of long hair. When the dress (covered her) Bhagavan turned around. Sadu Mata said: 'Well, here Maharaj.' 'Give me your word!' 'I promise!' Bhagavan said: 'Look, the matter is this, give me the *sakalp* of 23 Bagaravats with your hand.' She poured the *sakalp* of 23 Bagaravats with her hand. Then Sadu Mata thought: 'Now, why did this happen?' She grew a bit unresolved. Bhagavan said: 'Why are you afraid? Have you let down your promise?' 'I won't let down my word!' 'Well then? Give me the *sakalp*!' 'I'll give it to you, Maharaj!' 'Don't be afraid! Look, of the 24 brothers, one will be let off! One of them won't die.' Then Sadu Mata reflected to herself: 'If one of them is going to be let off, it'll be my husband who'll be let off.' Then Bhagavan said: 'Mata, it won't be the way you thought!' 'Then (how)?' 'You thought of your husband. (But) your husband will die. The eldest of (the brothers) Tej Simh, the Banya's child, will be let off! Your husband will surely die! And, you – you'll be immortal – your husband will die (in battle)! Give me the *sakalp*, or break your word!' 'Maharaj, I won't break my word.' Sadu Mata gave it to Bhagavan: 'Here you are Sri Maharaj, its yours. Do whatever you like (with it)!' Then he said: 'Mother, what do you want?' 'What should I ask for? I've no dearth of money, wealth – there's no dearth of anything. Now, what should I ask for?' 'Anything you desire.' 'Well, Maharaj, you give me your word too!' He as Bhagavan: 'I give you my word.' 'Well, then Maharaj, I want a son like you in my shoulder sash. I want you in my shoulder sash.' Then Bhagavan said: 'Mother, someone like me is myself. Who else is like me?' 'I want you – to feed you. I have no other desire (but) to feed you.' 'Mother, someone like me is myself, and you did a good thing in opening the shoulder sash. Otherwise I'm weak of my word. If you said come into my womb, then I'd have to come and suffer in the womb. That was a good thing you did (asking me) to come into the shoulder sash. I won't have to wallow in dirt and fat. When Bhoj's thirteenth day arrives after he dies, when his *sativada* takes place, on that day I'll take *avatar* with you on the Hill of Malasari.' This was Bhagavan's word: 'The others will die, be burnt. Don't you leave

> that place. Do *bhajan*, then your promise will be fulfilled.' So there was a pact between Sadu Mata and Bhagavan Dev for the thirteenth day. Bhagavan gave his word. Speak: Victory to Sri Dev Maharaj, victory!

By obeying Bhagavan's command to present herself 'as she is', Sadu Mata is able to impress Bhagavan of her 'knowledge' (*gyan*). Sadu Mata realises that the mendicant is Bhagavan, which is why she addresses him with the collective 'parents'. Her ability to recognise the mendicant's true nature arises also from her own asceticism-induced miraculous birth. But the alms the mendicant desires are truly awesome and foreboding: the lives of 23 of the 24 Bagaravats. Sadu Mata, thinking that the life of her husband Savai Bhoj will be spared, complies with the mendicant's wish. But he soon dissolves her illusions by telling her that her husband will die in battle, and that it is the eldest brother Teja, the son of a Banya woman, who will survive the 'Mahabharat'. However, after demanding the death of the 23 Bagaravats, Bhagavan reciprocates by granting Sadu Mata a boon. Sadu Mata wishes nothing more than to have Bhagavan be born to her as her son. Bhagavan agrees to her wish, promising to manifest himself on the thirteenth day after Savai Bhoj has been slain in battle. Whereas the Bagaravats are actively slain by Bhavani in the battle, it is Sadu Mata who initiates their deaths through her promise to Bhagavan. The word used here is *sakalp* which can mean 'an offering', 'the intention to offer', or 'a promise'. Sadu Mata thus utters the intention to offer, and Bhavani receives the offering in the sacred field of battle. Sadu Mata and Bhavani both play a decisive role in the slayings of the Bagaravats. Both are joined to the Bagaravats in a singular fashion: Sadu Mata as Savai Bhoj's wife, and Bhavani or Queen Jaimati as his lover. However, while Bhavani is overtly involved in their killings, Sadu Mata is covertly involved in the process that results in the Bagaravats' deaths. Bhavani and Sadu Mata represent two sides of the same feminine power. Both preside over life and death although Bhavani is the more pronouncedly divine of the two. In Sadu Mata's case it is her *bhakti* that characterises her role as the mother of Devnarayan. Her wish for a son echoes the fulfilment of a *bhakta*'s desire found elsewhere in religious narratives. She relinquishes her status as a married woman for the sake of a son 'like' Bhagavan. And, in doing so she violates the powerful norm of a widow's fate as *sati*. Even so she is called Sadu 'Satvanti' or 'Sati Mata' in the narrative, i.e., she is considered to embody the qualities of a Sati even though she has not committed the act of *sati*.

The third context in which images of women are embedded is that of divine power. Of all the women in the narrative it is Queen Jaimati who's directly connected to this context. She is considered to be an incarnation of the goddess Bhavani who has manifested herself in order to destroy the 24 Bagaravats. The episode describing her intention to destroy the brothers is paralleled by Puranic myths in which the gods, after declaring their inability or unwillingness to destroy a demon, summon the goddess to slay him. In the epic Bhavani explains that she will have to destroy the Bagaravats through deceit, since they cannot be defeated otherwise.

EPISODE IV

> In due course they meet their future enemy, the Rajput chieftain of Ran City whose name is Rana (or Ravji). The Rana and the Bagaravats become *dharam*-brothers. In an extended drinking session, they overturn jars laden with alcohol onto a hillside flooding the earth to such an extent that the alcohol actually flows down into the kingdom of Basak Nag, serpent lord of the underworld. Angered, Raja Basak deposits the Earth temporarily on a bull's horns and goes to Bhagavan's court to complain about the Bagaravats. But neither Basak, nor Hanuman, nor Bhagavan can do anything to remedy the situation because the Bagaravats are so powerful. Finally Bhagavan assumes the form of a mendicant (*jogi*) and visits Sadu Mata, the wife of Savai Bhoj, begging for alms. Sadu, who has just completed performing ablutions and bathing, appears in front of the mendicant covered only by her long tresses. Struck by her devotion, the mendicant (or Bhagavan) grants her a boon. Sadu desires that Bhagavan be born as her son. Bhagavan promises to be born as her son on the thirteenth day after the Bagaravats have been killed.
>
> After his return, Bhagavan requests Shakti to go to Earth to fulfil the task of destroying the Bagaravats. She manifests herself as an infant girl in a forest where she is discovered by the King of Bhual, who adopts her. Exactly at the time of her birth, her maidservant Hira Dasi is born in the house of a Mahajan. Shakti grows up unusually fast. And, soon Brahmans are sent out to find a suitable bridegroom for her. She insists that they find someone belonging to a family in which one father has 24 sons. After a long and frustrating search the Brahmans find the Bagaravats. They arrange to have the queen married to Savai Bhoj. But because they already have wives, the Bagaravats suggest that the queen be married to their *dharam*-brother, the Rana. Thus, arrangements are made for the Rana to marry Rani Jaimati, as the queen is called. When the marriage procession sets out, Savai Bhoj instead of the Rana, leads it. In the meanwhile Rani Jaimati orders the *toran* to be hung in a high place so that the Rana, who is old and feeble, cannot reach up to it. Instead of the Rana, Savai Bhoj strikes down the *toran*. When the marriage procession arrives, the queen pretends she has high fever. She asks her maidservant to bring Savai Bhoj's sword that is supposed to have healing powers. In the inner chambers of the palace she then circles the sword, thereby secretly marrying Savai Bhoj. In public, however, she marries the Rana. At the end of the ceremonies, when she is to accompany the Rana to her new home, she insists on staying with the Bagaravats. The Bagaravats coax her into going with the Rana, promising to fetch her after a period of six months. Upon arriving in the Rana's palace, however, the queen says she will not play dice with the Rana till he has

> constructed a new palace for her. The construction of the palace, of course, takes a long time, and six months are soon over. In the meanwhile, the Bagaravats — even against the advice of their wives — prepare to fetch the queen. The queen elopes with the Bagaravats. The Rana is patient, advising the Bagaravats in a brotherly manner to send the queen back to him. But, the Bagaravats stick to their decision. Finally, the Rana gathers together the armies of fifty-two forts on the banks of the Khari river. Bhavani, who now has assumed her true form, promises to accompany the Bagaravats only on the condition that they fight the Rana's army one at a time. She also demands that the brothers offer their heads to her. The Bagaravats willingly agree to her grotesque demands. A great war is fought on account of Rani Jaimati (or Bhavani). In the battle some of the brothers continue fighting even after their heads have been severed by the Goddess' discus. But in the end all of them are slain and the Rana is victorious. The Goddess assumes her awesome, terrifying form. Amidst the corpses of slain warriors, she squats on the battle ground, dripping with blood, stringing a necklace of the Bagaravats' heads. After their deaths, the heroes' wives with the exception of Savai Bhoj's wife, Sadu Mata, commit *sati*. Sadu Mata begins severe *tapas* on a hill near the battlefield. After eleven days, when her honour and life is about to be threatened by the Rana, she calls out to Bhagavan, who has promised to be born as her son. Devnarayan, who is playing a game of dice at that time with Raja Basak, lord of the underworld, rises up on a stream of water that splits apart the rock on which Sadu is seated. Borne on that jet of water in a lotus blossom, the infant Devnarayan falls into Sadu Mata's lap.

In the above episode Bhavani succeeds in slaying the Bagaravats by deceiving them. The means she uses to incite the Rana and the Bagaravats against each other are those of love and marriage, allowing each group to believe that she exclusively belongs to one of them. In reality she makes sure that neither marriage is actually consummated. Thus, in the six months spent with the Rana she refuses to play 'dice' (a euphemism for sex) with him, till he has built a new palace for her. Once she joins up with the Bagaravats, she incites the quarrel between them and the Rana, leading to the Bagaravats' death, once again avoiding intimate contact. The Bagaravats' willingness to go through with demands of the goddess is equal to an act of voluntary sacrifice, which in a sense is a continuation of the first episode in which they offer their bodies to satisfy Shiva's hunger. However, in contrast to Puranic myths in which demons often convert to become devotees of the god or goddess after their defeat or death, the Bagaravats are prior to their death great devotees of Shiva and Bhavani.

Conclusion

In this paper I have examined images of women in the epic of Devnarayan from the point of view of different women in different contexts. The contexts were those of marriage, devotion, and divine power. The social and religious identities of the women involved were formed by each of these contexts. Thus, they were successively wives, mothers, devotees, and goddesses. In their status as wives the women appeared predominantly in anonymous and passive characterisations. Notwithstanding this image, the women were shown to exercise an important influence in the domain of birth with regard to the qualities of their respective offspring. Moreover they also acted as integrators and assimilators of different social groups within the frame of the narrative and the cult. In the second example of Sadu Mata, we find that her identity is only partially determined through her status as the wife of Savai Bhoj. More prominent is the position and authority she derives from being a devotee of Bhagavan. As a devotee she is closer to her divine 'parent' than she is to her human husband. She is represented in a more independent and volitional manner than are the women in the first example. Her power is derived from her status as a devotee, and finally as mother of Devnarayan. In the third and last example we find the most extreme and overt expression of power issuing from the fact that Queen Jaimati is an incarnation of the goddess Bhavani. Although Queen Jaimati enters into marital relations with both the Rana and Savai Bhoj, her identity is least of all determined by marriage. In fact, as we have seen, she skillfully avoids the consummation of these marriages. Whereas in the first example, women are 'tricked' into marriage, in this case it is the Rana and the Bagaravats who are tricked into getting married by the goddess. Queen Jaimati represents the most independent, volitional woman in the epic, standing alone in her destructive power.

Taken together the examples outlined above point to a continuum of images. On one end of the continuum women's identities and the power they wield are derived from their status as wives. On the other end of the continuum a woman's identity is derived from her divine origin. Midway between these two extremes is the figure of Sadu Mata who represents a break from a complete identification with a human husband, to an identification with Bhagavan. This identification characterises her both as a devotee and as a mother of Devnarayan. Whereas in the first case women wield influence in the domain of birth, in the second and third case, women wield power over both birth (life) and death. In both the latter cases devotion (*bhakti*) is of central importance. In Sadu Mata's case it is devotion that brings forth creative powers that then result in the birth of Devnarayan. In the case of Bhavani the situation is reversed in that she is the focus of devotion. The Bagaravats' devotion to her, however, leads to the war between them and Rana, and to their destruction. But, it is their voluntary death that in turn elevates their status as heroes in the narrative and cult. Lastly the images of women discussed here mirror crucial concerns of the community of devotees articulated in the narrative: sociability (marriage), religious power (devotion), and religio-political solidarity and disparity (divine power).

Part III

Performers, Performance and Audience

15

The Pandav Lila of Uttarakhand

William S. Sax

Introduction

THE *Pandav lila*[1] is a tradition of ritual dramatisation and competitive bardic recitation of India's great epic, the *Mahabharata*. It is performed during the winter months in the villages of Garhwal, the former Hindu kingdom that is part of what is soon to become India's newest state, Uttarakhand in the west central Himalayas.

It would be very easy indeed to classify *Pandav lila* as a 'folk drama' based on the *Mahabharata*. However, I would like to resist the temptation to do so, first of all because, as I shall try to demonstrate, the *Mahabharata* is something other than what we normally think it is, and secondly because *Pandav lila* is something other than what we would normally understand as 'folk drama'. In what follows, I will first describe *Pandav lila* in some detail, and then make some literary, sociological, and theological observations about it. In the end, I hope to show that this ritual dramatisation of the epic is not a secondary derivation from a more fundamental source, not a vulgarisation of the Sanskrit text, but is itself an authentic, primary expression of the epic; and moreover that this sort of performative expression is characteristically Indian, so that categories of analysis derived from the Anglo-American tradition—categories like 'epic' and 'folk drama' —should only be used with great caution.

Description

Pandav lila is intimately associated with the Rajputs of Garhwal, who make up roughly 60 per cent of the local population, own roughly the same proportion of land, and are thus the locally dominant caste, to use M.N. Srinivas's term.

These Rajputs believe that they have descended from the Pandava brothers, so that when they perform a *Pandav lila*, they are in effect worshipping their ancestors. More specifically, *Pandav lila* is regarded as a *shraddha* (Hindu post-modern ritual) for the Pandavas' deceased father, King Pandu, and in many parts of Garhwal, it is referred to as a *shraddha*, so that people do not say they are going 'to see a *lila*' or 'to see the Pandavas dance' but rather that they are going 'to see the *shraddha*'.

The *Pandav lila* is better understood as ritual than as folk theatre, and this is so not only because it is regarded as a *shraddha*, but also because it is believed to be efficacious in a way that mere drama is not. *Pandav lilas* are performed in order to make the crops grow, to help women through the dangerous and difficult process of childbirth, to avert illness and calamity in the village, and especially for protection against foot-and-mouth disease among cattle. They are thus an example of *devakarya*, 'divine work' or 'the work of the gods', who are believed to be literally present during the performance. The semi-divine Pandavas are believed to dance in the bodies of the actors who play their parts, as are their mutual wife Draupadi, their mother Kunti, and other subsidiary characters in the performance. This possession by the gods is very important, and I shall return to it in my conclusion.

In order to prepare and maintain a suitable place for the deities to reside, a number of procedures must be followed. First, local ghosts, demons, and other disruptive spiritual beings are pacified, usually by offering them raw vegetables and uncooked grain, and once the drama has begun, such offerings are made at the beginning and end of each performance. Likewise the chief performers must remain pure by observing celibacy, following a strict vegetarian diet, avoiding intoxicants, limiting their sleep, and so on.

With one notable exception,[2] *Pandav lila* is a thoroughly amateur tradition: there are no printed scripts or paid performers of any sort. Like many other public rituals in Garhwal, performances are sponsored and organised by the village collectively. Every family has specific responsibilities in preparing for a performance: gathering firewood and foodstuffs, for example, or fashioning weapons and other stage props, making costumes, and clearing performance areas. The staging of a *Pandav lila* is an entirely collective affair, and the health and well-being generated by a successful performance is experienced by the whole village. In this way, villages constitute themselves as moral entities through the performance of collective rituals, a process that is typical of public ritual generally in Garhwal (Sax 1991b: 202-8).

The duration of *Pandav lilas* varies greatly, as does the time of the year in which they are performed and the episodes with which they culminate. In the far west of Garhwal in the Tons river basin, a typical performance lasts two to three days and is called a *shraddha.* These performances occur only in the months of *Magh* (January-February), *Shravan* (July-August), and *Margasheersh* (November-December). In the Mandakini river basin in Chamoli District, performances last up to six weeks, and culminate in the *chakravyuha* or 'circular array' which dramatises the encirclement and death of Arjuna's son Abhimanyu during the great battle. Here, performances occur only in the months of *Karttik* and *Margasheersh* (October-December), but in the neighbouring Alakananda and Pindar river basins, they occur only in the month of *Paush* (December-January). Full-length performances in the latter area include the *shami*-tree episode in which a large pine tree is ritually felled, dragged to the village square, and joyfully erected as a symbol of the Pandavas' ultimate victory (Sax 1991a); and the Rhinoceros (*gainda*) episode involving the killing by Arjuna of a rhinoceros belonging to his son Nagarjuna, followed by a battle between father and son (Sax 1997). In these performances, the *shami*-tree or the pond where the rhinoceros grazes may be at a distance of five or six kilo metres, making an effective performance area of dozens of square kilo metres.[3] Brief performances lasting up to three days occur annually in some areas, while the more elaborate, nine-day performances are performed less often, but at least once in a generation.

*Pandav lila*s incorporate at least five main features. The first of these is drumming. Garhwali folk drumming is a sophisticated art, and indispensable for virtually all public rituals (Chandola 1977). The musicians' esoteric knowledge, magically powerful utterances (*mantra*), and especially their drumming, are necessary not only to induce possession but also to provide the appropriate, highly charged ambience of a performance. Although the Das caste of musicians has a low rank, individual Das are often highly respected for their learning and artistic skill. Villagers from Taintura in Lobha Chandpur told me that the extended *Pandav lila* I attended there in 1990, was done for the benefit of Bhanu Ram, the local Das, in order to obtain his blessing; and during a *Pandav lila* in Dargan village in Singtur in 1994, I saw how Bhuli Das, an eminent local musician, was consistently addressed by his patrons as '*guruji*', a highly respectful epithet normally reserved for Brahmans.

Drumming cannot be separated from dancing, and indeed an alternative term for *Pandav lila is Pandav nritya*, the dance of the Pandavas. Each character dances with a specific weapon (Arjuna with a bow and arrow, Draupadi with a scythe, and so on), and their dance often incorporates characteristic actions (gluttonous Bhima gobbles huge amounts of food, Kaliya Lohar, the low-caste ironsmith who forged the Pandavas' weapons, circumambulates the fire, etc.). Moreover, what I have called 'possession' is conventionally understood as a kind of dance. Village gods and goddesses, along with the Pandavas, are said to enjoy 'dancing' in the bodies of human beings;[4] thus a common colloquial expression for staging a *Pandav lila* is 'causing the Pandavas to dance'.

Along with drumming and dancing, *Pandav lila*s include dramatised vignettes, or *lila*s, from the *Mahabharata*. These *lila*s cover a wide range of incidents and episodes, and are often humorous. Once, for example, I saw a *lila* depicting the Pandavas' exile: when they reach the court of King Virat *in cognito* and apply for work, they are given job interviews by his secretary. "What work can you do?", the secretary asks Arjuna. "Well," replies the latter, "I can teach singing and dancing." "Singing and dancing," replies the secretary. "Hmmm.

Things are pretty tough these days. I'll tell you what: don't call us, we'll call you." Seeing the great Pandavas thus treated like ordinary hillbillies, the audience responded with howls of laughter. But mainly, such *lila*s tend to focus on martial themes: the battle between Arjuna and his son, the slaying of the rhinoceros, the famous battle between Bhimsen and Hanuman, or the death of Abhimanyu.

A fourth characteristic of *Pandav lila* is the competitive bardic recitation of the *Mahabharata* story. This is done in a distinctive style, cupping one or both hands behind the ears, pacing back and forth across the flagstoned square, and chanting the relevant narrative in the local dialect. Sometimes the bard who is performing is politely and formally challenged by another to recall some obscure detail or the other from the *Mahabharata*. If he is able to do so, he continues his recitation; if not, the challenger takes over. Villagers encourage well-known local bards to attend their *lila*s, and modest cash prizes are sometimes awarded for superlative performances. Bardic recitation seems, however, to be something of a dying art: though it has many exponents in the Alakananda and Pindar basins, it is remembered only by very old men in the Mandakini basin, where newer forms of recitation (from handwritten scripts held by the performers) are more prestigious. I have not seen any such bardic recitation in the Tons basin.

The fifth noteworthy aspect of *Pandav lila* is the feasting and hospitality with which it is surrounded. In the Alakananda basin, all *Pandav lila*s involve a kind of sub-performance, a ritual within a ritual, known as *kadhai* or 'pot', in which the Pandavas are given festive foods by some or all of the families in a village.[5] Everywhere in Garhwal, successful performances of *Pandav lila* attract hundreds of relatives and friends from neighbouring villages, who must of course be fed and housed at considerable expense. Because villages tend to be dominated by single castes, this means that performances are in effect caste gatherings, where marriages and other sorts of alliances are negotiated, and matters of common political and social interest are discussed and acted upon.

Analysis

I would like to make three interrelated observations about *Pandav lila*. My first point is a sociological one: *Pandav lila* helps to define the community of Pahari Rajputs, and in so doing, it is typical of oral epics throughout India. How exactly does *Pandav lila* accomplish this task?

Anup Chandola has written that throughout Garhwal, the "most extensive body of folklore is that based on the Mahabharata tales" (Chandola 1977:18), and the importance of the *Mahabharata* extends to local customs and geography as well. The most important religious site in Garhwal, the high-altitude temple of Badrinath that was closely associated with the kings of Garhwal (Galey 1986) is clearly described in Sanskrit versions of the *Mahabharata* (where it is called *Badarikashrama*), and Garhwalis also believe that the Pandavas were born in the village of Pandukeshvar between Joshimath and Badrinath. The regional landscape is everywhere infused with the presence of the Pandavas,[6] and for Garhwalis this localisation has special importance, since they believe that they are direct lineal descendants of the Pandavas themselves. Therefore, *Pandav lila* is equivalent to a rite of ancestor worship, and indeed all *Pandav lila*s include a performance, authentic in every respect, of *shraddha*, the obligatory Hindu post-mortem ritual. The *shraddha* is performed for the benefit of the Pandavas' father, king Pandu, by a Brahman acting as a *purohit* for Sahadeva, who is regarded as the only biological son of Pandu (by Madri).[7]

There are many other reasons why *Pandav lila* may be considered as a fundamentally Rajput tradition. The villages that sponsor them are nearly always dominated by Rajputs, and thus they are also the main performers. Bards and pairs of dancers often come from elsewhere to participate, but they, too, are normally Rajputs. I have seen more than a dozen *Pandav lila*s, only one of which was sponsored by a Brahman village, and even then the three Rajput households of the village provided a greatly disproportionate number of bards and dancers. Nevertheless the performance was regarded as an aesthetic failure, a sham—what one of my friends called a *dhakosala-wali bat*, because a Brahman village is not thought capable of producing an authentic *Pandav lila*. The participation of low-caste musicians and Brahman priests is essential for a proper performance, but their activities are strictly limited to their respective ritual roles.

The main reason why it is felt that Rajputs should play the leading parts in *Pandav lila* is that it so strongly emphasises martial prowess. For example, the weapons with which the major characters dance—the bows and arrows of Arjuna and his son Nagarjuna, Bhima's club, Nakula's scythe, Sahadeva's slate, Yudhisthira's staff, Draupadi's dagger, and Krishna's discus—are the most ritually potent items in a performance. Actually there are two sets of weapons: the first is used by the main dancers and the second, which belonged to the previous generation of dancers (now mostly deceased), stays on the Pandavas' altar. At the conclusion of a performance this second set is buried along with the *shami* tree at a pure and holy spot, usually the village water-source. Meanwhile the weapons actually used by the performers are ceremonially hidden in a safe place, usually under the eaves of someone's roof, where they will remain until the next performance. All of this serves to emphasise the continuity of the Rajput community, living and dead, through the transmission of these specially powerful objects, which link the deceased ancestors with adult male heads of households, and in turn with their young sons.

Martial themes are also underscored by the episodes of the *Mahabharata* that are elaborated in *Pandav lila*. These emphasise the most Kshatriya-like qualities of the Pandavas: their martial and royal virtues (see Sax forthcoming). Elsewhere, I have described two very popular *lila*s: the hunting of the rhinoceros (Sax 1997) and the uprooting and erection of the *shami* tree (Sax 1991a). The first episode emphasises the Pandavas' bravery and skill by contrasting them with the cowardice and buffoonery of their reluctant guide, while the second episode can take place only after their victory over the Kauravas and royal accession, of which it is therefore a sign. In all *Pandav lila*s, Bhima's club is an object of particular veneration, and he uses it to great effect in defeating a variety of demons who block the Pandavas' way at various points. Other important *lila*s include the horse sacrifice (see Sax 1995: 140-1) and the *chakravyuha lila* which enacts the encirclement and death of Arjuna's son Abhimanyu: in these and other cases, the Rajputs of Garhwal are clearly celebrating the martial qualities they consider to be a fundamental aspect of their own identity.

In summary, then, the Rajputs of Garhwal define themselves in important ways by means of *Pandav lila*. They relate to the Pandavas as their own ancestors, whom they worship by means of performance. The landscape of Garhwal is inscribed with the heroic exploits of the Pandavas. Episodes that are dramatised in the *lila* celebrate the martial virtues of Rajputs, and the powerful weapons used in performance unite the community's youngest members with its deceased ancestors.

Such a close association of an oral epic with a particular community is common in India. In fact, Blackburn and Flueckiger have argued that oral epics in India are *defined* in terms of "the extent and intensity of a folklore community's identification with them; they help to shape a community's self-identity", and that "oral epics in India have that special ability to tell a community's own story and thus help create and maintain that community's self-identity".[8] This situation seems so characteristically Indian that we might ask if it hasn't something to do with India's traditional social structure. However that may be, the first point I wish to make is how deeply the *Mahabharata* is associated with Garhwal in general and Garhwali Rajputs in particular.

The second point follows from the first, and has to do with the way we think about the *Mahabharata*. My guess is that most scholars think of it as an epic written in Sanskrit, in other words, as a book. This is only natural for members of a bibliocentric profession, many of whom have bound copies of the *Mahabharata* on their office shelves. But the *Mahabharata* is much more than just a book. The story travelled throughout Asia as far as Vietnam (Desai 1970), and in many kingdoms along the way it functioned as a political model, as did the *Ramayana* in the old Thai kingdom of Ayutthaya. Elsewhere, the *Mahabharata* was received and understood as a form of dance or opera, or as a charter for personal identity. Even today a Javanese man, though probably Muslim, has a special name, his most intimate name, which is either Yudhishthira, or Bhima, or Arjuna, or Nakula or Sahadeva. Moreover, it has been known for a very long time that the *Mahabharata* did not originate as a book but rather as an oral epic, and the problems associated with establishing a critical edition proved so intractable that the editor of the critical edition, V.S. Sukthankar himself wrote that "[t]he essential fact in Mahabharata textual criticism is that the Mahabharata is not and never was a fixed rigid text, but is fluctuating epic tradition...." (1933-66, vol. 1:cii). I want to insist that books are just one part of this tradition; that they have no ontological or epistemological precedence; that for most South and Southeast Asians, the *Mahabharata* is first and foremost an oral tale, a bedtime story, or a performance seen by the flickering firelight; and that to think of it as a book is a monumental distortion, an artefact of the academic mode of production and not a reflection of what the *Mahabharata* really is. In Garhwal, the *Mahabharata* is an ancestral tale periodically enacted as a form of ancestor worship, and one that provides a basic — probably *the* basic — paradigm for what it is to be a Rajput. It proves that the *Mahabharata* is alive and well, a living tradition and not a frozen text in a dead language.

My final point is a theological one. It has to do with the relationship between humanity and the divine in Hinduism. By now it should be clear that performers in *Pandav lila* are often possessed by the characters they play. This kind of possession is common in popular Hinduism, and it is especially prevalent in Garhwal. In fact, first-time visitors to the area from elsewhere in India are invariably struck by the frequency of possession.

This has certain dramaturgical implications. Suresh Awasthi says that the most important feature in the theatre of roots, that is, the contemporary Indian theatre as it seeks to decolonise itself and reconnect with indigenous theatrical traditions, is its "rejection of the proscenium theatre" and its "use of a variety of performance spaces" (1989:50), and the religious dimensions of indigenous Indian theatre can help us understand why this is so. In the *Pandav lila* for example, one can never be sure where the stage ends and the audience begins, and this is true for a great deal of rural theatre of the type that I am calling 'ritual performance'. And just as one can never be sure where the stage ends and the audience begins, so one can never be certain of the boundaries between audience and actor, between actor and character, or between character and audience. How many times have I sat, in the middle of a Himalayan winter night, listening to the drums and watching the dances of the *Pandav lila*, when suddenly the person sitting next to me begins to tremble and shake, then bursts into the square to begin dancing the part of some character. And then, suddenly, they are finished, and take their seat again or perhaps begin to recite the next part of the story. As one of my teachers, the late and much lamented A.K. Ramanujan, put it:

> notions of possession are never far from the audience's mind . . . bard and character, bard and audience, bard and actor, actor and character are merged at crucial moments and separated at ordinary times. One goes to the theater/ritual to experience such mergers in different degrees. — 1986:69-70

I think that this closeness of the divine and the human, this permeability of the divine realm, is quite characteristic of Hinduism. Now in the Western monotheisms of Judaism, Christianity and Islam, there is an ontological gulf separating the divine and the human.

To assert the identity of god and man is a heresy which has sometimes been punished by excommunication and even death. On the one hand there are human beings, mortal and sinful, and on the other hand there is God, perfect and omnipotent; and the bridging of this vast gulf is the occasion for the singular, world-altering theophanies of the latter two traditions: the incarnation of Jesus Christ, the revelation of the Prophet.

In Hinduism on the other hand, we find a profusion of deities: gods and goddesses of particular places, lineages, communities, natural phenomena, sectarian groups, and meditative states, all ranged alongside the multitudinous deities of classical mythology. In mythology we have demons becoming gods and gods behaving like demons; in popular religion throughout India we have people who are regarded as gods, or gods who have temporarily become persons, which are of course one and the same thing.

The frequency of possession in *Pandav lila* is thus typical of popular Hinduism, and it reflects a wonderful idea: the immanence of the divine in the human, the proximity of the gods, the permeability of the divine and human realms. And yet there have always been those who would do away with this aspect of this religion; who would condemn possession as undignified and superstitious, banish the minor gods of village and field, and replace them with the great gods of the high tradition. This tension between polytheism and monotheism provides much of the creative energy of Hinduism. Think of the monotheism of the *Gita*, and the way it pokes fun at the materialistic ritualism of the Vedic sacrifice. Think of the contrasts, on the one hand, between the intellectual Advaita of the Brahmans with its monistic theology and its ethic of non-violence; on the other hand the blood sacrifices of the Kshatriyas, designed to secure victory in warfare; on the third hand the monotheism of the *Sant*s; and on the fourth hand the possession rituals of the peasants, polytheistic affairs like *Pandav lila*, intended to secure good health and bountiful crops, the very sort of thing against which Kabir and Nanak and all the rest railed so eloquently. There is nothing new in the tension between monotheism and polytheism: it is as old as the religion itself. *Pandav lila*, and other ritual performances like it, remind us of the popular side of this dialectic, according to which the human and the divine are each present in the other. I think that this is something worth remembering.

Notes

1. Also called *Pandav nritya, Pamval,* and by other terms as discussed below.
2. In Kaliphat between the Alakananda and Mandakini rivers, performances focus on the *chakravyuha* episode in which Abhimanyu is killed, and involve printed scripts and sometimes even semi-professional troupes of actors. These innovations are one object of my current research.
3. Compare Richard Schechner's remarks (1983, 1988) on *Ramlila* and environmental theatre.
4. Cf. Berreman 1964.

5. People in Chandpur, Distric Chamoli, connect this custom to Bhima's slaying of the demon Baka. The feast is said to be thanksgiving festival instituted by a grateful king.
6. This is an example of what A. K. Ramanujan (1986:67) has called the 'localisation' of epic figures in folk traditions.
7. It is said that Sahadeva (or Nakula, according to some) was conceived during King Pandu's fatal intercourse with Madri; cf. Hiltebeitel 1991:29 n. 26 where the Pandavas' younger sister Chankotari (a.k.a. Chankuvati) had the same parentage.
8. Blackburn and Flueckiger 1989: 6, 11. Further evidence for this sort of link can also be found in the recent works of Beck 1982, Blackburn 1988, Blackburn and Ramanujan 1989, Richman 1991, Smith 1980.

References

Awasthi, Suresh, 1989, 'Theatre of Roots: Encounter with Tradition', *The Drama Review*, 33: 48-69.

Beck, Brenda E.F., 1982, *The Three Twins: The Telling of a South Indian Folk Epic*, Bloomington, Indiana University Press.

Berreman, Gerald, 1964, 'Brahmins and Shamans in Pahari Religion', *Journal of Asian Studies*, 23 (suppl.): 53-69.

Blackburn, Stuart, 1988, *Singing of Birth and Death: Texts in Performance*, Philadelphia, University of Pennsylvania Press.

Blackburn, Stuart H. and Joyce B. Flueckiger, 1989, 'Introduction', In Blackburn, Stuart H., Claus, Peter J. and Joyce B. Flueckiger and Susan S. Wadley, eds., 1989, *Oral Epics in India*, Berkeley: University of California Press, 1-11.

Blackburn, Stuart and Ramanujan, A. K., eds., 1989, *Another Harmony: New Essays in the Folklore of India*, Berkeley, University of California Press.

Chandola, Anoop, 1977, *Folk Drumming in the Himalayas: A Linguistic Approach to Music*, New York, AMS.

Desai, Santosh N., 1970, 'Ramayana — An Instrument of Historical Contact and Cultural Transmission Between India and Asia', *Journal of Asian Studies*, 30: 5-20.

Galey, Jean-Claude, 1986, 'Totalite et hierarchie dans les sanctuaires royaux du Tehri-Garhwal' *Purusartha*, 10: 55-95.

Hiltebeitel, Alf, 1991, *The Cult of Draupadi*, Vol. II: *On HIndu Ritual and the Goddess*, Chicago, University of Chicago Press.

Ramanujan, A.K., 1986, 'Two Realms of Kannada Folklore', in Blackburn, Stuart and, Ramanujan, A.K. eds., *Another Harmony.*

Sax, William S., 1991a, 'Ritual and Performance in the Pandavalila of Uttarakhand', In Arvind Sharma, ed., *Essays on the Mahabharata*, Leiden, E.J. Brill, 274-95.

———, 1991b, *Mountain Goddess: Gender and Politics in a Himalayan Pilgrimage*, New York, Oxford University Press.

Sax, William S., 1995, Who's Who in Pandav Lila? In William S. Sax, ed., *The Gods at Play: Lila in South Asia*, New York, Oxford University Press.

Sax, William S., 1997, 'Fathers, Sons, and Rhinoceroses: Masculinity and Violence in the *Pandav Lila'*, *Journal of the American Oriental Society*.

Sax, William S., Forthcoming, 'Gender and the Representation of Violence in Pandav Lila', in Leslie, I. Julia, ed., *Gender and Social Position in South Asian Religions.*

Schechner, Richard, 1983, *Performative Circumstances, from the Avant Garde to Ramlila*, Calcutta, Seagull Books.

Schechner, Richard, 1988, *Performance theory* (rev. and expanded edn.), New York, Routledge.

Smith, John D., 1980, 'Old Indian: The Two Sanskrit Epics', In A. T. Hatto, ed., *Traditions of Heroic and Epic Poetry, Volume One: The Traditions,* London, Modern Humanities Research Association.

Sukthankar, Vishnu S., 1933-1966, *The Mahabharata*, Poona, Bhandarkar Oriental Research Institute (19 vols).

16

Pandava Dance
A Performance for Life

Richa Negi

Introduction

> Indian oral epics are better understood as traditions, as transmissions of story and performance that create cultural identity . . . only when we approach the epic as tradition handed down over centuries, are its fully accumulated meanings open to interpretation. (Blackburn *et. al.*, 1989: 15)

Garhwal, also popularly known as the *devabhoomi* (abode of Gods), is situated in the central Himalayas. An administrative division of Uttar Pradesh hills, it comprises the districts of Chamoli, Pauri, Tehri, Uttarkashi and Dehradun. The whole of Garhwal region reverberates with the *Mahabharata* epic tradition interwoven with the religious folk songs, ballads and dance-dramas. The presence of divinity is felt, transmitted and popularised through these expressions, preserving the continuity of a tradition through performative manifestations. Garhwal Himalayas is believed to be the land of birth and death of the Pandavas, the heroes of the great Indian epic *Mahabharata*. There are places that are identified and connected with the *Mahabharata* characters, elaborated through the local myths and legends strewn all over the Garhwal region. The epic tradition has been in the process of continuous adaptation over the ages, coalescing all the oral forms and traditions reflecting the perception of the indigenous people. Even to this day the traditional transmission continues to flow in the life stream of the Garhwali folk culture, manifesting itself in the form of the *Pandava* dance.

Nature of performance

Based on the episodes of the *Mahabharata* lore in its folk form through oral and performative art, the *Pandava* dance is more or less a community ritual. It is performed by the members of various segments of social hierarchy, who actively participate and intensify the whole performance. The *Pandava* dance is held during *Haribodhani aikadash* till the end of *Margasheersh* (mid-November to December), on the eleventh day, following the *Deepawali* festival. The exact date and time of the performance is fixed either by invoking one of the *Pandava* characters, who incarnates himself through *paswa* (medium) and declares an auspicious date, or by astrological calculations and by appeasing Bhumiyal, the land God. Duration of these performances may vary from fifteen days to three months. The date of occurrence, duration and frequency of the dance may vary from village to village or region to region. The *Pandava* dances are performed as the *shraddha* (mortuary rites) of King Pandu; for *dhan dhyan* (wealth and prosperity) of the village and also for the appeasement of the wandering souls of the Pandavas. According to a local legend, the Pandavas along with Draupadi, their consort, abandoned their kingdom after the great Mahabharata war, which culminated in great chaos, disaster and loss of human lives. They lost interest in their reign and proceeded towards the Himalayas in search of Lord Shiva for salvation. Shiva eluded them until the persistent search of the Pandavas won him over. The last leg of their eventful journey culminated at the Swargarohan Parvat (in Garhwal) where they perished one by one. But just before perishing, the Pandavas turned to take a last glimpse of the lush green land, which had been their abode for so long. They were moved by the sheer beauty of the land. Just then Arjuna is said to have shot his arrows at different landmarks to identify the places, so that their souls could return to wander again in their earthly abode and visit their devotees year after year to receive their offerings. Even to this day each brook, rivulet, tree, temple and mountain peak is identified with the Pandavas and have their names attached to it.

The *Pandava* dance is a community ritual, involving small children, women and elderly village folk alike, who participate collectively and enthusiastically. The dance is performed in an open arena, locally known as *mandan*. Fire is lit in one corner to provide light as the dances are usually held at night and also to provide warmth to the participants, audience and musicians. It also warms the drums making the hide soft and thus easy to play. Fire illuminates the whole arena and no other artificial lights or props are used. And according to local belief, fire also symbolises the birth of Draupadi who is said to have risen from the sacrificial flames of *agni* (fire). She symbolises *shakti* and is revered as Goddess Durga.

Prior to the dance performance, the local inhabitants proceed towards the *Pandava* temple in a huge procession where they worship the Pandavas and their weapons, locally known as *ban*. These weapons or attributes are then brought to the arena. Each night the weapons are worshipped and each character of the Pandava brothers picks up his respective weapons and performs the dance. Throughout the duration of the dance the weapons are kept on a makeshift altar near the *mandan*. After the culmination of the performance they are taken back to the temple and kept there till the next performance in the following year. The *Pandava* dance performance revolves around the main story of the epic *Mahabharata*. The five Pandava brothers braving the hardship in exile along with their mother Kunti and consort Draupati; their conflict with Kauravas, their cousins, resulting in the great battle of *Mahabharata*; and finally the main theme, that is, the victory of good over evil are depicted with the inclusion of local myths and legends.

Ritual as performance

The *Pandava* dance involves both ritual and theatrical episodes. While the theatrical form consists of interchange of dialogues along with musical accompaniment, it is the ritual aspect which is more important. Rituals are an integral part of the *Pandava* dance, which helps to achieve the objective of the performance and sanctifies it. A combination of varied rites and acts of ritual events following one after the other in a synchronised form is deeply embedded in the performative genres and cultural psyche of the people of Garhwal. Therefore, enactment of each episode in the *Pandava* dance involves ritualistic elements present in every act of the performance. Religious folk songs are sung in order to invoke the *paswa*, or the medium on whom it is believed that the souls of the Pandavas descend and take possession. *Paswas* are also the *dramatis personae* who personify the various Pandava characters. They are worshipped along with other deities including Bhumiyal, the land God, to protect the village from any evil and also to bestow prosperity and well-being. Rituals are also observed while lighting fire, playing drums and the other musical instruments, in the gyrating steps and tempo of the dance and also when the village community, in a huge procession, visits the Pandava temples to bring their attributes or weapons to the arena where they are kept and worshipped throughout the performance. Moreover, the augmentation through rituals helps the actors to reach a state of mind, enabling them to rise from the secular to the sacred level, which makes the performance more effective and sanctified.

Role of the character and identity of an actor

The role of the character, specially that of the five Pandava brothers, performed by the male members of the Rajput (warrior class) families, is a hereditary factor passed on from one generation to the next.

In the folk tradition of Garhwal Himalayas, it is strongly believed that the Pandavas were the ancestors of the local inhabitants. The local myths and legends add to this. Pandavas are said to be connected to the land of Garhwal through their birth and death. It is believed that they were born at the Pandukeshwar Parvat and perished at Swargarohan, both situated in Garhwal. *Pandava* dance is therefore a re-enactment of the past, re-lived through various performative events. An actor is accordingly believed to be a re-incarnation of the Pandavas through *paswa* (medium). An actor here is a performer for life and not just a one-show man momentarily satisfying his artistic urge. For instance, Arjuna is just Arjuna, he is not a character imitation of Arjuna. He is for real. This holds true for other characters as well. Even after the performances are over, the actors are addressed by the names of the characters they portray and not by their real names. They are looked upon with great reverence and people approach them for social as well as religious advice. An actor is also the medium for the divine spirit. When he speaks, he conveys the message for the community's well-being and advises abstinence from evil.

Significance of drums and the drummer

Any enactment is incomplete without music which enhances the performance. Although there are various other musical accompaniments, the drum locally known as *dhol* plays an important part in the *Pandava* dance performance. The drum and the drummer are the life-line of the *Pandava* dance. They play significant role in the rituals observed during the performance. The *ouji* (drummer) holds a very special place during the enactments. The drummers are ironsmiths called Dom or Mistri. They belong to the lowest order of the caste hierarchy but attain the highest position during the performance, acting as mediators between the human and the divine, establishing themselves as levellers between the two segments of the society. All caste distinctions and barriers are swept aside as caste disparity has no place during the performance.

The entire sequence of the *Pandava* dance runs in synchronisation with the drum beats. The *Pandava* dance consists of various beats and rhythms. Each character is introduced with different beat which is named after the character it is played for. Thus, the role played by the drummers is very prominent and vital throughout the performance as they are the true preservers of this age-old tradition. When the souls of the Pandavas descend on the human vehicle or medium, they first greet and offer obeisance to the *ouji* and address him as their *guru* or teacher.

The audience-actor relationship

Theatre cannot exist without an audience. In the *Pandava* dance performance the relationship of the actor and the audience is not that of the observer and the observed. It is rather a relationship of the performer and the participatory audience. The continuous intervention by the audience stimulates the flow and spontaneity of the performance. The accompanying cheers, shouts of slogans, laughter, cries and rapt silence shows the intense participation of the audience and enlivens the whole performance. The constant link and interchange of dialogues between the audience and the performers strengthen the emotional bond shared by the two. A rich tradition of offering feasts to the Pandava characters is widely practised. Each day during the performance the inhabitants invite them to visit various homes in the village and offer food to the Pandavas, who dine once a day. Towards the end of the performance the audience worships the Pandavas and prays for the appeasement of their wandering souls. They offer gifts and invite them again to their earthly abode in the following year. The parting is very emotional and moving. It culminates with the Pandavas bathing in the nearby river and returning the attributes to the temple, which remain there till the next performance. All through this the Pandava characters are accompanied by the people in large procession which shows their deep emotional involvement and active participation in the performance.

Overall, the *Pandava* dance performance is a part of everyday as well as religious life of the indigenous people. It is, therefore, a theatre of reality and a true reflection of their culture. It is not a mere enactment of the *Mahabharata* lore, but a sacred history re-actualised and re-lived through performance. *Pandava* dance, thus, acts as a locus of human expression. It reveals, moulds and transforms the personal as well as cultural identity individually and collectively, preserving the living continuance of a tradition.

References

Awasthi, Suresh, 1983, *Drama: Gift of Gods, Culture and Performance*, Tokyo, Institute for the Study of Languages and Cultures of Asia and Africa.

Blackburn, Stuart, H., *et. al.*, *Oral Epics in India*, 1989, Berkeley, University of California Press.

Chatak, Govind, 1958, *Garhwal Ki Lok Gathayen*, Dehradun, Mohini Prakashan.

——— 1966, *Garhwal Ke Lok Geet*, Dehradun, Jugal Kishor Pvt. Ltd.

Negi, Richa, 1998, *Pandava Dance as an Exponent of the Indigenous Folk Theatre of Garhwal and English Avantegarde Theatre: A Comparative Study*, Ph.D. thesis submitted to Garhwal University, Srinagar, Garhwal.

Srivastava, Sahablal, 1974, *Folk Culture and Oral Tradition*, New Delhi, Abhinav Publication.

Thakur, S.S.S., 1982, *Karyala: Folk Theatre of Himachal Pradesh*, New Delhi, Sangeet Natak Akademy.

Turner, Victor, 1969, *The Ritual Process*, Chicago, Aldine.

Vatsyayan, Kapila, 1976, *Traditions of Indian Folk Dance*, New Delhi, Clarion Books.

Walton, H.G., 1910, *Gazetteer of Garhwal Himalaya*, Allahabad, Government Press.

17

Loriki and its Singers

S.M. Pandey

THE oral epic *Loriki* or *Chanaini* [1] is sung by the Ahir singers of northern India in the Avadhi, Bhojpuri, Maithili, Magahi and Chattisgarhi dialects of Hindi. During my field work between 1965 and 1967, I could not find any version of this epic in the Braj or Rajasthani areas. We can say that the singers of the epic are found in the area extending from Allahabad in U.P. to Bhagalpur in Bihar.

Kavopadhyaya[2], Verrier Elwin[3], and S.C. Dube[4] have also written of a Chattisgarhi version of the epic in their books on Chattisgarhi grammar and on the folksongs of Chattisgarh, but I could not find the time to record a *Chattisgarhi* version. However, I have been told that singers are still alive in the area, although they are now quite old. I was also unable to record a Maithili version, but the tradition of singing this epic is still current in the Maithili region. The versions I have collected are from the Gonda, Allahabad, Varanasi, Mirzapur, Ballia and Patna districts. The singers are mostly Ahirs, who are either milkmen or farmers. They are called Gvalas; i.e., cowherds, as they keep cows. All these singers are male and hardly any of them can read or write. Women are generally not permitted to sing the epic, though in Mirzapur district there is a woman singer who can sing at least some of the episodes.[5]

The story of Loriki

The story of the *Loriki* is sung by different singers in different ways and the epic differs in all the versions. The four volumes that I have published so far are significantly different from each other. In fact, the same singer never repeats the same text verbatim in his subsequent recording, a detailed study of which I have already made in the second volume of the epic *The Hindi Oral Epic Canaini*. The story of the epic as I recorded in the Bhojpuri-speaking area of Varanasi runs as follows:

In Suhaval, there was an Ahir king Bamari who had seven sons among whom

Dasavamt and Bhimali were extremely valiant. He also had a daughter called Satiya. Bamari had taken a vow that his daughter should never marry, and had further forbidden, not only his own daughter, but all the girls in his kingdom to marry. This made the girls of the village very unhappy. His own daughter Satiya was herself also not willing to marry, for she knew through her divine power that her marriage would lead to great battles and the destruction of her whole family.

The hero of the epic, Lorik, the Ahir, had a step brother, Samvaru, who was both a warrior and a religious man. He lived in Boha, spending his time praying to Durga. He did not want to marry. Once Lorik went to play Holi[6] in Kusumapur, an outlying settlement of his village Gaura, where Chanva, the daughter of King Sahdev lived. Lorik threw coloured water on Chanva, ignoring the tradition of the village that coloured water may not be sprinkled on the girls of one's own village. Chanva felt insulted, and in anger she said: "Fool, you do not know the tradition. Go and get your brother married. He is getting old and nobody comes to him with a proposal of marriage. You can then play Holi with your sister-in-law."[7] Lorik returned home feeling insulted, and because of this he refused to eat for several days. He asked his mother Khoilani to persuade the unwilling Samvaru to marry, who finally gave his consent. Lorik came to know about the pious daughter of Bamari, through his friend Ajai's wife Vijaya, a washerwoman who came originally from Suhaval, and, deciding that she would be a suitable bride for his brother, he collected his warrior friends and set out from Gaura for Suhaval, determined to get Samvaru married. He prayed to Durga and to the local goddess Bansatti before setting out, and they assured him of their help. The marriage party consisted of warriors like Surjan, Bathava, Ajai and Devasi, all belonging to various untouchable castes. After a long journey they came to Suhaval and camped outside the village.

Satiya was worried when she came to know about this. She went to the temple of Shiva and after praying to him, asked why these warriors had come from Gaura and why they were beating the drums of battle. Shiva told her that she would soon be married and that the warriors would fight with her cruel father who did not allow the girls of his kingdom to marry. In the battle her whole family would be destroyed. Hearing this, she became very agitated and went to her friend Hardoiya, the serpent, and asked him to attack and bite the whole party. The serpent did attack everyone except Lorik, who escaped through the help of the goddess Durga. But in the meanwhile it had been revealed to Satiya that her marriage was inevitable, and at her insistence the serpent restored the whole marriage party to life. Bamari, Satiya's father, however, still opposed the marriage and as a result great battles broke out. The epic relates the following events:

(1) Satiya's father collects his army and sounds the trumpet for battle. The army

is equipped with elephants, horses and camels, and its warriors carry swords, spears and maces.

(2) Ajai, a great warrior and a friend of Lorik, fights bravely with his mace. Bamari's army is thrown into confusion, but later Ajai is captured.

(3) Samvaru wants to destroy the whole army by attacking it with flaming arrows, but Lorik stops him as he does not want to cause its complete destruction, fearing that in this event Satiya too may be killed.

(4) Lorik breaks the gate of Bamari's fort where Ajai is held captive, and sets him free. Bamari becomes anxious and writes to his warrior sons, who are in Slhat.

(5) His two sons, Bhimali and Dasavamt, who had received special powers from the gods, collect their warrior friends and come to Suhaval with their elephants. They go secretly and meet the distinguished warriors of Lorik's party, such as Surjan, Bathava, Ajai, Devasi and Sivgarh one by one in their tents. They also come to Samvaru and Lorik and realise that fierce battles are inevitable.

(6) The warriors of Gaura challenge Bamari's sons. Thereupon battles break out. First Dasavamt uses flaming arrows and for 28 miles around everything is on fire. Lorik is nearly burnt to death, but the goddess Durga brings him to the river Ganga and so saves his life. The fighting continues for seven days, and occasionally Lorik gets disheartened, but Durga keeps encouraging him to go on fighting. In the seventh battle Dasavamt is killed. Now Bamari's other sons come to fight, equipped with elephants and armed with all sorts of weapons. They are nevertheless defeated. Then Bamari himself comes with his army. Lorik, whose forces are now described as comprising twelve thousand Manglaits,[8] thirteen thousand Turks and sixteenth thousand Raghuvamshis (Rajputs), is finally victorious.

Satiya is now married to Samvaru, and the other girls of the kingdom are also free to marry. Samvaru, Lorik and other heroes come back to Gaura with Satiya. Samvaru then moves to Boha and lives there happily with Satiya.

Agori

The second chapter of the epic describes the marriage of Lorik and Majari. She is the daughter of Mahar, an Ahir of Agori, where a tyrant king, Molagat, rules. Molagat is a lustful man, who aims to marry or to seduce all the beautiful girls of his kingdom. It seems that it is almost impossible for Mahar to save his daughter from the king who is determined to marry her against their wish. But Majari is a strong character, and she writes a letter to Lorik appealing him to save her honour and that of the entire Ahir community by marrying her. Lorik reads the letter and his sense of honour is aroused.

He writes to her promising his help and tells her that he will come soon and marry her. He consults his mother Khoilani, his brother Samvaru and his friends. They all agree to this marriage even though they know that a great battle will have to be fought with Molagat. The party comes to Agori and the marriage ceremony of Majari is performed.

After the marriage the following events occur:

(1) When Molagat comes to know about the marriage of Majari he becomes very angry and sends for Bhat, a great warrior. He (Molagat) promises to give him half his kingdom for killing Lorik. Lorik's warrior friends have already returned to Gaura and Lorik is alone in Agori.

(2) Bhat goes to stop Lorik taking Majari away from Agori. Lorik breaks his bones.

(3) Molagat sends a fierce, maddened elephant to kill Lorik. It tries to crush Lorik under its feet but Durga intervenes and saves him. Lorik then kills the elephant.

(4) Molagat now asks for help from his sister's son Nirmal, a great warrior, who possesses five miraculous arrows which can kill any man.

(5) Majari is very much afraid of Nirmal, and thinks Lorik may not survive his attack. She invokes her chastity to come to her husband's aid.

(6) Nirmal attacks Lorik but Lorik is not killed. Then he uses a flaming arrow which causes the whole earth and sky to tremble. Lorik is almost killed. Durga takes him to the river Sursari, and he is revived again.

(7) Finally Lorik cuts off Nirmal's head with his sword, and the gods come to drink his blood. Nirmal's wife commits *sati*[9] with the dead body of her husband.

(8) Molagat comes with his army to fight. Lorik uses his powerful sword and kills Molagat and his warriors.

Haldi

The next episode of the epic tells how after these heroic battles Lorik settles down in his own village of Gaura. Chanva, the daughter of Sahdev, who meanwhile has been married to an impotent Ahir Shivadhar, rejects him and returns home. On her way home she meets Batha who tries to seduce her, but by her cleverness and strength she manages to save her honour. Batha, however, is a thorough villain and starts harassing her father, Sahdev. She appeals to Lorik for help, reminding him of the honour of the Ahir caste, and Lorik comes and beats Batha to death.

Gradually Chanva and Lorik start meeting each other secretly, and ultimately she becomes pregnant. Chanva persuades him to run away to Haldi. Chanva's husband Shivadhar comes to fight Lorik but is defeated. Later, a snake bites Chanva but Lorik invokes supernatural help and she is saved. In Haldi they are given shelter by Jamuni, a girl who sells liquor. Lorik works for Mahuvari, the ruler of Haldi, first as a cowherd and then as a wrestling instructor. But he does not do his job well and is a constant source of worry to everyone. He attacks some people in Haldi and kills two wrestlers. The ruler of Haldi cannot restrain him, as Lorik is very strong. Lorik meets some women in Haldi whose husbands have been made captive by the king of Neurapur. Lorik leaves Haldi to go and rescue them. Mahuvari offers him a fierce horse to take him to Neurapur, hoping that it may kill him. But Lorik and the horse become friendly. The whole of Haldi is surprised to find that the fierce horse has not killed Lorik. The following incidents then occur:

(1) The king of Neurapur, Hareva, prays to his goddess, and she sends evil spirits to kill Lorik, but Durga saves him.

(2) Hareva uses fierce dogs with poisonous fangs to kill Lorik and his horse, but he is saved.

(3) Then Hareva comes with his army to fight Lorik, but Lorik cuts off his head and the army flees.

(4) Lorik sets the prisoners free and they come back to Haldi with him.

The scene now returns to Lorik's village. After Lorik has run away from his village with Chanva, disastrous events take place in his family. Devasia of Pipari and Sahdev, Chanva's father, attack his brother Samvaru, kill him and take away all his wealth and cattle.

Lorik's wife Majari and mother Khoilani are reduced to extreme poverty, so much so that they are forced to perform the most menial tasks, such as grinding flour and spices for others. The people of the village do not give them any help as Lorik has disgraced his family by running away with Chanva. Majari sends a messenger, Jaggu Banjara in Haldi to Lorik to tell him of their sorry plight. Lorik comes secretly to Boha, a place near Gaura, and announces that he wants to buy milk and curd, offering a very high price.

All the milk-women of Gaura go to sell their milk and curd to him, and are paid handsomely. Majari also collects some milk from the neighbours and goes to Boha to sell it along with other women. On the way she has to cross a river and the ferryman struck by her beauty, tries to seduce her. Then Majari invokes the goddess of chastity and prays to her: "O goddess, if I am a chaste and truthful woman, make this river dry up." And the river dries up. The boatman is very distressed, for this deprives him of his livelihood. He falls at Majari's feet and begs for forgiveness.

In Boha Lorik recognises her. Later his old friends go to him and tell him about everything that has happened in his absence. Then he fights his enemies and recaptures his lost wealth. During this fight he discovers that he has lost his former strength. He gives all his wealth to his two sons and then burns himself to death in Gaura.

Loriki and Ahirs

It is important to notice the fundamental association of this text with the ethnic and social group called the Ahirs. The important characters in the story are Ahirs, and it is they who transmit this material from generation to generation and form its audience. In the Ballia district when I was recording this epic in 1965, more than a hundred people came to listen and one Ahir confessed to me that he used to come some ten miles on foot everyday to hear the performance. I think it may be taken as an indication that a very large audience indeed must have attended the recital of *Loriki* when proper festive performances were given and when the tradition was not yet dependent upon the chance visit of a field-worker. It is at night that the Ahir loves to relax and listen to the *Loriki*. Women do not come to recitals. It has been described above how the hero saved first the honour of an Ahir girl, and then that of the community as a whole from a wicked man. The epic constantly proclaims the hero as an Ahir and a saviour of the community. And of course the Ahirs take tremendous pride in Lorik's victories. The epic dimensions of the story are achieved by setting Lorik's acts of individual heroism constantly in a context of warfare on a grand scale. The constitution of the army — Mangalaits and Turks, elephants and camels, weapons of every sort, both familiar and completely unknown — has no bearing whatsoever on the historical realities of Ahir culture. The hero's acts of human valour always take place under the eye of the goddess, who has the power of leading the virtuous to success and the sinner to disaster. One episode draws a contrast between Lorik's alliance with the supreme Goddess and his opponent's alliance with a minor local divinity. Of course, the non-heroic elements of the story are very dear to the hearts of the Ahir audience. Lorik's brother, who combines great virtue and piety with a heroic defence of Lorik's interest during his absence, appeals greatly to the audience. They shed tears at the sufferings of Lorik's deserted wife and mother, and are greatly moved at the preservation of his wife's chastity when it is threatened by a boatman. In other words we can say that there is a common emotional reaction and certain common standards of appreciation among the people of the Ahir community to whom the hero and other important characters belong. The entire life of an Ahir hero has been described in the story. His birth, his marriage, his battles, his love and his sorrows are all of great interest to an Ahir audience.

Sir George Grierson, who in 1929 wrote two articles on the birth of Lorik,[10] has quoted a Bihari proverb:

ketano Ahira hohi sayana
Loriki char ṅa gave ana

However learned an Ahir be,
Nothing but *Loriki* singeth he.

In the Avadhi area I collected other versions of the proverb

ketano Ahira bace puranaa
Canaini chari na gave ana

However many times an Ahir may read the Puranas,
he will not sing anything but *Canaini.*

Ahirs have clung very strongly to the tradition of *Loriki* singing until recently. It was clear that the *Loriki* represented to the Ahirs what the Sanskrit epic tradition represented to most Indians.

Sometimes singers compare their epic with the *Ramayana*. Singers from the Ballia district in U.P. recited a verse to me:

sat kand Ramayan a sat kand Lorikayan
Ramayana *has seven cantos and so has the Lorikayan.*

The singers from the Patna district told me:

sat kand Ramayaṅ a caudah kand Lorikayan
The Ramayana *has seven cantos but the Lorikayan has fourteen.*

The singers and their background

The singers of this tale are illiterate, but they are not uneducated. They know the stories of the *Mahabharata*, the *Ramayana* and other Puranas. They know the stories of Harishchandra, Nala, Shravana Kumara and other important Puranic characters. Most of these epic singers sing the *viraha*, which is a kind of short song popular among the Ahirs, recounting some episodes from the *Mahabharata* and *Ramayana* and sometimes one can find traces of the *Mahabharata* and *Ramayana* in the versions of their epic as well. For example, the hero in the Gonda version of Orilal[11] does not burn himself to death in Varanasi or in his village but enters the ice just as the Pandavas did after the end of the *Mahabharata* battle.

All these singers tell us that they cannot recite these epics without supernatural help. Sivnath Chaudhari[12] told me that it is the goddess Sarasvati who helped him to sing. Without her help it was impossible to sing such a long epic. Panchu Bhagat[13] told me that it is with the help of Bansatti,[14] that he can sing the epic right to the end. Other singers also claim to receive divine aid.

None of these singers are professionals. They do not earn their livelihood by singing, though they get special rewards when they sing at weddings. The Ahirs invite these singers and treat them with utmost respect. But the singers can perform at anytime of the year and on any occasion — at the birth of a child, at festivals, or by the haystacks during harvest time or in big fairs. Sometimes Ahirs might gather without any special occasion if the singer is there and he is requested to sing. Hemp (*ganja*) is obtained at nearby shops and this keeps the party going. Gatherings take place mainly at night as most of the singers work during the day. Singers sing until very late at night, sometimes up to four or five o'clock in the morning. They begin at eight or nine in the evening. Since the story is very long and there is always room for improvisation or addition, the recitation may sometimes continue for a month. However when singers have to give a short performance they select one particular episode either of their own choice or that suggested by the audience. When I recorded the epic in 1965-7 all the singers used to smoke hemp. No singer could sing for long hours without the help of hemp and there were some shops where hemp was easily available.

None of these singers are literate, and in their childhood most of them used to graze and herd cattle. They learnt their art mostly during this period from their teachers, but for practice they sang regularly at gatherings of Ahirs, who encouraged the *Loriki* and the *viraha*. The teacher never charged any money for teaching the epic. He was satisfied with the knowledge that he was preserving the tradition and the fact that he had a great disciple through whom his name would be remembered in the community.

No musical instrument accompanied the singing of this epic. It was probably not practical to carry an instrument while grazing cattle in the forests or pastures. The audience consisted mostly of Ahirs, but other lower caste people, such as Telis (oilmen), Dhobis (washermen), Noniyas (manufacturers of saltpetre), Chamars (leather workers) and many other backward class people came to listen to it as well. There are sometimes Brahmans and Kshatriyas in the audience too, but they are few and mostly illiterate. However, Sivnath Chaudhari told me that in his childhood there was a Brahman who was very popular for his singing of the *Loriki*. The singers do not use any printed text as some singers of the epic *Alha* do. The *Loriki* is orally transmitted.

It has already been pointed out that this epic is especially popular among Ahirs. Lorik is their ideal hero. They enjoy listening to his loves and battles, victories and defeats. The singers think that the hero is a historical figure who actually lived and performed the acts which they describe. Like the singers, the listeners too believe in the historical existence of the hero, but neither the singers nor the audience know the actual place of the hero's birth. Of course, all of them believe it to be a place called Gaura, but there are several Gauras in U.P. and Bihar. Singers generally identify it with the place nearest to them. Like Gaura, all the other places, such as Suhaval, where

Lorik's brother Samvaru was married and where Lorik fought many battles, Pipari and Neurapur, where Lorik performed his many heroic feats, also remain unidentified. Singers believe that Agori is the Agori of Mirzapur district where the ruins of the Agori fort still exist. Sukkhudas[15] of Patna district suggested that most of the places connected with the epic are in the Gaya district of Bihar.

The names of the main characters, Lorik and his two wives Majari and Chanda (Chanva), Samvaru and his wife Satiya, and Lorik's enemy, Hareva are unknown to written histories nor are other characters like Ajai, Shivadhar, and the Mahar king of Agori, mentioned in the histories. However, a Hindi Sufi poet Maulana Da'ud who composed a Sufi work, *Chandayan*, in 1379 during the period of Firozshah Tughluq (1351-88) using the legend of Lorik and Chanda, alludes to some of these names. This at least shows that when Maulana Da'ud adapted this legend more than six hundred years ago, some of these characters existed in the oral tradition. Jyotirisvara, a scholar of Sanskrit and Maithili who is supposed to have lived in the early fourteenth century and perhaps before Maulana Da'ud,[16] refers to a dance called *Loriknacho* (*varnaratnakara* text, p.2). This suggests that there was a dance also current in the name of Lorik. All these references indicate that Lorik must have been a famous local hero and through the singing of bards his popularity might have increased.

Styles and themes

A notable feature of oral epic singing is that a singer never presents the same text twice. Every time he performs he presents a different text. In the *Hindi Oral Epic Canaini*, I have discussed this feature of oral epic singers not having a fixed text in their repertoire and their flexibility in narration in some detail. In fact singers do not even have any one specific style of singing. No two singers sing in a similar style even when they belong to the same area or are taught by the same teacher. When I recorded some parts of the epic sung by a disciple of Sivnath Chaudhari, I discovered that there were sharp differences between the versions of the teacher and the pupil, not only in the text but also in the style of singing. For example Sivnath Chaudhari begins his *Loriki* with a prayer, thus:

> *Ha, ha, ha, ha, he Ram, Ram, Ram Ram, ho Ram,*
> *aju Rame jiyani bari muvani ek din Rame le jiv ke hauni adhaar.*
> *je Ramabhajan na kariha parihani bhumi narak le gari*
> *Ji Ram bhajan jo karab to bani jai surdham,*
>
> (My life is lifeless, my life depends on Rama alone. If you do not repeat the name of Rama you will go to hell. If you worship Rama, You will attain heaven.)

Ramdev,[17] his disciple, begins his prayer thus:

ha, Ram, Ram, Ram, Ram, Ram ho Ram
kahalin ek din pance Ramalai ho lagali
ha uve, lai je lagali sanjhiya ho vi .... han
jei mukh Rame Rame ta nahi ave
u man jiyate holen he ardhangi
a muvale par sahas kumbhe narakave ke gari,
unka ke sarage sarniya nahi milal
na man chuve pavale je koi das.

(I tell you my audience, the love of Rama has arisen in me and it dwells in me night and day. The man who does not repeat the names of Rama in his heart may be alive but is truly half dead. He will go to the pits of hell. He will not get shelter in heaven).

Two singers of the same area may give two different accounts of the same episode. For example, Ramavatar[18] and Hira Lal came from neighbouring villages in the Allahabad district, but in Hira Lal's version unlike Ramavatar's, the hero burns himself to death in Varanasi. In Ramavatar's version he burns himself to death in his own village of Gaura.

Again, in Tulsi Yadav's[19] version (from the Mirzapur district) when the heroine runs away with Lorik to Haldi, a serpent bites her on the way and she dies; but through supernatural help she becomes alive again. In the version of Dadai Mallah[20] of the same area, this episode does not occur. In the fourteenth-century Sufi work of Maulana Dau'd this episode is found. Sivnath Chaudhari of Ballia and Sukkhudas of Patna also describe this episode. Though the singers try to remember the sequence of the events and some particular episodes and formulas as sung by their teacher, they do not reproduce the whole song in exactly the same manner. Disciples learn in the company of their teachers when they are performing, but in their free time they try to perfect it in their own way, exercising their originality and talents. Hence differences arise, as the example of Sivnath Chaudhari and Ramdev shows. There are other reasons for variations in transmission too. As already pointed out, singers do not have a fixed text in their repertoire. Therefore they produce different texts each time they perform, and though most of the singers claim that they are faithfully reproducing the versions of their respective teachers, in fact all of them use different styles of singing and different sets of descriptions. They never follow a single tradition. For example, Ramdev claimed that his teacher was Sivnath Chaudhari, but he went to other recitals of *Loriki* also and adopted those features of recitation of other singers which he liked most. Once in 1984 when Sivnath and Ramdev were performing together in my village Gothahuli in Ballia district, Ramdev deviated considerably from his teacher's version. Then his teacher publicly rebuked him and told the people that he was singing many things which were not part of the actual epic.

The audience also plays a significant role in the transmission and composition of an oral epic. When a singer is with his audience he is very lively and enthusiastic. At that time he gives the best performance of his epic with detailed descriptions, ornamenting his narration, and making his story more effective and interesting. Singers tend to change their versions in response to their audience. For example, Sivnath Chaudhari came to me in Agra in 1966 and when Professor Mata Prasad Gupta, who was then editing the Chandayan, asked him to sing the *Chanva ka Urhar* (elopement of Chanda) he sang a very different version in which the love making was described very modestly. Normally when he sang for his own audience in his own surroundings, he described the meeting of Lorik and Chanda and their love-making very openly with details of her beauty, body, breasts and so forth. When I asked Sivnath why he did not sing the original version, he told me that it was not nice to sing those things before educated and respected people (*are bar adami ka aga i kul na gaval jala nu*). This shows that singers tend to change versions and descriptions according to the situation and the audience.

Time is another factor which affects the performance. If a singer has to sing a longer version in a limited time he does it skillfully, omitting or shortening the episodes. He is a great artist in this respect, and knows exactly, the art of abbreviations, elaborations, and embellishments of narration and episodes.

Formulas

In my studies of oral epics I have discussed the formulas that appear in the texts frequently. They differ in their structure and metrical pattern each time they are used. Some examples are given here. In Sivnath Chaudhari's version the following lines are repeated time and again:

ab pance, hinu kare gangaa turuk kare gor
bhal kamili sang choralu mor
ab debi kaha giti bani gavat
kaha aju dilem paral bisbhor
dekh ab jevana din kar pujliy
tevani ghari gail niyarai.
ab debi kahi da kiratiya mardane ke
kekari karan bharath bhail taiyar

(A Hindu will go to Ganga river (after death) and a Muslim will go to the tomb. Good woman! (Durga) you have left me alone. O goddess! which episode am I singing now? I am lost. Why have you forgotten me? That day and time has arrived for which I worshipped you. O Goddess, tell us about the glorious deeds of the heroes. Who are the people for whom this Bharat (battle) is taking place.)

In the present formula, the *matra*s are 38, 38, 38, 44 respectively in each line. The singer remembers the goddess Durga and asks for her help when he feels he is in difficulty in his performance. *Ab pance* (O audience) is invocation and not a part of the line.

Another version of this formula is as follows:

> *are pance,*
> *aju hinnu karia ganga turuk kari gor*
> *bhali kamini sang chod luy mori*
> *ab debi kaha giti bani gavat*
> *kaha ab dilem paral bis bhor*
> *ab debi jevana din kari pujalimy*
> *ehija ghari gail niyarai*
> *debii kahi da kirratiya mardaanan ke*
> *jekari dese bajal tarvaar*
>
> (O audience, today a Hindu will go to Ganga and a Turk will go to the tomb. O good woman, Durga, you have left me alone. Where am I singing now? I have forgotten. The day and time has arrived now for which I worshipped you. My Goddess tell me the glorious deeds of these valiant people in whose country swords were drawn.)

The *matra*s in these stanzas are 36, 36, 36 and 38 in four lines. This formula in a previous performance had a metrical pattern of 38, 38, 38, 44. We can clearly see that the words differ in the two formulas. The vocative 'O audience today', *are pance aju* is not part of the main formula but is still different from the first in which the vocative is *ab pance*, 'audience now'.

All my singers use formulas and repetitions but they do not confirm totally to the principles of the theory propounded by A.B. Lord in his book, *The Singer of Tales* in which he defines a formula as "a group of words which is regularly employed under the same metrical conditions to express a given essential idea".[21]

The most important thing about the singers is that they are creative composers as well as singers. They can compose while they are singing.

They are *ashu kavi* who compose their poems as they go along. With this capacity, a good singer always adds new elements to his composition which keeps his audience spellbound by his singing. In classical Sanskrit literature good poetry with its implicit meanings and profound expressions and suggestions, intends to create freshness and newness every time one reads it. These folk singers recreate newness and freshness in their narration by additions and alterations in every performance and with this strategy they captivate the hearts of their audience. A folk singer is not only a preserver of a tradition; he is a creator of tradition too. This I have demonstrated, in my introductions to the four volumes of Loriki and Chanaini already published.[22]

Notes

1. The name of the hero of this epic is Lorik and the name of the heroine is Chanda. In the Bhojpuri, Magahi and Maithili areas this epic is called Loriki or Lorikayan, after the name of the hero and in the Avadhi and Chattisgarhi regions it is called Chanaini after the heroine. Hindi scholars believed that the *Loriki* and the *Chanaini* were not one and the same epic and that the singers in the Bhojpuri, Magahi, Maithili areas sang Lorik's entire life story and heroic deeds, whereas the singers in other regions sang only the part of the epic which was related to Chanda. In fact, this assumption was based on hearsay and on fragmentary versions collected and translated by scholars such as George Grierson, Verrier Elwin and S.C. Dube. My intensive fieldwork has now proved that throughout northern India good singers of the epic sing the complete Lorik story including the abduction of Chanda, although two different titles have been given to single epic.
2. Hira Lal Kavopadhyaya, 1921, *A Grammar of Chattisgarhi Dialect of Hindi*, tr. by George Grierson, Calcutta, 218-25.
3. Verrier Elwin, 1946, *Folk Songs of Chattisgarh,* London, 338-401.
4. S.C. Dube, 1947, *Field Songs of Chattisgarh*, Lucknow, 41-8.
5. I wanted to record a version sung by a woman. My assistant and I tried my best to persuade her to sing, but without success. The Ahir community of the area and more especially her relatives got angry with us and we had to give up the attempt.
6. Holi is a festival which is celebrated by Hindus in northern India in February and March. According to the Hindu calendar year this is the month of *Chaitra*. In the morning, on the day of *Holi* people come out of their homes and throw coloured water on each other. Merry making and shouting, abusing in fun disregarding all normal and traditional ways of behaving are significant features of this festival.

   In the evening people put on new clothes and visit both friends and enemies to mark their foreheads with red powder which is a sign of love and affection. For a detailed study, see Milton Singer (ed.), 1966, *Krishna: Myths, Rites and Attitudes,* Honolulu (U.S.A), 200-24 and William Crooke, 1968, *The Popular Religion and Folklore of Northern India,* New Delhi, vol.2, (Ist edn. 1896), 313-22.
7. One is permitted to play *Holi* with a sister-in-law, but a girl of one's village is like a sister and therefore one cannot play *Holi* with her.
8. The word used in the original text is Mangalait, the exact meaning of which is not very clear. Here it appears to refer to the Moghuls.
9. The ceremony of a widow burning herself on her husband's funeral pyre.
10. George Grierson, 1929, 'The Birth of Lorik', in *Indian Studies in Honour of Charles Rockwell Lanman,* Cambridge (Mass), 243-54.
11. Orilal, died about ten years ago. He was an Ahir and about fifty-five in 1966 when I first met him. He lived in the village Gujarpurava in the Gonda district of Uttar Pradesh. His teacher was still alive when Orilal performed for me, but six months later he died at the age of eighty-five. Orilal was a farmer and owned a few acres of land. His eldest son was twenty-six when I was recording the epic. The son had some schooling so he was looking for a job in the city. He did not want to learn singing. Orilal told me that he himself never sang *Chanaini* alone. At least

two persons were required to sing it together; but nowhere else was this kind of singing prevalent. The young man who was singing with him was most likely his disciple and Orilal wanted to train him. It was clear that wherever Orilal went he took this young singer with him in order to train him as a singer. I do not have the precise information now about the singers in that area but I was told recently that some singers were still alive in Gonda district. Orilal had been singing this epic for the last thirty years when I met him, but he could not read or write.

12. Sivnath, who died on 21 April 1982, was seventy when I recorded his version. He lived in a village called Bharauli in the Ballia district of U.P. Until the age of 65 he was a bullock cart driver and used to transport sacks of grain and other goods from Baxar and other districts of Bihar to U.P. and vice versa. Later he became a farmer and joined his brother Bhrigu as a farmer. He had no sons. He told me that he started learning his art at the age of 11 or 12, and it took him quite a few years before he was able to sing independently. When I first met him in 1965 he told me that he had been singing the *Loriki* for the last 50 years. He employed many more dramatic effects than other singers and gave detailed descriptions of the birth, love and battles of the hero. This made his version the longest one, about 48 hours recording on the tape. I have already published the first part of this version in *'Bhojpuri Loriki'* (Allahabad, 1995).

    This alone consists of 16 thousand lines. He left one disciple but Sivnath was not pleased when he went to him with a request to sing at least some parts of it for me. He complained that new singers did not learn the epic perfectly.

    I was surprised to discover that he had travelled by train, only twice in his life, the first time was thirty years before I met him. He had gone to visit his relatives from his nearest station Baxar to Jamania. The second journey took place when he came with me from Ballia to Agra. He was afraid to travel alone, so I had to persuade my relative Keshav Tivari who knew him well, to accompany him with me to Agra where I had my office and residence. In Agra I recorded the second part of the epic without the audience. The first part of his version I recorded in Ratsand in Ballia.

13. Panchu Bhagat is alive and still lives in his village Paranapur in Varanasi district near Chaubepur rail road station, not very far from Sarnath. In March 1966 when I recorded his version of *Loriki*, he was fifty-six. The name of his father was Rupnarayan, who had already died. Panchu Bhagat is a religious man and he worships Bansatti, a local goddess along with Durga and other gods and goddesses of the Hindu fold. If small pox breaks out in his area people come to him for help. They think he has miraculous powers and if he visits the small pox patients and invokes the deity Bansatti in the patient's home, the small pox will be cured. His religious temperament has not influenced the epic as such, but at least one erotic episode *'The abduction of Chanda'* in which the hero, who is married to Majari, meets his beloved Chanda (Chanva) secretly and makes love to her, has been described very delicately. Other singers describe this illicit love in some detail. It is worth mentioning here that most of these singers have two versions of this particular episode. Before an audience in which there are respected, old or educated people, they do not sing the original version in which the acts of love have been described openly. Panchu Bhagat, as he told me, sings only one version and that is not a very markedly erotic one. When I asked him the name of his teacher, he told me: "It was Lord Krishna himself". But in fact he learned this epic from someone in the Ghazipur

district in Eastern U.P. Bhagat had one son who had passed VIIIth class when I met them in 1966. Unfortunately he died a few years back of tetanus. Bhagat is a very influential leader of the Ahir community. He himself is a *Gval* Ahir. Since he is devoted to God he is called *bhagat*.

14. A local goddess. The word seems to be derived from the Sanskrit word *Vanaspati*, king of the wood.

15. Sukkhudas Yadav was the youngest of all the singers and was only forty-five when I met him in 1967. He learned his epic from his father Pannu, who had died 25 years earlier. He comes from a village Khanapur near Islampur in the Patna district of Bihar. I have lost contact with him now, but he was farming when I met him. He told me that the name of the epic is *Loriki* or *Lorikayan*. His version in Magahi dialect was the shortest in my collection, about six thousand lines. Sukkhudas could read elementary Hindi books but could not write. His sons went to school which was two miles away from their village but none of them could sing the *Loriki* although they knew the story of the epic.

16. Maulana Da'ud composed his work Chandayan in 781 A.H. (AD 1379). Important manuscripts of this work are in the K.M. Institute, Agra, India and in the John Ryland Library, Manchester, U.K. A critical edition of this work with a Hindi commentary and a long introduction was produced in Hindi by Mata Prasad Gupta in 1967. It has been reprinted by Visvavidyalay Prakasan, Varanasi in 1993. P.L. Gupta also published a text from Bombay in 1964. S. Chatterji and Babua Misra, *Varnaratnakara*, Calcutta, 1940.

    The story of Lorik and Chanda was adopted by a seventeenth-century Bengali poet, Daulat Kazi who called his work Lor *Chandrani*. Almost at the same time Maulana Gawwasi, writing in Dakhini, used this tale to compose his work *Maina Satwanti*. Another poet Sadhan whose dates are unknown, adapted this story for his work *Mainasat*. In this work the chastity of Lorik's wife has been described.

17. Ramdev was a young singer when I met him in 1965. He was learning Loriki as a disciple of Sivnath. He is now perhaps a little more than sixty years old. He lives in Pandavar, a small village of the Ahirs near Ratsand in Ballia district.

18. Ramavatar died on 13th February, 1979 at the age of about 85. He came from Ala nagari (miya ka pura) in the Allahabad district. In 1966 he was about seventy. People in the neighbouring village called him *virahiya* (a singer of the *viraha* song). Unlike other singers he was widely travelled and had spent quite a few years in Bombay, Karachi and Rangoon. He had been singing *Chanaini* since he was twelve. His first teacher was Bhairo *Gareriya* (shepherd) who lived in a neighbouring village. Later, when he went to Bombay, he met another singer from the Azamgarh district from Eastern U.P., where Bhojpuri is spoken. Ramavatar accepted him as his *guru* (teacher). Another man who influenced him in his singing was Aganu of Gariyar in the Varanasi district of U.P. The singer told me that he was not singing Chanaini in its original tune as he was too old to follow the rigorous, strenuous style of the *Chanaini* singing. On 13th September 1966 when I went to see him, he had gone to participate in a gathering of the singers of the *Alha*, which is another popular oral heroic epic in the Hindi area. The singer admitted that the tune of the *Alha* had influenced his singing. He had two wives but no children. One of his relatives told me that when he was young he had abducted some girls from other villages and brought them home but they did not stay with him for long. Ramavatar could not read or write. In 1965 or 1966 when he was elected a leader of the village community (*sarpanch*), his relatives taught him to sign his name. Like most of the

singers he smoked hemp (*ganja*) and he could not sing well unless he had smoked enough *ganja*.

19. Tulsi Yadav comes from a village Copan in the Mirzapur district of U.P. I could record only some episodes from his epic. He was very young when I met him in October 1966.

20. Unlike other singers Dadai Mallah belonged to the caste of boatmen (Kevat or Mallah) whose main occupation was rowing and fishing. He came from the village Kuruhul in the Mirzapur district.

    It was unusual to find a singer in a community other than the Ahir community, but the fact is that his teacher was an Ahir from his own village. In their young days they grazed cows in the forests nearby, and they used to leave the cows in the pastures and sing the *Loriki.* The teacher sang first and then the disciple repeated it, so that when he was alone he could sing the whole story and memorise the main themes and episodes. This apprenticeship continued for three years till he became an independent singer. Although his teacher was an Ahir, Dadai Mallah was very much influenced by the tunes of boatmen's folksongs. His version is particularly important because the hero of the epic *Loriki* fought many battles in Agori, which according to the popular traditions was only five miles from his village. The hero married a girl from Agori. The king of Agori was a tyrant and wanted to seduce Majari, but he was killed by *Lorik*. The ruins of Agori fort can still be seen there, but it may be difficult to prove any historical relationship of the hero with Agori. Still, the epic and the popular traditions very clearly refer to the battles of Lorik in Agori and his marriage with Majari, the daughter of Mahar. Dadai Mallah sang the marriage of Lorik and of his battles at Agori first, and did not place the marriage of his brother Samvaru with Satiya and battles of Lorik with Satiya's relatives first as some other singers do. Dadai Mallah was a farmer and was sixty-five years old when I recorded his version in 1966. He died on 22nd February 1970. In his youth he was connected with some dancers and singers of the area and he used to play musical instruments for them. Ahirs of the area attached very little importance to a non-Ahir singer like Dadai Mallah.

21. A.B. Lord, 1978, *The Singer of Tales,* New York, 30.

22. S.M. Pandey, 1979, *Hindi Oral Epic Loriki*, Allahabad.

    S.M. Pandey, 1982, *Hindi Oral Epic Canaini*, Allahabad.

    S.M. Pandey, 1986, *Hindi Oral Epic Lorrikayan*, Allahabad.

    S.M. Pandey, 1995, *Bhojpuri Loriki*, Allahabad.

18

Rajula-Malushahi: The Oral Epic (Ballad) of Kumaon

Mohan Upreti

RAJULA-MALUSHAHI is sung in Kumaon hills which comprise the northern tip of Uttar Pradesh. The region is situated along the southern slopes of the Himalayas, beyond which lies the land of Tibet. It is separated from Tibet by several snowy peaks, exceeding 20,000 ft in height. Towards the south, the higher ranges of hills abruptly descend, followed by a narrow stretch of low broken country called the Bhabar, and then by a gradual slope towards the great plain of upper India, the Tarai. The landscape of Kumaon is distinguished by its vastness; range after range of mountains fade away into blue horizon, crowned towards the north by the towering Himalayas with their well-defined peaks of Nandadevi, Nandakote, Panchchuli, Trishul, Chawkhamba and Badrinath. The mingled charms of forest, cliff, glen and distant snowy peaks lend the landscape a singular beauty and enchanting quality.

The population of the region presents great ethnic variety. It comprises the aborigines, the Khasas, the immigrants from the plains and Bhotiyas. The aborigines for centuries have been in a state of subjection to the caste Hindus. Most of the professional singers and dancers belong to this class. They believe themselves to be the original inhabitants of the country, who were employed by Mahadev as drummers when he adopted the Himalaya Mountain as his residence. The Khasas form the principal part of the population and are identified with the Aryan race hailing from central Asia. At one time widely spread over Northern India, they form a separate race or caste only in Kumaon and Garhwal, and are the main cultivators of the soil. The immigrants from the plains comprise those Brahman, Rajput and Shah families, and their descendents who came with the Chand Dynasty which was founded in the tenth century AD by Som Chand. The Bhotiyas inhabit the northern parts of the region. They used to carry on a two-way trade between Tibet and India, carrying wool, borax, rock salt, herbs and condiments and other commodities on the back of their sheep and goats over the high passes of the snowy ranges from Tibet. On their return journey, they took cloth, *gur*, and other items of daily use. This description of the Bhotiyas does not hold good now, particularly after Tibet's amalgamation with China. Nowadays they weave blankets and carpets which they bring down to the markets of the towns situated at lower altitudes.

Form and style

A secular romantic ballad, Rajula-Malushahi in all its existing variants takes on the narrative style. The narration is in verse, prose coming in-between long poetic chunks, to re-inforce a particular point in the story. It takes about ten to twelve hours of non-stop narration to finish the ballad. As the verse is being sung, the singing alternates between non-rhythmic and rhythmic passages. The singer is supported by two voices who provide vocal drone. As the rhythmic portions are longer in this ballad, they take on a rich musical colouring and tone, offering a wider variety of musical ideas and images than what the other ballads have to offer. This is one of the reasons for its popularity and appeal.

Considered from the point of view of the story, music and dialect the ballad has three major variants represented by three exponents of this form, all dead now: (1) Mohan Singh (2) Gopi Das (3)Jogaram. All these three versions use elaborate rhythmic narration, long or short musical stanzas, long musical phrases to begin or terminate a particular episode, and sudden rhythmic shifts to heighten the dramatic effect. What is significant in these singers is their ability to lace their storyline with appropriate melodic phrases and rhythmic figures. Each style has some marked musical bars which are repeated many times. But the singer, according to the mood of the narrated event, skillfully alternates them, keeping intact the dramatic power of his narration.

Another point that needs consideration is the relative flexibility of music and text. I have heard the same singer altering his text, using different words at different times, but he would never change or modify his music. The scope of taking liberty with the text also gets limited by the fact that one would dare not go as far as changing the main storyline or substituting the original situations or characters with new ones. But one would not expose oneself to ridicule, if the same situation is described in different textual stanzas. While describing the beauty of Rajula, the heroine of the ballad, the singer may invent a new metaphor or simile, adding to his usual vocabulary without risking his credibility with the audience. Whether he edits his narrative or makes it more elaborate, he would be doing that to suit the varied tastes of his audience. But he will certainly not compromise on his storyline and his music.

Other common factor discernible in the style of narration is the manner in which an event, the mental state of a character and the conversation between two characters are described. All happenings, whether a fight or a march, birth or wedding are described in third person. But when the singer describs the mental state of a character, he changes the form of his narration from third person to second person. For instance, "Rajula what steps are you now going to take to save your honour?" If it is a conversation between two characters, the form again changes from second person to first person. For example when Malushahi first meets Rajula, his words to her are put in first person: "Whose daughter are you? Where do you live? To whom are you betrothed?"

As far as the dialect is concerned, all the singers use Kumaoni. Some singers may introduce Hindi verse also in the middle of their narration. For instance Jogaram while narrating Rajula's escape from Tibet suddenly starts singing some Hindi couplets. His choice is appropriate in so far as the lines seem to contain portents of impending torture and humiliation which Rajula has to suffer. Very skillfully Jogaram finishes his Hindi couplet by joining a line in Kumaoni at the end. The Hindi couplet sung by Jogaram is

लकड़ी जल कोयला भई, कोयला जल भई राख,
मैं पापिन ऐसी हुई, ना कोयला रही ना राख,
घर की जलनी बन में गए, बन में लागी आग
बनो बिचारा क्या करे, तन में लागी आग।
गीदड़ बोले एक तो हे प्रभू . . . . . .

the line in Kumaoni

तू के बोलैली आज?

(what can you say to-day when the Jackal is howling?)

At the end of the narration, the singer gives his blessings to the audience, thanking his patron, and also the two vocalists (drone-singers). He introduces himself and his associates in his narration, and blesses Malushahi and Rajula, the hero and the heroine of the ballad, wishing them a long and happy married life.

Scope and content

Rajula-Malushahi ballad encompasses three distinct cultures, mainly dealing with the problems of the people, living in border areas, particularly when their economic prosperity and social stability is interlinked with continuance of brisk and vigorous trade between the two neighbouring countries or regions, in this case between Kumaon and Tibet. Since the story belongs to a period when India as a nation-state was non-existent and the region of Kumaon itself was ruled by petty warring kingdoms, it could be safely presumed that the borderland between Kumaon and Tibet must have been a no-man's land politically, inhabited by a pastoral community which carried on trade between

Tibet and Kumaon. This state of affairs continued to exist for many centuries, and even after Kumaon was annexed from the Gorkhas (Nepal) by the British in AD 1818, the Indo-Tibetan border was always kept open, the Bhotiyas continued to have free access to Tibet, Taklakote being the main centre for barter. During winter months, the Bhotiyas would migrate to warmer areas at lower altitudes, pitching their tents in marketing centres like Bageshwar, Almora and Dwarahat. This Indo-Tibetan border was closed only after Tibet was amalgamated with China.

In Rajula-Malushahi ballad, Rajula's father is called Shunapati-Shauka, Shauka being a local synonym for the Bhotiya. Tibet is mentioned as Hundesh, a land inhabited by the Huniyas (Huniya being a local synonym for the Tibetan). The dramatic conflict that Rajula-Malushahi ballad brings into focus has its basis in the dangerously close dependence of Shunapati-Shauka on the Tibetan rulers for his economic and social stability. His daughter Rajula falls in love with Malushahi, the Katyuria king ruling the small kingdom of Bairaath, situated in Kumaon. Shunapati could never agree to their marriage as his daughter was already betrothed to the Huniya prince, and going back on his word would invite the wrath of the Huniyas, leading ultimately to his ruination.

This dramatic conflict, and the events following therefrom highlight the same issue, and, that is the refusal of Shunapati to marry his daughter Rajula to Malushahi. He takes this position because he cannot afford to displease the Huniyas with whom his commercial and trade bonds are very strong. And this precarious position that the people living on volatile borders face is the underlying substance of all the versions. This is a universal problem which has often been responsible for the emergence of tragic situations. The story of the ballad unfolds itself in the background of this dramatic conflict. All said and done, the ballad remains a simple romantic tale but with epic dimensions. In all the three significant versions, the most interesting portions, both from the point of view of poetic imagery and music, are those related to the romantic aspect.

The central figure in the ballad is Rajula. She is endowed with an extraordinary beauty and a sharp intelligence. The singers compare her face to the full moon and her body with the hot sun of May. The appeal of her beauty is so overpowering that even the forces of nature like air and water stop in their course, the cows stop grazing, the traveller stops on his way. Her thighs are compared to the trunks of a banana tree, her breasts with the lemons of *Kartik* (October-November), the sharp bridge of her nose with the edge of a *khukri* (an indigenous dagger), her eyes with the twin water springs, the sheen of her black hair with the skin of a snake and so on. Singer Jogaram, compares her to a flaming rhododendron flower. As the story goes, Rajula is forcibly married to the Huniya prince, by her father Shunapati, from where she makes good her escape to meet Malushahi, whom she had suddenly left under Shunapati's orders.

Although all the versions sing more of Rajula than of Malushahi, they retain their romantic flavour in respect of him as well. All sing of him as a beautiful person, King of Bairaath, he has seven queens and he lives in a three-storied palace. When he learns about her betrothal to the Huniya, he does not get disheartened, but coaxes her to stay with him in his colourful Bairaath. Rajula comes under his spell in their very first meeting. Their meetings, clandestine though, come to an abrupt ending, when one night Shunapati decides to leave Bairaath. Rajula is forcibly married to the Tibetan prince. She manages to escape, and braving a hard journey reaches Malushahi's palace. The ballad takes a sudden turn at this point. Rajula stays with Malushahi for sometime, but one day, leaving a letter behind, she leaves his palace. She writes in that letter: "Since I had abruptly left you, I came to your Bairaath to atone for my guilt. Now if you really want me, you come to my land to take me. Remember, if a woman comes of her own, she is never respected. If you are the son of a living mother you will come to my land to take me; if of a dead one, you will remain lying inert in your Bairaath."

Thus, saying the Himalayan bird that she is, she flies back to the Himalayas. The lines quoted above carry the impress of the social mores and values of Kumaoni society. True love by itself is not enough. Once a woman loses her self-respect love will disappear. Rajula, the heroine of the ballad, is very sensitive to her self-respect. Hence the drastic step she takes of leaving Bairaath, even though she had undertaken so much pain and so many risks to reach there. All this she does to vindicate her honour.

When Malushahi reads her letter he rises to the occasion and makes up his mind to leave for Jalnar Desh/Hundesh. He is aware how hazardous his venture would be to go to the inaccessible and poisonous land of Shaunkiyana (the border land); but he accepts her challenge and reaches her land. There a fight ensues between the forces of Bairaath and Shaukiyana. Malushahi wins the battle, and returns to Bairaath with Rajula as his wife. A true love at last gets vindicated.

Music

It would not be an exaggeration to state that Rajula-Malushahi ballad offers the best and the richest in the folk musical repertoire of Kumaon. It breathes the air of Kumaon, not in fragments, but in totality. In its rhythm one can hear the heart beats of a highly emotional, self-respecting and virile community which has carved out its cultural contours under the shadow of awe-inspiring Himalayas. Their mighty presence has gone a long way in giving the music of this ballad an atmospheric quality, which seems to have captivated in ample measure, the various moods of nature, as manifested in the changing seasons and climate of Kumaon.

The names of various musical instruments occur again and again in the narration, particularly in those portions which are connected with vital preparations, like a march or a wedding or a fight. Some instruments are supposed to wield magical powers. The quality of music produced by some of these instruments is also indicated in the adjectives used, for instance: *udasi muruli* — the sad flute; *bairaag begul* — the other-wordly trumpet; *bidwanshi dagar* — the omniscient drum; *chaliya nagara* — the wavy drum.

Jogaram has at one place tried to communicate Malushahi's loneliness by using a musical motif. After Rajula has left Malushahi in his palace, he goes to a bamboo tree standing near his palace, and addressing it as his elder brother (*bansh dada*) asks it to produce for him a flute on which only sad music could be played. The tree obliges him by presenting him one.

All the singers use fixed musical stanzas comprising three to four lines, which are alternated as the narration proceeds. The composition of these stanzas differs from singer to singer. For instance Mohan Singh's stanzas are symmetrical as compared to those of Gopi Das. Gopi Das uses more stanzas of asymmetrical lines. One thing common to all the singers is the restricted range and tone content. No melody has a compass beyond three-fourth of an octave. The singers often try to make up this deficiency by resorting to augmented notes. For Gopi Das this is a normal practice. Jogaram has resorted to 'irrational' intervals also, particularly in the sequence dealing with magical fights. Since urban ears are accustomed to a different tone-system, his intervals sound irrational. Forming melodic peaks is Mohan Singh's speciality. He first ascends to one, two, or even three melodic peaks and then returns to the main level of the melody. Gopi Das's melodic contours are unusual. His elaborate ornamentation sometimes reminds one of the *tappa* style of singing.

The melodic content of Gopi Das is different from that of Mohan Singh and Jogaram in as much as he alone uses flat notes in his melodic lines. His *dhaivat* (DH) is generally flat and augmented.

The main singer is always accompanied by two male voices who provide the drone. They join him when he is finishing the last lines of a stanza. They just act as drones while the singer starts ornamenting his melodic structure by pure vocalisation, free from the burden of the textual lines. In Kumaon, this is a common practice in ballad singing. The two accompanists are known as *heynwars*. The singer after giving them his cue, sometimes stops, and they carry on the suggested ornamentation. The moment the singer resumes his narration, the *heynwars* stop.

The rhythmic organisation in Rajula-Malushahi ballad is more or less regular in all styles of narration. When there is metric uniformity of lines in the text, it is very clear: where there is lack of uniformity, the tune is often not based on a measure that runs through the melody. The pause, as a rhythmic device, is resorted to at the end of the line or tune. Together with long notes it marks a temporary close or finale. Long notes are often used as dramatic devices to bring or close a particular episode.

Before changing a tune, singers often resort to rhythmic shifts. Sometimes before passing on to a new tune, they stop the rhythmic accompaniment for a while, then start playing on the drum without singing any textual lines. This is done to break the monotony of a lengthy narration. Being a ballad, Rajula-Malushahi does not depend on a strictly structured rhythm, or a simple rhythm as is the case with other folk songs, particularly those which are closely connected with body movements. Rhythmic patterns, both intricate and simple, are alternated, corresponding to the subject matter of narration.

Rhythm is marked on the *hurka*, a small drum, which is used in other forms of folk singing as well. The singer himself plays the *hurka*, and through its modulations he tries to vary his accents and stresses. Clapping is often resorted to in those portions which narrate long marches. A listener may often go into a trance, while in the midst of narration, sometimes accompanied by frenzied movements. At such movements, the singer keeps elaborating on that particular sequence which is already on, until complete calm descends on the audience. He proceeds with his narration only after the trance has passed off.

An assessment

An assessment of the three versions of Rajula-Malushahi should be worthwhile for arriving at some generalisations with regard to the art of ballad singing in Kumaon. The most significant point that emerges from a study of its text, music and style of narration is that the predominant role is played by the singer himself, who with the main storyline and musical form gives a free reign to his imagination in depicting the events and characters, his socio-cultural background determining his approach. A Mohan Singh for instance would never condescend to giving so much status, power and influence to a Das Guru as a Gopi Das or a Jogaram would. Mohan Singh shows Malushahi going to Agniyari Devi Temple (where both the lovers first meet) with a rifle slung on his shoulder although, leave apart a rifle, even a primitive gun would be quite unthinkable to be existing then. He does not care to stick to the strict traditional text. He is more innovative and creative, as compared to the other two, but equally acceptable to the community.

Future

Rajula-Malushahi ballad seems to be breathing its last. The old generation of singers as also audiences is vanishing fast. One should not wait for a new ballad singer to be born to pick up the broken thread. That thread is broken for ever. The ballad is no longer going to be re-created and re-fashioned by the community in its old style. If it has to survive, it must find a place in the contemporary medium of artistic communication.

19

The Role of Audience in Balochi *Sher* Singing

Sabir Badalkhan

THE most famous and refined genre in Balochi oral poetry is *sher*. It is also the richest body and there are hundreds of *shers* current in every part of Balochistan. Basically, it is a narrative in verse; is always descriptive; has no refrain; and is sung in formal settings by professional or amateur minstrels. It is, however, never sung for group or individual dances.

There are no limits for the length of a *sher* — usually fifty lines are the minimum but there might be *shers* with fewer lines, while others may contain as many as several thousand lines. As a rule, it is in verse with irregular rhymes but with a number of lines of uniform metre[1], and with a fixed text based on memorisation — although different texts of a single poem show some textual alterations, no intentional changes are either admitted by the performer or tolerated by his listeners.

There are several *shers* composed about single events, for example, messages to or from important persons, on death or birth occasions, on journey accounts, on the occurrence of extreme famine or prosperity, praise poems to persons, animals, lands, trees, etc., and so on; or a series of *shers* composed about a sequence of events such as tribal wars, a chain of historical events, genealogical records, romantic episodes, etc. When sung, a *sher* is always accompanied by two types of musical instruments: one *suroz* (a type of violin played with a bow) played by a person called *surozi* (*suroz* player), and one or two *damburags* (a lute type of two to three stringed fretless instrument which is played with strumming the strings). The *damburag* with two strings is played by the singer himself and the other with three strings is played by his aid *damburagi* (*damburag* player), called *panjagi* (helping hand).[2] The *sher* is also recited or chanted by common men of any social background and status with no musical accompaniment. Its recitation is considered a *xanwadahi kar* (noble action) and a prestigious pastime. Therefore, it is considered respectful to memorise, recite and/or chant a *sher* with no musical accompaniment and almost every single Baloch knows some *sher*s, or few fragments, by heart.

The art of minstrelsy was hereditary and was transferred from father to son and thus from one generation to the other. If a man in a family of minstrels lacked a good voice, since the singing of a *sher* required one, then he would adopt the profession of musician — either accompanying minstrels or playing with other types of singers, e.g., *sot* singers, or would play music only, either just for musical entertainment or for leading dances.

The singer of a *sher* is male and traditionally belonged to the low caste of Ludis/ Dombs of Indian origin[3] who were artisans. They are known as Domb or Dom in eastern Balochistan (the regions bordering with Sind and the Panjab) (Dames 1907, I:xxxiv), and *pahlawan* (lit. 'the singer of heroic deeds') in the rest of Balochistan (see Badalkhan 1994a). The composers of *sher*s, on the other hand, were almost exclusively *aslzat* Baloch.[4]

During the first half of the twentieth century socio-economic conditions started undergoing great changes in Balochistan. In the western parts of Balochistan nomadism was being rapidly replaced by a sedentary way of life and new economic resources were being explored in trade and agriculture. As a result the tribal set-up started declining and thus a new conception of society emerged. New socio-economic necessities forced many people of *aslzat* background to adopt professions and activities which were traditionally reserved for low caste persons, e.g., playing music and singing *sher*; and in the absence of a strong tribal set-up individuals were not accountable to any tribal force for certain actions, so this made it easy for them to adopt other professions. In western Balochistan a group of *mulla*s (Quran-read persons), along with others with good voices from among the *aslzat* background, adopted the profession of singing with the accompaniment of musical instruments. This class of minstrels, however, limited themselves, like traditional *pahlawan*s, to the singing of *sher*s and did not sing short love poems of the *gazal* type or other wedding or entertaining songs. Neither did they sing with the accompaniment of musical instruments other than *suroz* and *damburag*, which they considered *pegumbari saz* ('instruments of prophets') and their playing as *xanwadahi* (noble). (Exceptions were the recordings for the Radio Pakistan where non-Baloch producers imposed their taste even while recording typical Balochi traditional songs.) These minstrels used the term *pahlawan* for low-caste minstrels and called themselves *shair*, a term usually reserved only for poets, and *shora*[5] to poets who composed poems. They argued that a *shair* is the one who belongs to the upper caste and sings only narratives, i.e., *sher*s, while a *pahlawan* is a low caste singer of *shers* who may also sing other short poems, like *gazal* and *sot* when asked.[6] However, no common Baloch accepted the term *shair* for these singers of *shers* and they are always called *pahlawan*, unless someone tries to use the term *shair* in the presence of a *pahlawan* in order to make him happy.

On the eastern borderlands of Balochistan, however, no changes were allowed to penetrate the tribal set-up. It was kept intact for geo-strategic and political purposes, first with the financial help and administrative powers given to the tribal chiefs by the British and then by successive governments in Pakistan. Here the tribal structure and mentality has remained unchanged for centuries.[7] In these regions the minstrels are till today almost exclusively those belonging to the low caste of Ludis, called Dombs or Doms. Mention is, nevertheless, to be made of some renowned minstrels coming from the high caste Baloch tribe of Bulaidis, now living in Sind.

The occasions for singing *shers* were various and in the past every occasion at which a congregation gathered was a good occasion to call a *pahlawan* to sing the glories of the ancestors and the heroic deeds and romantic adventures of the Baloch in general. However, formal occasions for *sher* singing included wedding and circumcision ceremonies; when a tribe returned victorious from a tribal war or from a hard task; during the *jirgas* (gatherings of elders headed by the tribal chief to solve conflicts); when two brothers, families or tribes made truce after a long-standing conflict; when one's dear ones recovered from a long illness; when a person returned from a long and risky journey, and other occasions. *Sher* singing gatherings (*diwwan*) were also arranged by tribal chiefs when someone of certain importance visited them or when a tribal chief visited another person of high status or another tribal chief. In most of such cases both the chiefs would have their tribal or family minstrels and each one would sing the glory of his tribe and poems about its genealogy. The outcome of such a poetic and artistic competition also left impressions on the morale of the tribe. Besides singing, *sher* reciting was also in vogue and there were *sherzant* (persons with a rich repertoire of *shers*) in every village who would compete with visiting guests. Even today when some aged Baloch get together in rural areas the best pastime is to recite poems from the heroic age of the Baloch and comment on them. Baloch are of the belief that the past Baloches have left guidelines for them with their actions preserved and transmitted to them in *shers*, and they find a great pleasure in reciting them. It seems that different societies under similar socio-economic conditions have similar notions about their national epics. For example, the following statement of Jensen expresses very much the real spirit behind the preservation and practice of oral epics and represents the Baloch mentality as well. He writes:

> The epic . . . is a very important genre for maintaining cultural identity, precisely because it ties the present to the past and thus supplies the

> listeners with a feeling that they share their culture with former generations. At the same time, the very broadness of the narrative enables the poet to encompass whatever is considered typical of the group concerned: its way of life, political and religious practices, material surroundings, etc., and to introduce a great variety of persons to set good or bad examples. . . . Add to this that the oral epic normally has a comprehensive audience (all men, all adult, or even the whole population), and it will be obvious that the epic is an especially important genre in this respect. (Jensen 1990:36)

The performance of a *sher* takes place in the open air, in the sitting of a village or at the place where the ceremony is being celebrated. A Baloch *pahlawan* is very conscious about the time of his performance and he never sings during day-time. The real time of the performance is the night-time starting at about 10:00 p.m. The method of arranging the *sher* gathering or *sheri-diwwan* in the past was that the minstrel used to sit in the centre. Carpets were spread for elders of noble birth in front facing the minstrel and mats were spread behind them for the common people, while children would sit behind all of them — only persons of high status would have their sons seated near them. Commoners would also sit all around the gathering thus surrounding the performers. The place for the minstrel and his musicians would be raised high by accumulating earth and placing on them mats, quilts and bolsters to make their place comfortable. Nowadays, however, there are loudspeakers and microphones and the performers take their place on a stage made for the purpose and the audience is seated in front of them.

A *sheri-diwwan* was started with a short poem in praise of the Baloch land, the Baloch as an ethnic group and their values, with a famous romantic episode of a famous Baloch hero or with a genealogical poem of the Baloch as a nation or of the host tribe. But since the beginning of this century when *mulla*s also adopted the profession of minstrelsy they start their *diwwans* by singing a religious poem and then enter into the main singing. After the introductory song the *pahlawan* continues singing less important and short *sher*s but as time goes on he enters into his repertoire of classical *sher*s and continues until day-break. Once he starts singing heroic and romantic *sher*s he never returns to sing religious or other types of poems except for inserting pieces of short love poems in Balochi or in Persian, and nowadays also in Urdu, to give a rest to his audience, leave them in suspense for the coming episode. After taking some sips of tea, having some pulls from his smoking-pipe (*chilimm*)[8], he enters into the second episode of the *sher*. As the night passes the strings of the instruments become tighter,[9] the voice of the minstrel clearer and sharper and the most attentive and selected audience remain. So it is the actual time to assist a good performance. It is for this reason that all the minstrels told me that the real performance begins around 2:00 in the morning and continues until day-break.

The study of oral traditions and its transmission has brought forward several interesting observations about the role of the audience and it has been attested, for the majority cases, that the listener's role is vital for the performance and the preservation of oral literature. It has been recorded in the majority of oral societies studied so far that the composition, revision and preservation of a piece of oral poetry is aimed at face-to-face performance in the presence of an audience,[10] whose function is similar to that of a critic of a written piece of literature. The more expert and interested the audience is, the more attentive and careful the performer becomes. A good audience brings the best out of a performer and a skilled performer involves his listeners and holds their undivided attention. In the words of Reichl (1992:114), "a good singer transports his audience, and a good audience influences and furthers the singer's performance". Finnegan (1988:72) observes that

> each piece of oral literature is realised in its actual performance and . . . before a particular audience. It is directly influenced, and thus moulded, by the audience as well as by the composer. The listeners may even take a direct part in the performance, and altogether make a more obvious contribution than with written literature.

Similarly, Trypanis (1977:62) writes that

> the poet's consideration for his hearer is a basic factor in oral poetry, and it has to a great extent an influence on the narrative technique itself. The poet's primary concern is to keep a firm hold of his hearer's attention.

And Pandey (1982:31) reports that

> when a singer is with his audience he is very lively and enthusiastic. At that time he gives the best performance of his epic with detailed descriptions, ornamenting his narrations and making his story more interesting. If one asks a good singer to sing his epic without an audience he gives a shortened version and very often omits the embellishments and ornamentations which are the life of the performance.

He concludes that "it is the audience which brings out the best in the singer".[11]

Like other oral societies, studied so far and as can be gathered from examples available to us, the audience here has a very essential role in a Balochi *sher* singing gathering as well as for the performance of other type of oral poems. A Baloch minstrel rightly told me that the audience is the breath of a singer (*diwwan pahlawane sah int*). As without breath a person dies, he explained to me, in the same way a singer cannot perform perfectly without an audience in front.[12] Another *pahlawan* compared the audience with the salt in food. "As without salt there is no flavour in food, in the same way there is no taste in a performance in the absence of a proper audience," he told me.[13]

Both the singer and his audience believe that the stories versified in poems tell the truth, and a good performer and his listeners, at the peak of the performance, take themselves back to the time when heroic actions were carried out, and these poems were composed and sung. It is not only the listener who finds himself in the characters of the poems but also the singer. A modern Baloch singer, *Ustad* Abdul Sattar told me how he tries to convert himself in his imagination into earlier Baloches when he sings a national poem. In his words:

> When I start singing Balochi national poems (i.e., modern nationalist songs) I imagine myself in the time of Rustom and Suhrab.[14] I start from them because they were Baloch and the first mention of Baloch power as excellent swordsmen, valorous combatants and unparalleled fighters come from them — if there were other Baloch of such a great fame before Rustom and Suhrab, we know nothing about them. Starting with Rustom and Suhrab I then enter into the period of Mir Chakar Rind and Mir Gwahram Lashari because they were the nation builders of the Baloch. This was the second period of the mighty power of the Baloch when they unified Balochistan and gave it a central administration. I imagine and try to understand how the singers of the heroic poems of the period of Rustom and Suhrab and later on those of Chakar and Gwahram had sung these poems of national characters in the presence of the heroes of the time. I try to take myself to that period and put myself in their place. When I see that the audience is warmed up and full of enthusiasm I then enter into the romantic episode of Hani and Shey Murid,[15] because it is again the other extreme of Baloch literary culture. I try to represent both aspects of Baloch way of life which was full of heroic deeds and romantic episodes. When I see that my listeners are completely merged in the singing then I start singing modern nationalist songs (*komi sot*).[16]

The presence of an audience and musical accompaniment are two basic requirements for a good performance. For example, when I visited a *pahlawan* in Nigwar (Dasht in Pakistani Makran) and asked him to bring his *damburag* and sing some famous *sher*s cycles for me, he replied: *to badshahen mardee. tara zor baz man. sher chusen chizz et ki besaz o be diwwana janag bi bitt* ("You [behave] like a monarch. What an unreasonable person you are! Can poems be sung without an audience and with no musical accompaniment?") On another occasion he told me:

> Bring me my *damburag*, call some aged listeners (who understand and appreciate old poetry) and then see how the poems come in my mind like the writings on the pages of an open book.

Comparing various versions of texts recorded during public performances, i.e., in the presence of an audience, and those recorded only for individuals, either for scribes or for tape-recordings, one does not fail to note that the texts performed for an audience are full of detailed descriptions, ample explanations, extended comments, and constant repetitions, while the versions recited/sung for individuals, and thus with no proper audience, are colourless and lack any vitality.

One of the remarkable distinctions of a Balochi *sher* singing in the presence of an audience are the explanations and repetitions. When a *pahlawan* is facing his listeners he makes extensive explanations and continued repetitions to make the story more understandable, to emphasise certain actions and episodes, give more importance to some characters, and authenticate certain claims.[17] The *pahlawan*, in the course of his singing, repeats certain lines or parts of the poem once, twice, thrice or even four times, depending upon the content of the episode. He first takes some lines and sings them in *dapgal* (semi-recitation), then he takes the same lines and sings them, depending upon the content of the lines, in *zahirok* (melodious) tune or in *chihal* ('with the highest pitch of the voice', sometimes repeating a single line in *chihal* three or four times and then taking several minutes before proceeding on). After singing the same lines for two or more times the singer once again sings them in *er-rech* (singing in a chanting way) and goes onward without stressing or stopping at any line or name. When this process is finished the singer stops for a while and lets the *surozi* play and anticipate the coming lines and the episode. In the meanwhile the singer takes some sips from his cup of tea, takes a few pulls from the smoking-pipe (*chilimm*) amidst the strumming of his instrument; the audience relax themselves, discuss the content of the episode just sung and wait attentively for the coming episode or lines. For the next episode the same rules are observed unless it is one of the least important parts of the poem or the contents are less interesting to the audience. In such a situation the minstrel sings the lines in a chanting way (*er-rech*) and proceeds to the next episode or lines. In the absence of an attentive and critical audience, on the other hand, the *pahlawan* does not feel the necessity to imply all these styles — he simply recites or sings poem after poem just to pass the time and earn his money.

It can be easily observed that in the early part of the night, when the audience is composed of persons of all ages and from any status, the singer sings short poems, uses less repetition, and only occasionally sings any *chihal* or *zahirok*. But by midnight when the audience becomes more selective, the strings of instruments warmer and thus tighter, his voice clearer, he enters into the best poems in his repertoire, and he uses repetitions and sings *zahirok* after *zahirok* and *chihal* after *chihal* — such a situation is expressed as: *pahlawana jok jatag ant o chihal pa chihal kutag* ("the *pahlawan* is sitting on his knees and is singing at the highest pitch of his voice").

Another feature while singing a *sher* for an audience is the suspension of the main *sher* at certain points to leave the audience in suspense and let them imagine the outcome. The method is that he suspends the poem at a crucial point[18] and starts singing some lines from a modern *gazal* or some lines from a short Balochi, Persian, or an Urdu poem. After that he lets only the musicians play for a couple of minutes. After 10 to 15 minutes' detachment from the main poem he then enters into the poem from the line where he left.

On important occasions or at the ceremonies of well-to-do families there are always more than one *pahlawan* to sing in competition — but never more than two were asked to compete on a single night. In such circumstances each one would try to win the sympathies of the gathering and have more compensation in cash as well as in compliments from the audience. The audience of a competitive performance would also be divided accordingly — one group would support the *pahlawan* who sang heroic poems of their tribe, or of the tribe or characters dear to them, and the other backed the competing *pahlawan* singing the rejoinders. If the audience was not made of only the tribe's men from either side they would divide themselves on the basis of the area or preferring one *pahlawan* over the other. In any case, the competition between the supporters of the two *pahlawan*s was felt, and is still felt, in areas where *pahlawan*s are asked to sing in competitions, so much so that they behave like two warring tribes or belligerent parties. On some occasions they start shouting at each other, shooting gun-fires in the air, and reaching a point where they even challenge each other. Bowra's observation that "after all, national pride is a legitimate pleasure, and heroic poetry cannot fail at times to promote it" (1952:30) seems to represent the mentality and behaviour of the Baloch audience in such situations.

The role of the audience is also decisive in the selection of poems to be sung in a particular setting as well as in determining whether certain names, characters, or places should be excluded or sung with much stress or sung with a suppressed voice. Making changes in the text of a Balochi poem is never tolerated by its listeners but under some extreme necessities a Baloch minstrel is also forced to make minor changes in the text in order not to offend any of his listeners. For example, I obtained the recording of a Baloch minstrel from Iranian Balochistan who has sung a famous poem about the migration of the Rind and Lashar tribes from the present-day Iranian Balochistan during the fifteenth century, their occupation and settlement in the Sibi and Kachchi plains in the extreme east of Pakistani Balochistan, and their fratricidal wars that resulted in the dismemberment of the newly-formed Baloch principality with its capital at Sibi during the fifteenth and sixteenth centuries. Listening to the cassette one cannot fail to note how the singer alters an epithet related to a Baloch tribe in the poem. For example, when it comes to mentioning the name of the Bamadi tribe, who are called *bekaren* (useless) in other versions of the same singer, he calls them *namdaren* (renowned, famous), because on this occasion he is singing at the wedding ceremony of a Bamadi chief. Here he modifies the text and quickly completes the line without repeating it, giving no time to the audience to note the change in the text.

Maximilian Braun specifies another function of the audience for the Serbo-Croatian singer — that the listeners are "the 'real' carriers of the tradition in so far as their taste determines the choice of poems and thereby acts as a selective mechanism for the survival of particular songs." (quoted in Reichl 1992:113). This is very much true for the Balochi oral poetic tradition as for many other traditions. The taste of Baloch listeners has made possible the preservation and survival of certain poems as old as from the fifteenth and sixteenth centuries while a number of other poems, composed before and after, have been lost with no traces or only with a few surviving pieces. For example, there are certain heroic poems from the Rind and Lashar epic cycle of the fifteenth and sixteenth centuries which are essential in the repertoire of any professional or amateur minstrel since no singing gathering is considered complete without the singing of one or more poems from this cycle. Love romance of Hani and Shey Murid of the same period, heroic and romantic poems about Mir Bibagr Rind, love romances of Miran, and some other poems of the fifteenth and sixteenth centuries have also a similar position in Baloch society. A *pahlawan* from Makran is also expected to be able to sing some poems about the romantic and heroic deeds of Mir Hammal Jiand, who is famous for his fights against the Portuguese invasion of Makran during the sixteenth century[19] as well as his fight with a lion; poems about the eighteenth-century hero Balach Gorgej; the heroic epic about Mir Kambar (eighteenth century); one or more poems about Dadshah's fight against the Iranian regime (twentieth century)[20], to give a few examples.[21] Similarly, if the singer is singing in front of an audience in eastern Balochistan then he must know some poems of the most famous poets of that region, like Mast Taukali (nineteenth century), Jam Durrak (eighteenth century), Rahmali Mari (nineteenth-twentieth centuries), Jawansal Bugti (twentieth century), and so on. And the people living in these areas know the majority of these famous epic cycles in whole or in part or at least something about the story in general and poems composed by poets of their areas. Both the performer and his listeners have a similar repertoire of songs, and they bring shared knowledge, sentiments and ideas to the song. They can remain in harmony as far as they work according to the expectations of one another. As such, lapse of memory may put the singer in a difficult situation since an attentive audience never tolerates it. But since most of the *pahlawan*s of certain reputation and experience never admit that they make mistakes, even if they do, either in the wordings of a *sher* or in the sequence of its lines, sometimes heated discussions are carried on between the minstrel and his listeners about the originality of his version.

In same way the listeners have their preferences and if the minstrel is not in a position to sing some of the most famous *sher*s or *sheri-dastan*s (prosimetrics) then he is not accepted as a first-rate minstrel. To prove their command most minstrels proudly say that they sing what the audience wants to hear (*ma diwwane taba sher janan*).[22] In this way the choice of the audience determines the survival of certain poems and their more stable texts while some other poems get partly or completely lost and undergo more textual variations if not asked for by listeners for a long time.

When a *pahlawan* is singing in front of an audience with a little or no tradition of *sher* listening then he is relaxed and makes changes when and where he feels the need. If he forgets a name, word, or a line he skips it without thinking twice. He does the same with particular melodies aimed at accompanying different parts of a *sher*. I have been told several times that an expert *pahlawan* is the one who first observes the audience and then selects *sher*s and melodies. For example, *pahlawan* Alimahmad Sadbadi (d. 1992) explained it to me in the following words:

> You must have noted when the food is served to a great gathering. In such occasions the person in charge of serving the food to persons first watches the status of a person and then orders a plate for him: if he is an important person his plate will be full of meat, but if he is a layman then he would be given a plate with only one or two pieces of meat. We adopt the same method: first we examine the audience and then we select our poems and melodies for that audience.

Ragam (1990:46) reports that once Pahlawan Mazar had performed for an audience at the Cultural Centre at Quetta. The audience had comprised, for the majority, of Baloch and non-Baloch bureaucrats and middle-class city dwellers who had little or no knowledge of the basic rules of *sher* singing. Mazar, knowing that his audience was not in a position to judge his performance, had cared little for traditional rules while singing a famous epic. The audience had applauded the performer, but he (Ragam), watching the video cassette of the performance, had noticed many mistakes made by the singer. He had, later on, inquired of Mazar why he had trampled the rules to that extent. Mazar, says Ragam, had replied to him in a very relaxed way: *ludichaion kutag* ("I have behaved like a Ludi"), i.e., presenting one thing for the other and not taking the audience into any proper consideration. It shows that when there is no attentive and expert audience then the performer does not care much about the originality of his performance.[23]

I was present at the performance of Pahlawan Mazar in Turbat for a mixed audience at Turbat College's auditorium. The performance was arranged in 1994 on the occasion of the fourteenth anniversary of the inauguration of Radio Pakistan's Turbat station. In the front row I was sitting with persons who had a good knowledge of Balochi *sher* singing techniques. Pahlawan Mazar was well aware of our presence and it seemed that he was singing only for us. He frequently looked at us for admiration and sometimes even addressed me saying, *waja Badalxan dilgosh* (Badalkhan, sir, listen attentively). Or in order to show that he had a great knowledge of *sher* singing he pronounced the names of different melodies and explained different characters of a very famous epic from the fifteenth century which is universally known among the Baloch. All this shows that the performer was very much conditioned by the presence of a group of persons who could challenge him if he confused the sequence of lines, the wordings of the poem or even if he made mistakes in choosing correct melodies for different parts of a *sher*. At one point he was even shouted at and challenged by an aged man who was sitting behind for not being successful in playing a famous tune.

As has been stated earlier the text of a Balochi *sher* has the primary importance and no minstrel is ever allowed to make any changes in it or make any attempt to improvise it.[24] In some parts of Balochistan he is treated very harshly if he makes any changes in it. During my research tours in Pakistani and Iranian Makran I learnt that in the Baho and Dashtyari regions in Iranian Makran, in Dasht region in Pakistani Makran and in Koshkalat in Turbat, the audience is so severe with the performer that if he makes any mistake either in the wordings, in the sequence of lines or with the tunes of some famous *shers* he is beaten physically or sent out of the stage amidst shouts and abuses. Interviewing an aged *pahlawan*, originally from Iranian Makran but now living in Dasht Makran, I was told:

> In my area (i.e., in Baho and Dashtiari) if a *pahlawan* does not sing perfectly or if he tries to pass time with stupid things then the people attack him physically and the audience does not hesitate to extract his eyes (*diwwane mardum aigi telagan kashshant*). Because there sit expert persons and the vast majority of listeners know more *shers* by heart than the so-called (*richi-pichi*) *pahlawans* and they can tolerate anything but the mishandling of classical poems (*ahdi sher*).

I was also told of cases where *pahlawans* had literally been beaten by the audience or even by their musicians on forgetting or omitting lines or words in continuation.

In 1991 I recorded Karamhan, one of the most famous minstrels among the Bugtis in eastern Balochistan, who was unfortunately killed in a tribal conflict in 1995. I was very much impressed by the richness of his repertoire and by his command on *sher* singing. He was suffering from chronic bronchitis and thus could not sing with a melodious voice but he performed with actions and by colouring his songs. I was recording him in front of the guest house of a friend and the audience consisted of some school teachers and employees of the Sui Gas Company, who had little or no interest in Balochi classical poetry. At one point, when it was very late in the night and the singer noticed that he was performing only for my recorder and that the listeners were all talking to each other and discussing politics or other issues, he rebuked them. Several times he urged them to listen to him attentively because he was giving the traces of the Baloch and the register of their heroic deeds to me but it did not seem to be working and after a few minutes they again started talking to each other which was very disheartening to the performer. At one point he said that the Baloch of the past have passed and the young now had no values. At another point he recited an Urdu song which meant: "O heart take me to some place where there is no one, no friend or stranger, no one kind or unkind to me, neither any one who knows me." Then he told me that the gathering was not suitable for the singing/recitation of classical poems and if I was interested to record poems from his repertoire and to know about the past Baloch then I was to invite him somewhere where there could be some people who admire Baloch values.

Like the listeners of a Serbo-Croatian singer (cf. Reichl 1992:113) the Baloch *pahlawans*' audience also forms a kind of 'resonator' for the singer's performance with their shouts and hurrahs, and influences the quality of the singing by their behaviour (cf. also Finnegan 1977:228-35). They express their likings with shouts like *ji bat tara* (health be to you), *her biginde* (peace be upon you), *hao pahlawan, hao* (well-done *pahlawan*, well-done), *shabash pahlawan, shabash* (bravo *pahlawan*, bravo), *Allahe bahote* (be in the protection of God) *hudae mayare* (may God protect you).[25]

The minstrel also understands very well when he is to abstain from singing. He realises without any help from outside whether the people facing him are willing to listen further to him or not, and whether it is the right place to perform or not, or whether he is singing the right poem for the right audience or not. If he has the slightest feeling that he is not with his traditional listeners he desists from singing.

It was probably in 1984 when the *Balochi Labzanki Diwwan* (a literary organisation) had organised a musical programme on the occasion of the oath taking ceremony of its newly-elected office-bearers. Most of the famous Baloch singers of Karachi were invited for the occasion and the performance was to begin with *pahlawan* Saleh Mahmad Gorgej, one of the most famous minstrels who died in 1992. With a formidable introduction by the stage announcer, and attired in his traditional Balochi dress with cap and turban (*pag o top*), Saleh Mahmad walked on the stage amongst the unceasing applause of the audience. He and his musicians tuned their instruments and he started singing the famous epic about the Baloch migration from Kirman in Iran, their conquest of the present-day eastern Balochistan and their settlement in Sibi and Kachchi regions and their further penetration into the Sind and the Panjab areas. The audience had adopted a pin-drop silence and was listening to him with admiration and attention, when about an hour later, a young boy from the back seats shouted at him, saying "Stop braying, leave the stage for other singers (he meant for modern singers)." It seemed that Saleh Mahmad was split into two, his voiced slowed down, and his fingers seemed to have stuck with the strings of his *damburag*. He struggled for a while with his emotions and then shouted in reply,

> You son of a disco mother, come and shake your buttocks at disco songs. I am leaving the stage to you (*disko mate chukk, bya diskoe sara wati kunna bisuren. Man jagaha parto yala dayagaon*).

After saying this, soaked in sweat, in anger and rage, and with the impression of having suffered humiliation, he left the stage. People from among the audience requested him to continue but he refused and added: "The Baloch of early times have put their heads towards north (meaning that they are sleeping in graves having their heads towards north) and these modern Baloch, sons of disco mothers, do not understand what we sing. Please do not call us to dishonour us (*mąra pa kamm-sharapp kanaga malotainit*)."

The singers of *sher*s, whether belonging to the low caste Ludis and Dombs or to the common Baloch background, depend on the generosity of their listeners. If the listeners are content the performer returns to his house with a pocket full of money but if the audience is not satisfied with the singing then the minstrel's earning is also limited. In general, Baloch listeners are very generous towards their minstrels. In the past the minstrels were given horses, camels, new dresses and turbans — this last was necessarily given to the minstrel and his musicians by the host — apart from money. In modern times they are given money in cash and if the performance of the minstrel is satisfactory then he is showered with bank notes. *Pahlawan* Mulla Kamalan of Iranian Balcohistan told me that he receives around 50,000 Pakistani Rupees — i.e., almost twice the annual salary of a primary teacher or an office clerk in Pakistan — per night from the public in his audience. Some less important minstrels get less but all this depends on how they perform. In the past a whole family — comprising parents, siblings and their families, children and their families if they were married — could live on the earnings of a single *pahlawan* in the family, I have been told by *pahlawan*s interviewed so far. Another *pahlawan* told me that from their performance the listeners decide whether to shower them with bank-notes or abuses. It is not only the economic benefit which the minstrel receives from his audience for a good performance but also glorious fame which makes him famous and thus in demand for ceremonies. The name of a famous *pahlawan* would attract listeners from distant villages and a big gathering would always mean a good compensation in return. Some *pahlawan*s told me that they were engaged throughout the year and people paid them weeks before in advance to secure their performance in their ceremonies.

Since the early 1970s the socio-economic conditions in Balochistan have undergone great changes. The people of Makran have discovered the riches of the Arabian Gulf and the youth *en masse* have gone there to work as labourers. From there they send cash money, electronic goods like audio- and video-cassette players, and as such have changed the social outlook and cultural values of the people in Balochistan. With the help of the money sent from the Gulf states a whole generation has been attending schools and education has attained an important status among the Baloches. With education and exposure to the outside world on the one hand, and with the introduction of new electronic mass media and new tools of entertainment (for example, the satellite television facility is available in every corner of the Baloch land and majority of families have televisions and dish antennas in their houses) on the other hand, the traditional listeners and admirers of *pahlawan*s are diminishing very fast, and the art of minstrelsy in particular and the oral tradition in general are dying out. Most of the *pahlawan*s told me that they have not performed at any public gathering for the last ten to fifteen years and that they are forgetting their songs. The same is the case with good *suroz* players, another very important component in *sher* singing — very few of them among the living *surozis* can play the tunes for the accompaniment of a *sher* singing.[26] As the demand for this art is fading and admirers as well as critical listeners wanting, there are no new minstrels emerging. I have met only one minstrel in his thirties in all of Balochistan; while four of the minstrels have expired since I started my research works on Balochi oral tradition in 1988, the rest are mostly in their late-fifties and sixties. It shows that there is no future for Balochi oral literature nor can one do anything to save it from the unmerciful hands of socio-economic progress.

Notes

1. The forms adopted in versification owe, observes Dames (1907:xxix), "little or nothing to the literary forms of Persian poetry which have generally been adopted in neighbouring countries . . . every poem of whatsoever length consists simply of a number of lines of uniform metre, with or without rhyme".
2. There are also *damburag*s with four strings but they are played for dance music and not for *sher* singing since their music is strong and, as explained to me by musicians and minstrels, dominates the voice of the singer.
3. Dames (1904:17) states that "the Loris are the same as the Doms, the hereditary minstrels of Indian origin, known in Persia and Balochistan under the name Lori, or Luri" (cf. also Dames 1902:253; Basham 1954:514-15; Baluch, 1984:472-3; Barker and Mengal, 1969, I:320). During (1981:74) maintains that the Dombs are "une ancienne caste de musiciens professionnels d'origine indienne appelée *dombha* est mentionnée dans des textes bouddhistes sogdiens." Darmesteter (1888-90:cxciii-cxciv) writing about the Doms in Afghanistan mentions that "le mot *dum* . . . c'est un mot hindoustani qui désigne la caste des musiciens; c'est le même mot qui, sous les formes *Dom, Lom et Rom*, désigne les chanteurs bohémiens ou gipsies de Perse, d'Asie Mineure et d'Europe". Neither Domb nor Ludi is a title for minstrels among the Baloch but these are two different names for the same caste of handicraftsmen (*ustakar*). Besides many other activities, which they carry out, they also function as musicians and minstrels, but all persons of this caste are not necessarily minstrels though drum beating and oboe (*surna*) playing, along with blacksmithery and circumcising, is one of their traditional professions. It cannot be said with any certainty when the Dombs/Ludis were first introduced in Balochistan but the *Shahname* of Firdausi has an interesting story about the arrival of Ludis in Iran. It says

that the Mobeds reported to Bahram Gur that "the poor complained of their hard lot while the rich were enjoying themselves with eating and drinking to the sound of pleasant music, he writes to Shangal [the king of India] to send him 10,000 Luris, who play the lute and sing, in order to make agriculturalists of them, and when they come gives each a bullock, an ass and corn for the purpose, stipulating that they should play and sing to amuse the poor: they, however, eat the bullock and the corn and present themselves at the end of the year with yellow cheeks. . . . They accordingly wander in the world singing and playing, to steel day and night." (Rogers 1973:436-7)

4. Baloch usually use the terms *aslzaten Baloch* or *hanzaten Baloch* (Baloch of pure or noble origin) for upper caste Baloch, while the others of dark skin, or those who are believed to have migrated either from the African continent or the Indian sub-continent, are called *kamzat* (low-caste). In the past people belonging to this latter caste were either engaged in serfdom, slavery for the ruling class (*hakim*), or in different activities of craftsmanship like blacksmithery, carpentry, music playing, singing, circumcising, providing manual help to their masters (*wazdar*) on the occasions of birth, circumcision, wedding and death. Although this caste difference is not valid anymore and new economic opportunities and political institutions have made all castes equal or closer to each other, there are still some professions reserved for people of certain class or caste background. For example, it is almost impossible to find an *aslzat* Baloch who is a blacksmith, or has adopted the profession of singing wedding/circumcision songs and short love songs, called *sot*, and hence is called *soti*. Even if he does sing, along with other songs, wedding/circumcision songs and *sots*, he would be called a *gwashinda* (lit. one who says or sings) and not a *soti*, which is reserved for low caste singers of *sot*.
5. The term is simply the plural of *shair* (poet) in Arabic.
6. Traditionally *pahlawans* sang only *shers* with the accompaniment of stringed instruments but now one can meet a *pahlawan*, forced by economic necessities, who also sings *sot* accompanied by different musical instruments.
7. Another reason has also been the geographical situation of these tribal lands since they have been borderlands and in order to protect their land and interests from those across the borders, they have clung to their tribal force and have kept it intact.
8. During my field work of many years in Balochistan I have learnt that almost all the minstrels smoke the smoking-pipe during the performance, which they consider good for warming up the throat. But the tobacco of their smoking-pipes does not contain any addictive drug and I have not heard of any minstrel making use of any drug to help his performance. On the contrary all of the singers recorded by S.M. Pandey in India made use of hemp. He reports that "the singer . . . could not sing without smoking *Ganja* (hemp). In fact, all the singers of Loriki smoke *Ganja*. They say it was not possible to sing for four or five hours without smoking" (1987:31-2). Cf. also Pandey 1995:24, for another instance of a singer's use of hemp. He writes: "It was impossible for him to sing for so many hours without smoking. There were always some people in the audience who were ready to prepare the hemp or *chilam* for the singer." (See also Pandey's paper in present volume).
9. The famous *surozi* Rasul Baksh of Rask in Iranian Balochistan told me that his *suroz* has 12 tunings and the twelfth tuning is given just before the dawn. With that the *suroz* reaches its highest pitch and then is the peak of singing and music accompaniment. He told me that for short performances or for radio and television recordings they do not have much time to warm

their strings by playing them this long so they cannot perform at their best.

10. Exceptions are some kind of religious poetry aimed at individual recitation either in heart or loudly. However, even in that case God Himself and His angels are present in the reciter's mind as his audience and he is very careful to ensure the correct recitation of sacred poems or formulae.

11. A number of other examples have been given directly or indirectly about the important and rather inevitable role of the audience in an oral performance during the course of this workshop. For example, Dr. M.M. Mishra noted that even if you provide food and money to a singer he will not perform unless there is a proper audience to listen to and appreciate his performance. And Dr. M. Meitei remarked that "as a teller our singer knew what was his role: to please the audience, first and foremost". See also the paper presented by S.M. Pandey.

12. There are occasions when a singer performs in the absence of an audience, for example, while recording for the radio or for a cassette recording company but even on these occasions there is an audience in his mind who will listen to his songs for decades to come and give their judgement. For example, during my recordings from different *pahlawan*s in Balochistan I always noticed that all of them would be more attentive and conscious when they saw my tape-recorder or the note-book. Some of them expressed their preoccupations by saying that *diwwane sheran gwat bart, tai sher daptar bant* ("the song sung in front of a gathering will be blown away by the wind while your [recorded] songs will become history"), meaning that they gave more importance to my recordings since they considered that they were performing for a permanent audience who would give their judgement for decades to come; and that the poems would bear the stamp of their names. So they tried their best to recite/sing only the poems they could remember well and of which they had the correct and authentic versions.

13. Cf. Abdulkadir (1975:151) for the Hausa/Fulani oral tradition where the audience is often referred to as "salt of the performance".

14. Two heroes, father and son, in the *shahname* of Firdausi, who according to the Balochi folk tradition were Baloch.

15. Female and male, respectively, chief characters of a romance in the fifteenth century.

16. A passage from his interview in Balochi recorded in 1992, in his music club at Chakiwada, Karachi.

    The identification of the narrator with his protagonists has been aptly termed "breakthrough into performance" by Dell Hymes in his studies of American Indian narrators, who at particular points in the telling of a story switch from the language of the story into the language of the character (quoted in Reichl 1992:116).

17. Wadley (1986:229) points out that "if there is no audience, no evaluative statements are necessary. And any audience will react subjectively as well as analytically, believing or not believing, laughing or not laughing, as their own personal reality demands". In the same way, Abdulkadir (1975:171) opines that "it appears that the oral singers use repetition in oral composition to make orally presented works more immediately understable (sic) [understandable?] and retainable by the chorus as well as their audience".

18. An expert *pahlawan*, when singing before an audience, behaves like a television novel produced in a series of plays: he suspends a poem in a place which is full of suspense and the audience

is held by excitement at what happens further, by anticipation of what will come next, and to know the result of a dialogue or an encounter. For example, I noted from the singing of *pahlawan* Bashsham that he suspended the main story several times and sang parts of other short poems or drank some sips of tea or took some puffs from the smoking-pipe. But each time he left the poem at certain points when the curiosity of the audience was very high. On one occasion he suspended the poem at the point when it was being stated that the messenger went running to inform Mir Chakar that the enemy had attacked their herds and villages, and that Chakar was about to speak: *Mira jawab gardentagat* (Mir replied thus). Now the audience was curious to know what would be the reaction of Mir Chakar after that important news but he left the poem there for a couple of minutes. In another poem I noticed that he suspended the main story when the hero was informed that robbers had looted some neighbouring villages, imprisoning women and merchants, and were proceeding towards their area without any fear or consideration. The hero orders his servants to saddle his horse, bring his arms and he goes to seek the permission from his mother and have her benediction. When he relates the happening to his mother and asks for permission and when the mother is about to speak the singer suspends the poem and goes on to sing some lines from a Persian poem, then leaves the instrumentalists to play for a while and lets the audience wait anxiously to know what will be the reaction of the mother — although the majority of the listeners know the poem by heart, word by word or at least the main story, they do not want to miss it from the mouth of the singer to listen to whom they have gathered. Bowra (1952:31) observes that "in primitive societies the audiences who listen to him partake in their imaginations of the events related, as they themselves were spectators of them". It can be said without any doubt that exactly the same atmosphere can be seen among the listeners of a Baloch minstrel.

19. For details see Badalkhan, 1994b.
20. For Dadshah's episode see Shahbakhsh, 1994.
21. Some of the verses from these poems have become proverbial among the Baloch and are frequently quoted to solve disputes on various issues about Baloch life, its history or in order to justify a conduct of certain type.
22. There are also less equipped minstrels with a poor repertoire who make it clear at the very beginning of any performance that they do not sing on the audience's request and that the audience may not ask for particular *sher*s or cycles.
23. It should, however, be made clear that not all performers behave in this manner. For example, when I recorded *pahlawan* Saleh Mahmad Gorgej in Karachi in 1988 and then Hot Shahdad in Dasht Makran in 1989, both were very conscious of the texts of the poems they were either singing or reciting for me. They would not recite any poem they did not remember completely, saying that versions recorded by me would become part of history and someday somebody may challenge the authenticity of the texts recited by them, and as such, their reputation as authentic *pahlawan*s would be challenged.
24. Dr. M.K. Mishra's paper in the present volume gives an interesting example about the importance of verbal memorisation in Kalahandi epics. He says that the singer sings an already composed fixed text and does not make any changes either in the wordings or in the sequence of lines or episodes.
25. I have been told that some *pahlawan*s in the past were also accompanied by persons who

were to shout or act according to the singing and mimic the scenes in order to evoke the sentiments of the listeners and make them participate to their best.

26. On the contrary, the number of *surozis* playing trance music (*gwati saz*) has increased considerably since the practice of curing with music is spreading widely, especially among the poor families and the low caste (for details see During 1981; Sultana 1996).

References

Andrzejewski, B.W. and Lewis, I.M., 1964, *Somali Poetry: An Introduction*, Oxford.

Badalkhan, S., 1994a, *Poesia Epica e Tradizioni Orali Balochi: I Menestrelli Pahlawan del Makran*, Ph.D. thesis, Naples.

———, 1994b, 'Portuguese presence in Coastal Makran: Some accounts from an oral epic', paper presented at the international seminar on *I Portoghesi e i mari: incontro tra le culture*, held in Naples, December. (in press)

Baluch, M.S.K., 1984, *A Literary History of the Baluchis*, vol. II, Quetta.

Barker, M.A.R. and Mengal, A.K., 1969, *A Course in Baluchi*, 2 vols, Montreal.

Basham, A.L., 1954, *The Wonder that was India*, London (reprinted 1969).

Bowra, C.M., 1952, *Heroic Poetry*, London.

Dames, L.M., 1902, 'Balochi Folklore', *Folklore*, 13/3:252-274.

———, 1904, *The Baloch Race. A Historical and Ethnological Sketch*, London.

———, 1907, *Popular Poetry of the Baloches*, 2 vols., London.

Dandatti, Abdulkadir, 1975, *The Role of an Oral Singer in Hausa/Fulani Society: A Case Study of Mamman Shata*, Ph.D. dissertation, Indiana University.

Darmesteter, James, 1880-90, *Chants Populaires des Afghans*, Philo Press, Amsterdam, (Reimpression de L'edition Paris, printed in the Netherlands, 1888-90).

During, J., 1981, *Musique d'extase et de guerison du Baloutchistan. Anthologie de la musique traditionelle iranienne*, Paris.

Finnegan, Ruth, 1977, *Oral Poetry: Its Nature, Significance and Social Context*, Cambridge University Press, Cambridge.

———, 1988, *Literacy and Orality. Studies in the Technology of Communication*, Basil Blackwell Ltd. Oxford.

Jensen, M.S., 1990, 'The Homeric Epics and Greek Cultural Identity', in Honko, L. (ed.), *Religion, Myth and Folklore in the World's Epics: The Kalevala and its Predecessors*, Monton de Grayter, New York, pp. 29-48.

Pandey, S.M., 1982, *The Hindi Oral Epic Canaini*, Allahabad.

———, 1987, *The Hindi Oral Epic Lorikayan* (*The Tale of Lorik and Canda*), Allahabad.

———, 1995, *The Hindi Oral Epic Tradition: Bhojpuri Loriki*, Allahabad.

Ragam, S., 1990, 'Gind o nind gon Se Ragama', *Balochi*, 5/51:21-47.

Reichl, K., 1992, *Turkic Oral Epic Poetry: Traditions, Forms, Poetic Structure*, Garland Publishing Inc., New York and London.

Rogers, A., 1973, *The Shah-Nama of Firdausi. Translated from the Original Persian*, Heritage Publishers, Delhi

Shahbakhsh, Azim, 1373/1994, *Dadsah: pazohasi dar tarix-i mu'asir Balocistan,* Teheran.

Sultana, Farhat, 1996, '*Gwat* and *Gwat-i-leb:* Spirit Healing and Social Change in Makran', in Titus, P. (ed.), *Marginality and Modernity: Ethnicity and Change in Post-Colonial Balochistan*, Oxford University Press, Karachi, pp. 28-50.

Trypanis, C.A., 1977, *The Homeric Epics,* Aris and Phillip Ltd., Wiltshire.

Wadley, Susan S., 1986, 'The Katha of Sakat: Two Tellings', in Blackburn, S. and A.K. Ramanujan (eds.), *Another Harmony. New Essays on the Folklore of India,* University of California Press, California, pp. 195-232.

Yildiray, E., 1987, *Duelling Singers: Strategies and Interaction Processes among Turkish Minstrels*, Ph.D. dissertation, Indiana University.

20

Verbal Narratives
Performance and Gender of the Padma Purana

Nabin Chandra Sarma

Introduction

The paper aims to show the relation between text, performance and gender in one of the well-known oral epics of Assam, *Padma Purana*. The transmission of the epic is not confined only to Assam but extends up to Bihar, West Bengal, Bangladesh, Tripura and so forth. It is also popular among most of the tribes of Assam. The epic is based on songs, sung by men and women folk either in a ritualistic or non-ritualistic context. Gender plays an important role in the performance of this epic.

The term *Padma Purana* is a formation of two words *Padma* and *Purana*. The word *Padma* is one of the many names of the snake goddess Manasa. She was born of Shiva-Mahadeva's semen left on a leaf of lotus. As such she is known as Padma or Padma Devi. The word *Purana* means stories, particularly the old stories that include myths, legends and tales. The *Padma Purana* contains stories related to the snake deity Padma or Manasa or Bishahari. The epic consists of three major parts which are closely connected to form a composite whole. These segments contain various mythical and legendary songs which are sung during the worship of the snake goddess Manasa/ Padma or Bishahari. Initially these songs were transmitted orally by bards who were responsible for spreading them to different areas. As a result various versions and variants of these songs emerged. Later on, some of these versions and variants were compiled into written texts. However these songs are still preserved in the oral tradition. The written text of the *Padma Purana* attributed to Narayanadeva is still found in oral tradition in various regions of lower Assam. The singers of the songs of the *Padma Purana* claim that their songs are based on the manuscript of the *Padma Purana* composed by Narayanadeva. However, in actual practice, these songs are not based on the manuscript but belong to the oral tradition.

It is very difficult to establish Narayanadeva as a historical figure. Narayanadeva is popular in Bihar, West Bengal, Bangladesh, Tripura and Assam. He is equally popular among the tribals of Assam such as the Rabhas, the Boros, the Hazongs and the tribals of Bengal, Bihar and Bangladesh. His songs are popular even amongst the Muslims of Assam, Bengal and Bangladesh and it is not possible to place him according to any specific area or time.

Summary of the epic

The *Padma Purana* is a narrative that describes the conflict between the mother goddess Chandi or Durga and the new goddess Manasa-Padmavati. Manasa of course is victorious in the end. The first part of the epic describes the creation of gods and goddesses including Manasa and Neta. it also contains a detailed description of the creation of the world and all the beings. The second part narrates the efforts of Manasa and her friend, guide and philosopher Neta to spread the popularity of Manasa. To begin with, she was worshipped by a few cowherds. Then, Hasan and Hussain, two Muslim rulers began to worship her. Having seen the extraordinary powers of Manasa, Jalo and Malo, two fishermen brothers, worshipped the goddess in pots by beating cymbals and drums. Their entire community became prosperous with the blessings of the goddess. On hearing this news, Soneka, the wife of Chando, and her six daughters-in-law began to worship the goddess in a pot. Chando, who was a devout follower of Chandi and Shiva, did not consider Manasa as a goddess. He was given a magical cudgel by Chandi and with that cudgel he gave a big blow to the pot at the instigation of Chandi and as a result the waist of Manasa was broken. Being angry with Chando, Manasa killed all his six sons by sending snakes. However Chando did not relent. The third part narrates about Manasa's efforts at defeating Chando. Manasa brought Usha and Aniruddha from Indra's heaven as per the advice of Neta. Both Usha and Aniruddha gave up their life in heaven and their souls were carried away by Manasa. The goddess inserted the souls of Aniruddha and Usha into the wombs of Soneka, the wife of Chando, and Sumitra, the wife of Saheraja respectively. Soneka gave birth to a male child whose name was Lakhindar and Sumitra gave birth to a female child who was named Beula. After twelve long years, Chando came back home from trading. He forgot all his sufferings upon seeing his young son Lakhindar. Chando wanted to solemnise the marriage ceremony of Lakhindar. He tried to find a suitable match for Lakhindar and selected Beula as his daughter-in-law. Accordingly the marriage ceremony of Lakhindar and Beula was performed.

Lakhindar was bitten by *Kali naga* (Black snake) at the behest of Manasa, on his first night in the bridal bed. Lakhindar breathed his last. Then Beula decided to go to *deva-puri* (realm of gods) on a raft along with the corpse of Lakhindar. Chando made futile attempts to dissuade Beula. But she was determined. Finding no other alternative,

Chando gave permission to Beula. She started her voyage on a raft along with her husband's corpse. The raft was swiftly carried by the current. She had to face various difficulties in her journey, but she overcame them all by the grace of Manasa. Ultimately, she found a washerwoman, who used to wash the garments of gods and goddesses. She was Neta, the elder sister of Padma or Manasa. Beula took shelter at the feet of Neta and told her the sad story. Neta promised to help Beula.

In accordance with the advice of Neta, Beula performed a dance at *deva-puri* to please Shiva. He was very much impressed by her performance and was moved by the story of her tragic life on earth and heaven. Chandi also helped Beula to some extent. At last, Narada was sent by Shiva to summon Manasa. Manasa vehemently denied that she was responsible for the tragedy of Beula. However, Beula succeeded in producing definite evidence. But Manasa insisted that she was not responsible for the sad plight of Beula, and it was Chando who was responsible, because he always abused Manasa and did not consider her to be a goddess worthy of worship. Manasa then told Beula that if Chando were to worship her, she would bring Lakhindar back to life. Beula agreed. Manasa then brought Lakhindar and his six brothers back to life by uttering spells. At the request of Beula, Manasa recovered Chando's fourteen boats along with the cargo and crew that had been submerged by her. She thus fulfilled the desire of Beula. With the help of her ardent devotion to Manasa/Padma, Beula rescued the lost sons and property of her father-in-law. They along with Manasa and Neta sailed for Champaka city. Chando was requested to worship Manasa by Soneka, all the six widowed daughters-in-law, priest Somai and all his well wishers. But he did not agree. Then Manasa decided to go back along with Beula and Lakhindar. At this critical juncture, an old man of Chando's family threatened to behead him if he did not worship Manasa. Overcome with fright Chando gave his consent to worship the deity. Manasa was worshipped by him with offerings of various fruits and animals. The goddess blessed him. Chando realised that there was none except Manasa in these three worlds. It was Chandi who had made him antagonistic to Manasa by her ill-advice.

Thus, a devout follower of Chandi changed his religious ideals and became one of the staunch followers of the Manasa-cult.

The epic is replete with descriptions which focus on various aspects of life and culture of the medieval Assamese society. Various gods and goddesses alongwith human beings figure here. The epic lays special emphasis on the characters of Beula and Soneka, who are sympathetically depicted (Sarma 1993 : 361-7).

Context of the epic

The actual ritual context of the epic is the worship of the snake goddess Manasa or

Padma. Generally, the worship takes place in the rainy season of the year particularly in the month of *Shaon*, i.e., *Shravan* (July-August). However, the worship may take place round the year. The worship of the snake goddess Manasa may be celebrated for one day or it may last two weeks. The worship that concludes within a day is called *phul-puja* and if it lasts for a couple of days it is termed as *gota-puja* or *rang-puja*. The worship that continues for three days or more than three days is called *mare* (or *marai* or *marai-puja*). The term *mare* (or *marai*) may have come from the Assamese phrase *mari-maraka*, i.e., epidemic diseases. Belief has it that Manasa is the presiding deity of epidemic diseases. Hence, she is called *mare* or *marai* or *maraidevi*. If she is appeased by worship, epidemic diseases may not break out. The worship aims to expel the malevolent force and to welcome the benevolent force. Manasa-worship is also observed on the eve of the marriage ceremony. In some areas this worship is also celebrated in the context of pre- and post-cultivation or pre- and post-harvest festivals. In this sense the goddess may rightly be equated with the fertility goddess. In the drought season, the snake-goddess Manasa is worshipped in order to get rains. Thus she may also be called rain-goddess. Amongst the Pati Rabhas of Assam, the snake goddess is not known as Manasa, but as Padmavati or Bishahari or Barmani. In the Goalpara regions, particularly among the Rajbanshis, the goddess is known as Padda or Kani[1] Padda, i.e., blind Padma or Mancha, i.e., Manasa. The worship of Manasa is prevalent among the Hinduised Garos. They celebrate the worship as *rakhowal-puja*, i.e., the worship performed by the cowherds for the well-being of the cattle.

The Muslims, in a few limited pockets, also worship the deity. Her worship is also prevalent among the tea-garden communities of Assam. The womenfolk of the districts of Darrang, Kamrup, Nalbari, Barpeta, Goalpara, Dhubri and Kokrajhar observe the *Manasa-vrata* or *Bishahari-vrata* particularly in the rainy season. The fishermen community, the snake charmers and the cultivators propitiate the goddess irrespective of caste and religion. Even some rich and powerful people worship the snake goddess Manasa.

Performance

The worship of the snake goddess or the snake god performed in Assam and other parts of India is always associated with *geet-vadya-nritya* (song-music-dance) and some kind of *abhinaya* (dramatic performance). Scholars like J.Ph.Vogel (1972 : 232-3, 259, 275), William Crooke (1968 : 138). P.K. Maity (1966 : 312-14) described it in their works.

In Assam various performances take place as part of the worship of Manasa. The scripture related to the Manasa cult emphasises that the goddess should be propitiated by both Vedic and *Pauranic*, as well as *laukik* (local/folk) modes accompanied by *geet-*

vadya-nritya and *abhinaya*. The *vidhi*, i.e., the handbook of Manasa-worship states that *geet-vadya-nritya* are part of the worship of Manasa (Sarma 1929 : 4-5).[2] Even the *Padma Purana* states that the worship of Manasa cannot be complete without the *geet-vadya-nritya* performance (Kalita : 1931 : 10). Listening to myths, legends and tales associated with the goddess Manasa is part of the worship.

The artforms related to *geet-vadya-nritya* and *abhinaya* in the context of the worship of Manasa are known as *ojapali*, *gan* and *deodha* or *deodhani*. The term *ojapali* is popular in the Kamrup region and in the district of Darrang . The term *gan* (*Mare-gan, Padda-puranar-gan*) is current in the Goalpara regions. The word *gan* includes both song and dance as well as some kind of a drama. The term *ojapali* consists of two words, *oja* and *pali*. The word *oja* has its roots in the Sanskrit term *upadhyaya*, and it means the chief singer of the *ojapali* chorus. The word *pali* is a Sanskrit term meaning the assistants of the *oja*.

According to prevailing custom the *ojapali* should be performed at the time of Manasa worship. The *ojapali* performance is essential in the context of the worship of Manasa.[3] The *ojapali* associated with the worship of Manasa-Bishahari may be sub-divided into the following genres according to thematic differences:

(i) *Sukanani ojapali* or *rang-gowa ojapali*,

(ii) *Bishahari-gan*,

(iii) *Mare-pujar-gan* or *mare-gan*,

(iv) *Padda-puranar gan*,

(v) *Gitalu-git* or *gahan*,

(vi) *Rakhowal-gan*,

(vii) *Tukuriya ojapali* (Sarma 1996 : 42).

The *Sukanani, Mare-gan, Padda-puranar-gan* and *Gitalu-gahan* forms of *ojapali* consist of one *oja* and more than two *pali*s. A group of the *ojapali* is generally confined only to menfolk, though female *ojapali* is also not uncommon. The *oja* sets the refrains and the songs with dance-movements and the *pali*s repeat the refrains as well as songs to the accompaniment of cymbals along with dance movements. In the context of *shastric* worship (according to scriptures) of goddess Manasa, the *ojapali* sings various mythical ballads relating to the origin and creation of the world, gods and goddesses including Manasa and Neta. Ballads about the origin of such items of performance, as the jute fibre with which the cymbals are held, arecanut and betel leaves, *dhenki* — the vehicle of Narada, earthen pot and pounded rice are also sung during the performance. These songs are sung in sitting position according to the advice of the priest. At the end of the *shastric* mode of worship, the *ojapali* sing songs from the *Padma Purana* in standing position in the traditional dress like *dhoti, chadar, gamocha,* headgear and so on. The *oja* does not use cymbals, but each *pali* plays on a pair of cymbals by holding them in one hand. The *oja* begins the *alapa* or *svara sadhana* which commences with such syllables as *ha, ta, na, ri(r)*, *rita* (*rta*) (Sarma 1974 : 122).[4] The *alapa* follows *vandana*, i.e., invocation, or *mangalacharana*, i.e., prologue, which begins with the syllables *ha, ta, na ri(r)* and *rita* (*rta*). After this the *ojapali* sings a *vandana*, i.e., prayer song. The repertoire of *vandana* songs includes prayers to Ganesha, Dasavatara (ten incarnations of Vishnu), Rama, Shiva, Padma, and Manasa (*Ibid.*). A stanza of a *vandana-geet* is given below as a specimen:

Prayer to Padmavati

Refrain:

We adore the supreme goddess Padmavati
Daughter of Siva, the Ultimate Reality.

Verse:

Thou art born out of the semen of Siva, who is
worshipped by gods, snakes and human beings.
The three eyes of thou represent moon, sun and
fire and the four hands represent the four Vedas. . . .
(Sarma1993:3)

The *vandana* singing is followed by the singing of *diha*, i.e., refrain. Every song of the *Padma Purana* is connected with a *diha* in a particular *raga* or tune and the *palis* repeat it.

At the end of the singing of a *diha*, the *oja* sets the first and the first half of the second line of a particular *pada* or song, then the *palis* sing the second half of the second line along with the *diha*. In this way the *ojapali* sings the entire content of the *Padma Purana* to the accompaniment of cymbals, dance movements and occasional play-acting. The content of a song is explained in prose by the *oja* with the help of the *dainapali*, i.e., the principal assistant and chief partner of *oja*. There is an exchange of dialogues between the two. These dialogues not only explain the events described in the narrative singing but also provide an opportunity for the *dainapali* to regale the audience with wit and humour. (Datta 1996:26) As a specimen, a stanza of a song taken from the *Padma Purana* is given below:

Refrain: O lotus faced beloved! awake

For how long are you sleeping happily?

Verse: The moment of separation of you and me is impending,

I am extremely distressed due to the venom,
I am setting off to the city of Yama,
O merchant's daughter (i.e., Beula) awake
Why are you sleeping happily?
Fetch the Priest immediately,
You and I are sleeping in the fortified building happily,
But I do not know the god
Who did bite me?
The little finger of my left leg is covered by venom,
I do not know who bites me?
I am going to the city of Yama. . . .
(Sarma 1993: 27-8)

The last stage of the *ojapali* performance is known as *samarani*, i.e., epilogue and at this stage the *oja* and the *palis* give farewell to the goddess by singing a song from the *Padma Purana* in a sitting position.

For the *mare-puja* that continues for more than three days, at least two or three troupes of *ojapali* are essential. On each day of the *mare-puja*, the *ojapali* performance continues day and night. The last day of the *mare-puja* is commonly known as *bhardak*, when female shamans present ritual dances and dramatic performances along with the *palis*. During these dances the *palis* beat *joy-dhol*, i.e., a kind of drum used strictly in the context of the worship of Manasa, and *bhor-tal*, i.e., large size cymbals. However, the female shamans are not an essential part of the *ojapali* artform. The performance can take place without them. The female or male shaman or shamans appear to be optional in the context of the *sukanani ojapali*.

The *ojapali* troupe formed by womenfolk on the model of the traditional *ojapali* is known as *api-ojapali* or *likiri ojapali*. They may perform in the context of Manasa worship, though the phenomenon is not accepted by all the sections of the society. The members of the *api-ojapali* troupe have to observe some taboos. For example they cannot perform the *ojapali* during their menstrual period. They cannot play on drums, and in the context of *mare-puja*, they cannot take active part like male *oja* or *palis*.

In the *Manasa-vrata* the womenfolk sing songs from the *Padma Purana*, particularly those songs which depict the sad plight of Beula. In such *vratas*, an expert female story-teller (called *kathati* or *ojeni* or *ojheni*) narrates stories from the *Padma Purana*.

Gender aspect of the performance

Performance of a particular artform may reflect the nature and norms of gender distinction of a given society. The *ojapali* performance throws light on the gender aspects, particularly in lower Assam. Tradition has it that a woman cannot take part in the *ojapali* artform. The *api-ojapali* is a modern phenomenon and this kind of *ojapali* is only meant for stage. A woman may take part in this performance only as a shaman. A female shaman shall have to remain a virgin. According to the prevailing tradition a woman cannot play on the *joy-dhol* or the cymbal used by the *palis* of the *ojapali*.

Although the womenfolk have no right to act as *oja* or *palis* and perform in the context of the worship of Manasa celebrated privately or publicly, nevertheless they can sing songs from the *Padma Purana* in the context of the *Manasa-vrata* in sitting position without beating cymbal or playing on drum. The total number of female singers in the *vrata* are usually more than ten. But three or four female singers may also give the performance. The leader of the troupe is called *ojeni* or *ojheni* or *pattheni*. The assistant singers are known as *dhareti*. The men-folk do not take part in the performance. Even in the context of the worship of Manasa, the womenfolk perform chorals (i.e., *Manasanam*) simply to the accompaniment of the rhythmic clapping of hands. The aim of such choral singing is to offer obeisance and to seek blessings from goddess Manasa.

However the gender distinction is not observed in the singing that takes place at the time of drawing water from the pond or river for worship, and at the time of the immersion of the idol of the deity. Both the men and women sing songs connected with the goddess.

Men sing a few episodic songs while working in the paddy fields. The purpose of this singing is to forget physical labour. Women do not sing these songs as work-songs.

Male singers use both verse and prose in communicating the content of the epic. They first sing in verse and then explain the content in prose. Female singers do not use prose. The male singing is accompanied by dance movements and dramatic performances. Female singers do not perform dance or present any drama while singing.

The performance, that takes place in the context of worship, is strictly restricted to male singers. However the women predominate as audience.

The performance held in the context of the *vrata* is strictly restricted to women singers. The audience of this performance are also women. Men never participate as audience.

The male performance gives emphasis to the entire story, but the female performance gives emphasis to the description of Beula's purity, devotion, courage and chastity.

Stories from *Padma Purana*, are narrated as tales in a family gathering. The telling of a tale is an important social event. The tale-telling event is generally held in a family, but children from other families also participate. The teller may be either male or female. The listeners are mostly children of both sexes. In such events episodes from the Manasa-lore, particularly from the *Padma Purana*, are told with appropriate gestures and postures and some sort of a dramatic performance. This kind of tale-telling is performed in a non-ritual context.

Although the general outline of the story is same, the details of the text seem to be different in the male and female performances.

Conclusion

The performance of the *Padma Purana* is a social phenomenon. As such, both the male and the female are more or less associated with the performance. But the males have been dominating the performance from the beginning. The *ojapali* is an open air performance. The use of microphone and other modern accessories is totally absent in this artform. Hence, the *oja* and the *palis* have to sing in a high-pitched voice. The women singers do not have such high-pitched voice and are hence not encouraged to learn the art of *ojapali* music. Playing on cymbals and beating of drums by women is a taboo. A.K. Ramanujam rightly observes; "The world of the women is not the world of men" (Appadurai, *et al.* 1991 : 53). He describes the two categories of *akam* and *puram* as ethnic genres. *Akam* is domestic and *puram* is public in terms of the teller and the audience. In the performance of the *Padma Purana* it has been observed that the female performance is for women and centres around women. On the other hand, the male performance is for both the male and the female but is centred around the male. The female performance may be termed as *akam* genre and the male performance may be called *puram* genre. Here it should be noted that the songs sung by the female singers are not similar to those of the male singers, though both of them claim that they sing songs from the *Padma Purana*.

Notes

1. Chandi, a stepmother of Manasa, made her blind by striking her with her bangle, suspecting her to be the new wife that Shiva, her lascivious husband might have brought.
2. Vaidika-Pauranika-laukikadi vividha prakaraih devim pujayet.
3. Informants: Late Nareswar Sarma Barua (80), Dipila, Darrang,
   data collected on 7-12-81.
   Late Bhadrakanta Sarma (83), Baladevapara,
   Darrang, data collected on 6-3-84.
4. *ha* stands for Ganapati,
   ta stands for Sadashiva,
   na stands for Mahamaya,
   r(*ri*) stands for Krishna,
   rta (*rita*) stands for Gandharva.

References

Appadurai, Arjun; Korom, Frank J & Mills, Margaret (eds.), 1991, *Gender, Genre and Power in South Asia Expressive Tradition*, U.S.A., University of Pennsylvania Press.

Blackburn, S.H. , *et al.*, 1986, *Another Harmony*, Delhi, Oxford University Press.

Crook, W., 1968, *The Popular Religion and Folklore of Northern India*, Vol. II, Delhi.

Datta, B., 1996, 'Indigenous Narrative Forms in Assamese' in *Bulletin of the Department of Folklore Research*, ed. N.C. Sarma *et al.*, Department of Folklore Research, Gawahati: Gauhati University.

Ramanujam, A.K., 1986, 'Two Realms of Kannada Folklore' in ed. S.H. Blackburn, *et al.*, *Another Harmony*.

Sarma, N.C., 1974, *Asamiya Loka Samskritir Abhasa*, Guwahati.

———, (ed.), 1993, *Padma Purana*, Guwahati.

———, 1996, *et al.*, *Bulletin of the Department of Folklore Research*, No.4, Gauhati University.

———, 1996, *Asamar Parivesya Kala Ojapali*, Guwahati.

Vogel, J.Ph., 1972, *Indian Serpent Lore*, Delhi.

Unpublished Manuscripts

Kalita, Phatik (copyist), 1931, *Padma Purana, Puja Khanda*, Pithakhowapara, Darrang, Assam.

Sarma, Indranath (owner), 1929, *Manasa-Pujar Vidhi*, Hazarikapara, Darrang, Assam.

21

Gender, Genre and Narrative
Case of Junjappa Epic

T.N. Shankaranarayana

Introduction

THE impact of gender and genre on folk narrative has been the subject of research by scholars in recent years, particularly in relation to Indian folklore, which is rich in variety. *Another Harmony* (ed. Blackburn and Ramanujan, 1986), *Oral Epics in India* (ed. Blackburn *et al.* 1989) and *Gender, Genre and Power in South Asian Expressive Tradition* (Appadurai, Arjun *et al.*, 1991) are pioneering works in this area. "The division of social roles along gender lines is of course nothing new to social sciences but the role that gender plays in performance is still a fertile area of exploration." (Appadurai, Arjun *et al* 1991:7)

Late Prof. A.K. Ramanujan has identified South Indian native genre categories called *akam* and *puram* and has analysed the impact of gender on these genres. "*Akam* is interior, private, familial in terms of teller and audience and *Puram* is exterior and public of the Genres." (ed. Blackburn and Ramanujan, 1986:46) Ramanujan explains these concepts in the context of folktales and also says "Genders are Genres. The world of women is not the world of men." (ed. Appadurai, Arjun *et al.* 1991:53). Prof. Susan Wadley in her research paper titled "Why Does Ram Swarup Sing?" (*Ibid.*, 201-23) has made a detailed analysis of the function of genres in the performance of a North Indian secular folk epic called *Dhola* which is performed for entertainment. Keeping these developments in view this paper discusses the role of gender, genre and narrative in the performance of a South Indian religious folk epic called *Junjappa*.

Junjappa is a popular deity and cultural hero of the Kadugollas who are a Kannada-speaking community, which is in transition from pastoralism to agriculture, living in south-central part of Kạrnataka State. Kadugollas live separately in a settlement called *hatty*, which is surrounded by a fence of thorns, away from the village. Earlier they were cowherds when there were abundant pasture lands for grazing the cattle; but because during the past decades the pasture lands have been converted into agricultural fields, they have become mainly shepherds and agriculturists. They still maintain their tribal identity to the possible extent. Their tribal deities are Chithra *devaru*, Katama *devaru*, Kethe *devaru*, Pathe *devaru*, Ethappa, Junjappa and many more deities like Veeranaganna, Veerakariyanna, etc. They also worship different female deities like Maramma and male deities like Puralahalli Bhuthappa, etc., which are worshipped by other communities also. Junjappa is a deity of Kadugollas in general and Maranavaru and Kambiyavaru clans in particular. Junjappa has become their deity by 'Death and Deification process'. An elaborate epic on Junjappa has been developed and an annual fair called *jathre* is also held. The epic of Junjappa does not exist in any written form. It is oral in composition, performance and transmission. The narrative of Junjappa is considered an epic as an analytical category for academic purpose, but as an ethnic genre it is called *Junjappa pada/hadu* (Song of Junjappa) or *Junjappana kathe* (Story of Junjappa). Usually some episodes of this narrative are performed, but some singers perform the entire epic.

Summary of the epic

The epic of *Junjappa* is concerned with the intra-tribal conflict between two clans of Kadugollas, viz., Maranavaru and Kambiyavaru and also inter-tribal conflict between Kadugollas and Myasabedas (hunters). It is a story of three generations: the life of Junjappa, his father Kenguri Mallegowda and his grandfather Devara Dayamara who belong to Maranavaru clan. The story begins with the life of Devara Dayamara. In the story about the first generation, Devara Dayamara married Kambakka of Ajjiyavaru clan. But his concern for his cattle was irresistible and he left his wife and went to the grazing lands to take care of his cattle. Unable to bear the torture of the members in the joint family, Kambakka left her home and could join her husband with great difficulty. She spent sometime with him and became pregnant. Both of them went to a thick forest. Kambakka gave birth to a male child. Both husband and wife died of starvation as they could not get any food. The child was blessed by Isvara and Parvathi and was nurtured by Badachithama, the child's maternal aunt. The child was named Kenguri Mallappa. Being an orphan, he was also ill-treated by his own uncles and aunts and was driven out of the house. Fortunately, he was supported by Honnahatti Alegowda, an agriculturist of Aluvinavara Vokkaliga caste. Honnahatti Alegowda developed confidence in Kenguri Mallegowda and entrusted him with the responsibility of taking care of his cattle. In the process, both Alegowda and Kenguri Mallegowda became very prosperous. Kenguri Mallegowda married Chinnamma belonging to Kambiyavaru clan. By the blessing of Lord Isvara, through the mediation of a female deity called

Gowrasandrada Marakka, Junjappa was born to him in an unusual way, out of the backbone of his mother Chinnamma. He performed miracles while in the womb of his mother and also after his birth. Chinnamma gave birth to two more male children called Maranna and Mylanna and a female child called Marakka in the natural course. The birth of Marakka was believed to be inauspicious and Kenguri Mallegowda died because of a breach of tribal convention.

Junjappa became an adult. Because he was poor, his seven maternal uncles patronised him by giving him seven calves. Junjappa worked hard and his cattle wealth was increased to seven hundred cows. The maternal uncles became jealous and planned to kill his cattle by poisoning the water in a tank. They took the help of a sorcerer who had buried a calf alive as part of the ritual. Junjappa found out that the calf belonged to his maternal uncles. But they refused to accept it as their own calf. Junjappa brought back the calf and nurtured it with love and affection. It became a very powerful bull and was named Badamyla by Junjappa and this bull became his assistant. Since Junjappa was believed to be an incarnation of Veerabhadra (classical Hindu deity and son of Isvara) he became very powerful and aggressive. He competed with his maternal uncles and was successful in increasing his cattle wealth. The maternal uncles became very jealous and thought of various methods to pull him down. They instigated the local chieftains called *palaygars* like Sira Ranganna, Cheluru Ranganna, Maradi Ranganna, etc., of Myasabeda tribe. Junjappa fought and won the battles against them. The maternal uncles finally thought of killing him by means of food poisoning. Junjappa's sister was married to the last of the maternal uncles. The maternal uncles invited Junjappa to attend a festival in their home and forced Marakka to serve the poisoned food to him much against her conscience. Junjappa knew this. He told the people gathered there that his maternal uncles have planned to kill him by food poisoning and ate the food. After that, he went inside a haystack, and by the fire of his third eye burnt the maternal uncles and their settlement and finally burnt himself to death. To honour the request of his mother, he did not burn his sister Marakka and blessed that her progeny would continue to prosper. After his death Junjappa was deified by Maranavaru and Kambiyavaru clans and they began to worship him. Even after death he performed many miracles. His own paternal grandfathers became his priests and gradually other clans among Kadugollas also began to worship the deity Junjappa.

This epic is full of descriptions which are valuable from the point of view of cultural and literary studies. The hardship of the female characters, and the jealousy and conspiracy of the maternal uncles are all described in the epic in detail. Paramashiviah (1971) is the first scholar in Kannada who has collected and introduced this epic to the readers. He has also analysed two versions of male singers of this epic from literary and cultural point of view (1979). The present author (1982) and Dr. Kalegowda

Nagavara (1985) have also worked on this epic.

Context and performance

The tradition of Junjappa includes a ritual performance during annual fairs and also narrative performance of the epic. The religious bards of Junjappa epic called *ganeyavaru* or *kanikeyavaru* go from place to place collecting offerings from the devotees in the form of money called *kanike* and also small images of the serpents and scorpions made of gold and silver plates called *harake*. They follow the bull of Junjappa called *Junjappana basava* and carry the image of Junjappa which is in the form of an ornamented *gane*, the top of which is covered by the image of serpent-hood made of silver plate and decorated with peacock feathers and coloured cloth. *Gane* is a three-feet long and one-inch wide bamboo flute.

Junjappa is believed to cure snake and scorpion bites. People take a vow that they would offer *kanike* or *harake* if they are cured of snake or scorpion bites. *Ganeyavaru/ kanikeyavaru* are supposed to be helping the devotees by taking their *kanike* and *harake*, an act that would relieve them of their burden. The bull is identified with the bull Badamyla described in the epic. The devotees treat both the bull and *ganeyavaru* with respect. *Ganeyavaru* sing a portion of this epic while staying in the devotees' houses.

Annual *jathres* (fairs) are held at Bevinahalli and Hagalavadi, two important centres of this tradition, in Tumkur district. During the fairs *asadis*, bards of untouchable caste, play on a leather instrument called *urume*, while the Kadugollas chant songs praising the heroic ways of Junjappa. These songs are called *kaggada padagalu*. Sometimes Kadugollas play holding sticks in their hands. The performance is called *kolata* and the song is called *kolatada pada*. Women sing songs of Junjappa at Kudugolla *hatties*. Whenever a person is bitten by a snake or a scorpion, the singer is requested to perform the epic during the whole night. Whenever there are no rains in a particular year the singers are requested to sing this epic. This is based on the belief that after singing this epic there would be abundant rainfall. Women sing portions of this epic while planting the seedlings and grinding the millets. Special performances are also arranged by patrons in Kadugolla community in their *hatties*. Semi-professional singers sing this epic.

The performance of the epic is done in a religious atmosphere. They worship the deity and then start the performance. The performance starts with invocation songs to different deities such as *Bhumi-taayi* (mother earth) and *Bidiramma* (Bamboo deity) after which the story of the three generations is narrated. Episodes narrated are: the life of Devara Dayamara, the life of Kenguri Mallegowda, the life of Junjappa, which includes his birth, the episode of Cheluru Ranganna, Sira Ranganna, Maradi Ranganna, the episode of Talyadadurgi, Hulikunte Tammanna, the episode of Mathodu Kavalu and also the death episode of Junjappa. The post-death adventures of Junjappa include the episodes of *pujari* Chithaiah, Giddiregowda and Thigala Balegowda, Badachithamma and Meke Bikkanna. The performance ends with the concluding song *mangalarathi hadugalu* showing reverence to Junjappa and other deities. Only a few singers perform all the episodes in an elaborate manner. In the usual performance the singers sing invocation song, one or two episodes pertaining to the life of Junjappa and conclude with *mangalarathi hadugalu*. The performance of *Junjappa* epic varies from an hour to fourteen hours. The delivery styles include poetry and a mixed form of prose and poetry. Some performances are accompanied by the traditional musical instrument *gane* and some are not.

Impact of gender on the performance

So far I have dealt with certain general features of the performance of the epic. Now let me concentrate on gender differences in this performance. They are listed below:

	MALE SINGERS	FEMALE SINGERS
1.	Male Singers sing this epic accompanied by a *gane* player One person sings while the other person plays on *gane* simultaneously. This is the usual practice. The maximum number of performers is two. *Gane* creates a pleasant background music. Sometimes a singer sings without the accompaniment of the *gane* player.	Female singers sing this epic either in part or as a whole in lead duet and duet chorus. The total number of singers is usually four. Sometimes there may be three or four chorus singers. Though there are two lead singers one will be more prominent. Female singing is not accompanied by any musical instrument.
2.	During the fairs male singers sing the praise songs of Junjappa called *kaggada padagalu* followed by the playing of a musical instrument called *urume*. *Urume* is a drumlike leather instrument, the sound of which evokes emotions of heroism. This is not played by	During the fairs the female singers sit near the deity in a corner and sing the song of Junjappa in a group as explained earlier. They also sing while moving in the procession. But they do not sing the *kolatha* songs and the songs with the accompaniment of *urume* or *gane.*

	Kadugollas but by an untouchable caste Asadigalu.	
3.	*Ganeyavaru/kanikeyavaru* are from male singers only. This is because it is basically a male dominated tradition.	Women are not initiated to serve this purpose.
4.	Male singers sing the epic in public. Their purpose is to communicate the story.	Women sing portions of this epic while planting seedlings and grinding millets. The purpose of doing this is to forget physical pain and to get relief from boredom. The song of *Junjappa* is one among so many other songs that they sing. In the case of female singers it is the singing which is more important than communication of the story.
5	Male singers use poetry as well as prose mixed with poetry and use a large number of oral formulae of which most are not refrains.	But in female performance the musical aspect is more important and hence female performance is more poetic. Female singers use only poetry as delivery style and repetition of refrains is the major portion of their performance.
6.	In the case of male singing the performers are strictly male singers.	In the case of female singers the performers are strictly female singers.
7.	The emphasis in male performance is on the adventure and heroism of Junjappa and also the conspiracy of maternal uncles and *palaygars*.	The emphasis in female singers is on the description of the beauty of the child Junjappa, the sorrows and turmoil of Kambakka and Chinnamma and the pathos expressed in the death episode of Junjappa.
8.	Though the broad outline of the story is the same, the details of the text are different in male versions.	Though the broad outline of the story is the same, the details of the text are different in female versions.

Analysis of an episode

Let us take a particular episode and take one version each from male singing and female singing and analyse the contents. In this paper the episode of the poisoning of Junjappa is taken as an example. The versions from a semi-professional male singer Shivanna and from a female singer Mangajji are analysed here. The episode of the poisoning of Junjappa consists of the following incidents:

1. Maternal uncles invite Junjappa.
2. Preparation of poisonous food.
3. Serving poisonous food to Junjappa by his own sister Marakka and his acceptance.
4. Junjappa taking revenge on his maternal uncles and his death.

The maternal uncles do not meet Junjappa directly and invite him to their place. Instead they put pressure on their sister. This is common in both versions. But in the female version it is described that Chinnamma feels very happy on seeing her brothers and treats them well. She expresses her helplessness in persuading Junjappa and requests them to meet Junjappa directly and invite him to their place. Her love for her brothers and the attachment she has towards her kinsmen is important here. But in the male version Chinnamma treats her brothers in a casual way, tells them that if Junjappa is ready to come he may be taken to their home. This approach is very formal and not intimate. In the traditional Indian context parent's house (*thavaru mane*) is very dear to women and they are emotionally so much attached to it that they are ready to forget any ill-treatment they may have met from their father's or brother's house. This is clearly expressed in the female versions, which is quite obvious in the traditional Indian context.

Her joy is expressed as follows in the verse sung by Mangajji:

> Oh brothers mine, that you should come
> To grace your forlorn sister's home!
> Truly blessed, this home coming
> God's mercies will glad tidings bring.

But in the male version this incident is described as follows: The maternal uncles pressurised their sister Chinnamma, but she said that Junjappa does not listen to her and hence Junjappa may be approached directly. The maternal uncles did as she said and they were successful in inviting Junjappa to their place.

In another incident Marakka was forced by her husband and his brothers to serve the poisonous food to her own brother much against her conscience. In the female performance the attention is concentrated on the feeling of sorrow and helplessness experienced by Marakka. She tries her best to avoid telling Junjappa that the food is poisoned. She keeps it a secret until Junjappa actually starts taking the poisonous food. Unable to hide her secret any longer, she says:

> Oh brother dear, God spare your life!
> Ah brother mine, survive this strife!
> Ah precious one, God spare your life!
> There is poison in your food!

She indirectly suggests to him not to take the food. But Junjappa accepts the poison by saying:

> Peace be with you! God rest your soul!
> So put your mind at rest!
> I know such poison takes its toil;
> I will eat it now and pass the test!

Emphasis here is not on the feelings of Junjappa nor is he highlighted as a tragic hero.

In the male version Junjappa immediately understands that the food is poisoned just by smelling it and seeing the tears of his sister Marakka. He consoles Marakka and tells her to act according to the dictates of her husband and his brothers. He addresses the people gathered there and delivers his speech pointing out the crookedness of his maternal uncles and declares that he is going to consume the poisonous food. While consoling Marakka he advises her with the responsibility of an elder brother by saying:

> Sister Marakka, you stayed in your parents' house for thirteen years. You are married to your husband and now it is your duty to follow their orders and now you should not worry about your mother's house. . . .

After consoling her like this he addresses the gathering and says:

> My maternal uncles have prepared special food for me in which they have put poison. That is why I requested you to take food first because I was sure the food served to me only was poisoned. Hence, I thought it better for you to have the food first, as it would have been wrong on my part to have stopped you from taking food after having taken it myself. I would have died and you couldn't have taken food. . . .

Here in the male version, though the sorrow of Marakka is described, the emphasis is on the personality of Junjappa. His responsibility as an elder brother and the way he consoles Marakka and his concern for the gathering and his intelligence in handling the whole tragic situation and his boldness in accepting death are all emphasised here.

By analysing the above two incidents we come to know that in the male version male personalities are highlighted, whereas in the female version the women's helplessness, and their intimacy towards their brother is highlighted.

The male and female versions analysed here run to ten pages and six pages respectively. In the male versions the description of purchasing poison, the way in which Junjappa comes to know of food poisoning and Junjappa's address to the gathering are described in two pages each and the other four pages are concerned with his death and revenge. But in the female version the whole episode is stated in twelve lines and is elaborated with refrains of three lines and two lines repeated several times. Here singing becomes very important.

In the male version the mode of preparing and procuring poison is described in detail. This is because it is the men who go out and are exposed to the outside world. Since women in Kadugolla community are not so much exposed to the outside world it is quite obvious that in the female version it is only stated that the burning poison has slipped into the food spread on banana leaf. They do not know how it is prepared and obviously it is not described.

After the death of Junjappa, in the male version, Chinnamma comes to know that her son is dead and she comes running and cries. But in the female version, as soon as Chinnamma comes to know of the death of Junjappa, she immediately faints. There is emphasis on fainting.

Genre difference

In this section an effort has been made to find out what happens to the text and performance when male singers perform with and without instrument and also to find out the function of prose narration and singing in the form of poetry.

The epic of *Junappa* is performed by male singers in two types of genres: (1) song (2) mixed forms of song and prose. Male singers who perform in the form of song and prose are usually accompanied by a flute like musical instrument called *gane*. Some singers can sing only when they are accompanied by the *gane* player. But some other singers sing independently without the *gane* player. The background music of *gane* imposes restriction and discipline on the performer. He cannot deviate from the main story and cannot afford to be very light or humorous in his presentation style, because *gane* produces a solemn and serious religious atmosphere. *Gane* itself is considered sacred in this tradition. Singers worship the *gane* before commencing their performance. And hence if the performer is accompanied by the *gane* player he will not take any liberty to make changes in the performance of the text. But if he is not accompanied by a *gane* player he will have the freedom to add some humorous or spicy items in his presentation or he may sing a particular portion and after that he may give his own commentary also. This type of liberty is possible only when he performs in a style that uses both the forms, song as well as prose. This type of narration is similar to classical native genres called *Harikatha* and *Gamaka* in Karnataka. In this paper I have taken the versions of two male singers: one is the version of *pujari* Eranna who sings only when accompanied by a *gane* player and second one is the version of Shivanna who sings independently and is not accompanied by a *gane* player.

Let us take the example of the incident of preparation or procurement of poison. *Pujari* Eranna, who is traditional and serious by nature, describes how the poison was prepared from a poisonous plant. Shivanna also describes this when he sings. But after singing he shifts to prose. He says:

> One of the maternal uncles of Junjappa went to a shop and asked the shopkeeper to give him poison. The shopkeeper obviously asked what sort of poison he needed, whether it was a rat poison, cockroach poison or some other poison. The maternal uncle did not expect this type of reply and was confused. He moved out of the shop immediately as he was afraid that people may see him purchasing poison and doubt his intentions. In total confusion and anxiety he asked the shopkeeper to give him a mixture of all sorts of poisons.

When Shivanna says this there is laughter in the audience. Here the purpose of Shivanna is to impress the audience. When Shivanna sings he conforms to the tradition and his mood is serious but when he shifts to prose he can cut jokes, give examples and provide commentary. That is how the performance of Shivanna continues. He sings for a while and then explains whatever he has sung along with his own commentary. This is not possible in a performance accompanied by *gane*. Here we have two different types of presentation styles. The personality of the performers is also of equal importance. Singers who are more devoted to the deity and who are more serious in their nature sing accompanied by the *gane* player. *Pujari* Eranna is an introvert and religious by nature. He is more devoted to the deity. He takes his performance to be a kind of service to the deity. His objective is not to please the audience. In comparison Shivanna is an extrovert and a seasoned public performer. His intention is to impress the audience. And for that reason he uses prose. But he also wants to show by singing that he adheres to the tradition. Here song helps him identify himself with the tradition and also establish his text as authentic. Prose helps him display his individual talent. Since he is a semi-professional performer, it is necessary for him to keep the audience in good humour. The impact of individual personality on the performance is worth investigating in detail. This type of work has been done in a systematic manner by Anna-Leena-Siikala in her work *Interpreting Oral Narratives* (1990). Such type of studies are needed in the context of Indian folk epics.

Conclusion

On the basis of the analysis presented above a few observations may be made. In the performance of *Junjappa* epic, it is observed that the female version is in the form of a song and is sung by women. It centres around them and its audience are also women. Hence it is of *akam* genre. It is only recently that some women singers have started giving public performances like male singers. This is a recent development in the changing situation of Kadugolla community. Need for money, popularity and also competition with male singers is the reason for this development. With this exception, the traditional female performance is domestic in nature and earlier only female listeners were the audience. But recently men also form part of the audience. Male performances are intended both for male and female audiences and it has been traditionally a *puram* genre. Ramanujan cites examples from secular tales where there is lot of scope and freedom for the performers to make changes in the text and performance. But the performance of *Junjappa* epic is religious and there is less scope for the performer to make changes. It is observed that male and female versions of the epic are different in text and performance, in spite of religious restrictions. This paper supports Ramanujan's observations on gender and genre in the context of Kannada folk narratives.

Susan Wadley has analysed an episode from a north Indian secular folk epic called *Dhola* which is performed for entertainment and she has rightly observed the role of prose in the presentation style of the performer. In the present paper an effort has been made to show that prose is used to interpret the song in serious as well as humorous manner in the performance of a religious epic. It is observed that performance of the religious epic *Junjappa* is strictly religious when sung accompanied by a *gane* player but when the epic performer is not accompanied by a *gane* player, he uses song to maintain seriousness, religious atmosphere and conformity to the tradition; he uses prose to display his individual talent and impress the audience by creating a secular and humorous atmosphere.

References

Appadurai, Arjun, Korom, Frank J. and Mills, Margaret ed., 1991, *Gender, Genre and Power in South Asian Expressive Traditions*, U.S.A., University of Pennsylvania Press.

Blackburn, Stuart H., 1960, *Singing of Birth and Death: Text in Performance*, Philadelphia, University of Pennsylvania Press.

Blackburn, Stuart H. and Ramanujan, A.K., 1986, *Another Harmony*, Delhi, Oxford University Press.

Blackburn, Stuart H., *et al.*, 1989, *Oral Epics in India*, Berkeley, University of California Press.

Beck, Brenda E.F., 1982, *The Three Twins: The Telling of a South Indian Folk Epic*, Bloomington, Indiana University Press.

Claus, Peter J., 1987, *Tuluva Darshana* (Vision of Tulu Culture) by Navada A.V. and Subhash Chandra, Kundapura: Pradeshika Vyasaga.

Claus, Peter J., 1993, unpublished report titled *A Study of Social Structure and Epic Songs of the Gollas*.

Claus, Peter J. and Korom, Frank, 1991, *Folkloristics and Indian Folklore*, India, Regional Resources Centre for Folk Performing Arts, Udupi.

Claus, Peter, J., Handoo, Jawaharlal and Pattnayak, D.P., 1980, *Indian Folklore*, vol. II, Mysore, Central Institute of Indian Languages.

Nanjundaiah, H.V. and Aiyer, Anantha Krishna, 1926, *The Mysore Tribes and Castes*, vol. III, Bangalore, Mysore Government Press.

Nagavara Kalegowda, 1985, *Ondu Budakattina Hatti* (Settlement of A Tribe), unpublished Ph.D. thesis, Bangalore University.

Paramashivaiah, J.S., 1971, *Janapada Kavya Kathegalu* (Folk Narrative Poetry), Mysore, Suruchi Prakashana.

Paramashivaiah, J.S., Dakshina, 1979, *Karnataka Janapada Kaavya Prakaragalu* (genres of South Karnataka Folk Poetry), Mysore, Prasaranga, University of Mysore.

Roghair, Gene H., 1982, *The Epic of Palnadu: A Study and Translation of Palnati virula Katha, A Telugu Oral Tradition from Andhra Pradesh, India*, New York, Oxford University Press.

Shankaranarayana, T.N., 1982, *Kadugollara Sampradayagalu Mattu Nambikegalu* (Customs and Beliefs of Kadugollas), Mysore, Prasaranya, University of Mysore.

Sontheimer, Gunther Dietz, 1989, *Pastoral Deities in Western India*, New York, Oxford University Press.

22

Performance Situation of the Khamba-Thoibi Folk Epic

M. Mani Meitei

An introductory note

RECENTLY the Manipuri folk epic *Khamba-Thoibi* has received warm critical attention. The diverse aspects of this oral epic are being explored today. It has been defined and its genre identified (*see* Sanatombi & Meitei 1996: 133-42). It has been transmitted orally over the centuries; but it is distinguished from other tales in our oral tradition by its enormous length, romance and heroic exploits of the hero (whose deep love for the heroine incurs the wrath and hostility of the villain), and above all by its style. These are the characteristic features of a folk epic internationally accepted. A folk epic, according to Oinas, is a long narrative composed of songs "in formulaic and ornamental style dealing with the adventures of extraordinary people", and the songs "are traditional, that are handed down by word of mouth, as distinguished from literary epics, attributed to definite authors" (Oinas 1972:99). Again Albert B. Lord says in his definition of the term,

> ... oral epic song is narrative poetry composed in a manner evolved over many generations by singers of tales who did not know how to write; it consists of the building of metrical lines and half lines by means of formulas and formulaic expressions and by the use of themes. — Lord 1981:4

In our context, however, we take into consideration the particular form of folklore, how it exists in the culture concerned, the mode of transmission, the linguistic and metalinguistic factors, and the (mental) text. All these are crucial "*internal* criteria", as Alan Dundes rightly puts (Dundes 1978:23), that contribute to the definition of any given aspect of folklore. The study of folklore involves one or two or all of the three levels of analysis (*Ibid.*:25). All three can be taken up when a study on the performance situation of *Khamba-Thoibi* folk epic is attempted.

From initial situation to performance

The study of Manipuri folklore is slowly gaining momentum. Structuralism, psychoanalytical treatment of tales, and contextual studies have recently attracted the attention of some folklorists. What is necessary is the application of new theories to the already existing forms of folklore. In this paper an investigation into the performance situation of the Khamba-Thoibi epic will be made by selecting only a part of the epic. This study not only concentrates on the textual part of the epic but also takes into consideration other factors governing a performance situation, outside the text. However, both text and context are welded together as body and soul. Text alone without the contextual background is a soulless body; context or performance infuses soul into the text — that is, living conditions are added to the text. About their interdependence and interrelationship Blackburn writes:

> Context is the sum total of factors from both the cultural and the more immediate situations that impinge upon an oral presentation. Performance, on the other hand, is the delivery and stylization of a story within a context; it tells not "what" but "how". Though different, context and performance methodologies are supplementary: contextual data are necessary but not sufficient for a performance analysis, since the latter encompasses both context and text. Performance, in other words, is what happens to a text in a context.
> — Blackburn 1986:168

Despite their interrelationship text precedes context, and can even live independently in one form or another. In our study, however, a synthesis of the two is most emphatic. In this connection what Blackburn says is worth noting: "any effective analysis of performance begins its work from inside the story, proceeds outward, and returns to it cyclically". (Blackburn 1986:168)

It is equally important to understand the pre-performance rites. The performance is by no means restricted to any particular time and place. It means that on any day or days of the year a performance can be conducted. However, events relating to birth, marriage, death, religious festivals, seasonal festivals, social and communal gatherings, etc., are often associated with the singing of the epic. The occasions may be secular or sacred. Whatever the occasion, a formal invitation in the form of three pieces of *kom kwa* (raw betel fruit) and two or three *pan* (betel) leaves placed on a round banana leaf are presented to the singer as a prelude to the performance. In the villages the appropriate time for performance to take place is after dusk, for after a day's hard work the villagers look forward to some entertainment. They come to listen to the romance and heroism of the characters, as well as gossip and pass time leisurely. As a rule the actual place of performance is in front of a house, in the open or in a *shangoi* (an outhouse in front of the main house). The place is properly lighted. One singing session lasts three to four hours depending upon the part being sung. The choice of the part is always unanimous. The singing time, however, is not governed by the episode, for episodes can be stretched. The singer is a mastercraftman, who scrutinises the time, situation and episode, all of which determine the actual performance time. For instance, the *kao* portion takes about two to three sessions under normal situations, but it can be performed in about two hours if the situation so demands. The oral epic text has no fixed length; it can be contracted or expanded by eliminating or adding details. In a broader sense, performance and performative text alone do not constitute a particular situation, but a number of factors such as audience, performer, reception and delivery do certainly mould the context. Indeed, the study of an oral epic performance encounters complex relations between sets of artistic, non-artistic, human and non-human elements, all of which attribute to the totality of a performance situation. Musical instruments, place and time of the performance are some of the non-human elements that play an important role here. All these factors are what Lauri and Anneli Honko call "the units of epic discourse" that is, "multiforms" (Honko and Honko 1995:209). Their explanations cannot escape the attention of a researcher who is interested in oral epic performance situation. They write:

> We contend that an oral epic breathes through multiforms. The 'breathing' metaphor refers, firstly, to the fact that an oral epic has no fixed length, i.e., its text may appear in shorter or longer form depending on such factors as the situational context, mode of performance and performative style. Secondly, shorter or greater length is essentially produced by resorting to multiforms. Although easily perceived as fairly constant elements of epic discourse, multiforms are largely responsible for variability in the epic because their presence or lack, as well as their different manifestations offer the singer different strategic solutions. Another feature of multiforms is their mobility: they may be transferred from one epic to another, or from one textual position to another within one and the same epic. This co-textual variation makes multiforms polysemantic.
>
> — Honko and Honko 1995:211

Every epic singer is in his or her own right a creative poet. No two singers perform the same text in the same manner, for each has different methods to grapple with the immediate situation at hand. But neither is left uninfluenced by multiforms. Even the same singer acts differently on two different occasions.

After discussing some of the fundamental issues of performance theory and performance oriented practical problems, my aim is to deal with a performance situation, as proposed earlier.

* * *

It was at 4 pm, January 4, 1997 that the 85-year-old Moirangsaion singer, Heisnam Mangoljao Singh, popularly known as Thanga Mangoljao alighted from a passenger bus at a place 45 km from Imphal. We (my wife and I) greeted him by touching his feet before we took him to my native village, Wabagai (Manipur) in a car. We had invited the singer a week ago. The part of the epic he was to sing was 'kao phaba' (catching of the bull). Before his arrival we hired a *dholak* for his use during the performance. Every epic singer has to sing the story to the accompaniment of either *pena* or *dholak*. A video camera and megaphone facilities were properly installed for the occasion. The session started exactly at 6.25 pm as the singer settled on his seat, made of two weed mats kept one on top of the other. They were covered with woolen blankets for warmth. Sitting arrangements were made in the *shangoi*, just in front of the house, and the place was lit up with big oil lamps. To begin with there were about forty people, but the number increased in about half an hour. People came from as far as three kilometres braving the severe cold. On the right side of the singer sat the women, and on his left and in front of him, the menfolk. Not far from him a charcoal stove was burning. The sitting arrangements were done in a way that the singer could have a better contact with his audience physically, metaphysically and psychologically, each feeling the other's presence — all within a hearing distance. Sitting position is of vital importance so far as the performance is concerned, because in such a performance situation the singer is the epicentre, from whom tremors of thrill, delight, anxiety and suspense are released endlessly. In return, he gets the "audience's input" (Stotter 1994:71). As a teller our singer knew what his role was: to please the audience, first and foremost.

The first part of the narrative is invariably an invocation. Our singer, too, started his singing by praising the four gods of Manipur governing four different directions: Thangjing in the west, Koubru in the north, Marjing in the east, and Wanghrel in the south. Subsequently the narrative that followed began with recounting Thoibi's earlier births. She is linked with Leimarel, the Supreme Mother in the Creation myth, who reincarnated herself into Nongthangleima, Leinaotabi, Panthoibi, Phououileima, and lastly, as Thoibi. Both Thoibi and Khamba are believed to have been sent by God Thangjing to complete the sixth cycle of the Incarnation story. The epic singer knew what was going to make his narration more artistic. An epic singer's talent lies not only in his ability to present the story in the sung form; but he is also a poet *par excellence*, following the rules of composition. Besides, he is the man of the show, the stage manager simultaneously opening all channels of communication, transmission and entertainment. This way he shares with his audience the "emotional experience and adventures" (Stotter 1994:71) evoked by the cumulative effect of text, texture and context. The choice of a particular episode, say from the middle of the story, does not, however, preclude the teller from bringing in, for example, the parentage of the major characters in the epic. Our singer of the epic was adept at this art; his description of the bull's past history and its being kept by Khamba's father, and its offering help to Khamba and Khamnu after the premature death of their parents can be evidently cited. Such a descriptive part, like the *protasis* in a Greek tragedy, gives information about the characters. This part of the narrative is essential before the opening of the plot.

While studying a performance situation, the singer-audience relationship takes precedence over most of the other related issues and questions. Singer's voice, gesture, eye contact, kinesic movement of his body as well as poetry, music and musical instrument play a vital role in establishing the singer-audience relationship. The success of a performance lies in establishing such a relationship. There is an unending process of give and take on the part of the singer and his audience. The singer, in order to attract the attention of his audience, has to draw upon a number of devices. If the audience applauds him with laughter, clapping of hands, and others sounds of approval, then to sustain the moment of joy, the jubilant tale-teller uses a variety of techniques like sudden change of pitch, beating of the drum with different sound patterns and repetitions. Besides, when humour, pathos, ironic descriptions, exaggerations, distortion of truth to evoke laughter and anecdotes, are presented with a poetic power, the singer and audience come very close to each other.

A performance situation, however, is not necessarily always governed by similar conditions. For example, there is no guarantee of a continued good response from the audience: the coming and going away of people, gossiping and whispering disturbs the performance. When things become unbearable the elderly people shout back and ask others to keep quiet. This happened several times during our performance. At times some noisy people in the audience were directly handled by the singer himself in more than one way. To begin with, he criticised his own voice, which he said was failing due to old age. Later he got agitated and in a strong and pungent attack cautioned a jabbering group of people against mistaking high pitched shouting for a song. He rebuked a man for getting up and leaving in the middle of the epic telling session by saying: "Those of you who have little inclination to listen to the story should not suffer here any longer". A story-teller/singer is simultaneously a performer and an observer. His role, therefore, is not confined to displaying his skills; he must also maintain constant contact with his immediate environment. He is both a poet and a critic who moves in and out of the text almost intuitively and instinctively. He has all the necessary tools and mechanism for grappling with any unforeseen situation. He can entertain and he can chasten his audience without offending them. He can talk about his health, about himself, his musical instrument, sip tea and comment on the weather when the situation so demands. This has been experienced by many folklore scholars. In his paper, 'The African Heroic Epic', Deniel P. Biebuyck writes thus:

> Each performance has its own flavour of originality. The bard is not bound by a rigid text that he must follow with precision. He can introduce into the narrative certain episodes or characters, and leave others out. He inserts personal reflections, proverbs, statements. He digresses to speak about himself, his ancestors, his experiences, his clan or caste, his artistry, his musical instrument, his teachers and predecessors, or about certain members of the audience. The narrative may be interspersed with longer pauses, to eat or drink, for dance performances, for dramatic action, for musical interludes, for praises. — 1978:352

The oral text and its relationship with the performance context is closely knit. The earlier notion that text alone is the most important element in a tale-telling session no longer holds true; text responds differently in different situations, which may even bring about a semantic change in it. Factors that influence the performative text must be taken into account by the scholar.

Narrative technique

It is true that every creative artist has certain problems that need to be sorted out first. In our context, the epic singer's problem is how to present a story that is already known to the audience. As a sensitive artist Mangoljao, perhaps, knew that the art of telling his story lay not necessarily in repetition but in improvisation. The success of a performance lies in the presentation of the story in an ever refreshing manner, by using rhetorical devices such as comparisons, similes, metaphors, innuendos, images, epithets, anecdotes, sayings and proverbs, hyperboles and litotes. A sense of humour, wit, personal comments, musical rendering, ability to create tempo through acceleration and deceleration of speed, and above all, the amiable personality of the singer are some other important factors. While singing the 'kao' portion Mangoljao displayed his skill and rare charisma as a minstrel. Before going into the details of the narrative techniques he employed, let us first get to know the story. What follows is a brief summary of the 'kao' portion. The episode is a sequel to the earlier defeat of Nongban, the villain, by Khamba in the *kangjei* (an old game of the Meiteis that looks like the modern hockey game) match.

> Thus with the fall of Nongban his reputation as a champion of Moirang for seven years also died, but still worse was his possible loss of the prospects of taking Thoibi, the beautiful daughter of Yubaraj Chingkhu Akhuba, in marriage. So Nongban's wicked plan was to remove Khamba, his earthly obstacle, at the earliest opportunity available. One evening when he was returning home he chanced on two women at a marketplace who were crying. He accosted them and on enquiring he came to know that they were from Khuman land, which was then ravaged by a ferocious bull that proved to be stronger than the strongest man in Khuman land, and they

> were gripped with fear at the thought of returning home as evening approached. Much pleased with this piece of information Nongban awarded them with money, and boasted that he was the strongest man in Moirang and his name was Angom Nongban Kongyamba, the mere mention of which was enough to terrify the bull.
>
> Nongban worked out a wicked plan to entrap Khamba. He feigned that he was possessed by God Thangjing who had entered him and wanted the bull to be caught so that peace and prosperity may prevail in Moirang. He added that his friend Khamba had volunteered for the task. However, Khamba contested his having said so. At this Nongban teased Khamba by saying that he was being a worthy son of a twister father. The disrespectful reference to his father made Khamba red with anger, and in an instant he pounced upon Nongban. A scuffle followed between the two. Later Khamba agreed to catch the bull in a manner befitting his family name. For his father alone had caught seven tigers.
>
> The task, however, was not an easy one. But Khamba, at the instance of Thonglen, the general of Moirang, came to know that his sister Khamnu had the secret knowledge about capturing the bull, which in fact belonged to their family, and even looked after the brother and sister (Khamba and Khamnu) after the death of their parents. So with Khamnu's secret knowledge, Khamba introduced himself to the bull as the son of Puremba, the bull's master. At this the wild and ferocious bull, as if hypnotised, became so tame that it not only obeyed Khamba but also shed tears from its eyes like a human being. On seeing Khamba coming with the bull, the villain Nongban planned to take the bull away from him, for the king had made an announcement that he who caught the bull would be married to Thoibi. So he made a futile attempt at snatching the bull away from Khamba. The bull charged at Nongban making him run for his life. However, nearing the crowd, he protested strongly that the bull caught by him was forcibly snatched away by Khamba, and that justice should be meted out to him. Just then Khamba, too, arrived with the bull, and denied the claim of Nongban before the king and his ministers. So, now to prove their prowess and stand trial for the charges each made against the other, they had to catch the bull before the public. It was Nongban's turn to face the bull. But after his initial advantage over the bull he withdrew, and the animal charged at him wounding him badly. In his utter helplessness Nongban yelled out: 'Help me, Khamba, my friend. Help me!' However, Thonglen, the general, insisted that he must first confess that what he had said earlier was motivated by his desire to marry Thoibi, and that the bull was actually caught by Khamba. Nongban did as was demanded and he did so by running inside the arena. Only then was Khamba allowed to save Nongban's life from the fierce bull.

While this becomes the story of 'kao', the narrative is enriched by a number of literary, semi-literary, linguistic, paralinguistic, kinesic devices; by additions, digressions, anecdotes, similes, metaphors, imagery, dramatic monologues, dialogues, epithets, proverbs, dialects, incantations, laments, maxims, paradoxes, aphorisms, rhetorical questions and so on. It is these elements that make the whole rendering so poetical. When Mangoljao sang the 'kao' portion, his narrative moved back and forth in time: the present moment slipping into the past or future and vice versa. Hence, the plot development was not always linear. The narrative was not governed by the arithmatical progression of time; instead, there was a blend of the arithmatical and geometrical progression of time.

At certain points the singer's presence became unnoticeable almost to the extent of being non-present. At such moments we easily forgot him as a separate entity; by losing his self in the process he became the character whose voice and role he imitated or performed. In short, he became the *dramatis personae* changed from both within and without. He could change the narrative voice from third person to first or second person with ease. Dialogues were used frequently to build a dramatic situation. The dialogue substitutes for action in the play. For a solo performer impersonation helps in creating vivid characters. Without these devices the narrative will not remain so attractive and poetic. Mangoljao's performance made use of these devices several times. A few of them are cited here:

Simile: Nongban's eyes shone with fear from under the bed like a rat's whose head is above a crevice in a field cursed by the scorching heat of the sun.

In foolishness women are like the cow; in fickleness they are like the movement of a snake; in their uncertain destination they are like the birds that perch on any branch of a tree at dusk.

Metaphor: Nongban, you're your father's morning sun and evening moon.

Chaoba Nongthon is the sun of Moirang Kangla.

Imagery: That's just a calf as big as an elephant (Khamba describes the size of the bull he is going to catch).

Chaoba just closes his eyes, and sees two *nganap* (very small long slippery species of fish) fish, husband and wife, talk four fathom and a half deep down the surface of the Loktak lake between Thanga and Karang hills (to indicate the shrewdness of Chaoba, who can instinctively smell right and wrong as a politician).

Maxim: Is there anybody who doesn't want money? Money is all powerful.

For children parents are the real gods; for a wife the husband is her god. Of all virtues *vakti* (devotion) is considered most highly.

Proverb: A crying baby grows faster.

A lion breeds a lion; a tiger breeds a tiger; a fox breeds a fox.

Epithet: *Khuman chanu ponjenbi nongyai chanu yaithibi* (to call Khamnu); *Nongyai Khamba* (to call Khamba); *Angom Nongban Kongyamba Angom Ningthou Mapari Khuraileima Naoyokhei* (to call Nongban); *Ngangba ningthi pamheiba* (to call the bull).

Folk speech: *napchari* (flattery), *sono* (silliness), *lya, sabas, bhalo.*

The narrative movement from one idea to another and from one theme to another is often marked by pauses, beating of the drum, etc. However, a change in the stanza is usually indicated by words such as: '*ngasina lairel nongjada*' (today), '*makha tabana kamdouba*' (what comes next), 'Asomdana Kamdouri' (what happens there), and so forth. The narrative speech is replete with 'formula', 'formulaic expression', and themes. In this connection what Albert B. Lord writes may be quoted:

> By formula I mean "a group of words which is regularly employed under the same metrical conditions to express a given essential idea". . . . By formulaic expression I denote a line or half line constructed on the pattern of the formulas. By theme I refer to the repeated incidents and descriptive passages in the songs.
>
> — Lord 1981:4

Mangoljao profusely makes use of these devices. Given below are some examples:

Formula	Formulaic expression	Theme
1. *kallk-i-da kallak-i*	1. *ho nongban achanba kallak-i-da*	1. The king's summons are served
2. *kege moirang*	2. *mapu ibungo moirang ningthou*	2. Gathering of people
3. *khuman ibungo*	3. *pelle pelle achanba changshillak-u*	3. Dispersal of people

Another characteristic feature of the singing performance is the shift in *tal* (rhythm). Mangoljao changes the rhythm of his song movement from one *tal* to another, showing his mastery in handling three *tal*s, namely *khemtal, loital* and *choukatal*. The first of these is expressive of dance rhythm; the second is grave and plaintive; and the third is used when description of nature or a person is made and also when a new theme is presented. Poise, craft, innovation, humour, placidity, serenity, variety, colloquialism made Mangoljao's performance both familiar and unique in flavour and style.

Gender and the epic

"In the process of folk narrative production," says Bottigheimer, "every component and every analytic process is fundamentally conditioned by gender. Whose voice we hear *in* tales depends to a very great extent on whose voice tells a tale" (Bottigheimer 1995:356). Further she adds: "Storyteller itself is highly sensitive to gender issues" (*Ibid.*:357). This is true of my experience as a field researcher. The singer was a male; the audience was composed of men, women and children. The men and women sat separately: women were seated on the right side of the singer and behind the menfolk, who clustered themselves on the left of the singer as also in front of the singer. The episode itself was about male prowess — catching of a wild bull. Folklorists agree that epics dealing with heroic actions, fights and battles belong to the male world and genres such as chants and laments to the female. Nenola holds the view: "Some genres of folklore, such as long epic in Kalevala metre, were the property of bearded males while others, such as laments, were markedly women's tradition." (1991:2)

It is true that ours is a patriarchal society, and in our folklore women are often a picture of the suffering class — widows, helpless mothers, girls ill-treated by step mothers and step sisters. Even the highly placed girl like Thoibi, who is a princess in the epic is forced to go into exile by her father for her refusal to marry the person chosen by him. Yet she stands firmly by Khamba through thick and thin, and is always found by his side at crucial moments, specially when he is being unduly tortured by her father and the villain Nongban. Thus, with courage she brushes aside all the mores of the society. She becomes one of the earliest women characters in our folklore who revolts against patriarchal authority.

However, my purpose here is to show the extent to which gender biased ideas govern a performance. The tale-tellers generally have a gender bias, as also revealed by our singer. He commented upon women with derision. For instance, the two women, whom Nongban meets at a market late in the evening and who inform him about the fierce bull that had attacked their Khuman kingdom, instead of being praised for providing the relevant information, are rebuked for their timidity, foolishness and nervousness. They are compared to cows. In Manipuri society the other meaning of the cow is invariably derogatory. This unkind comparison between the two, however, is drawn not by Nongban who rebukes them in the tale, but by the singer. He may have inherited that misconception either from his teachers or from his environment.

The singer more than once turned to the women in the audience and assailed them for their heartless decision to leave their parents at the time of marriage, and then their endless demands on their parents after marriage. He did not spare the educated women either. The epic portrays man's position as sacrosanct: the practice of polygamy, was openly given moral sanction. Nongban who already had five wives was dying for the hand of Thoibi. The fact of his having five wives is of no consequence. Similarly divorce is portrayed as changing one's unwanted clothes. Nongban's father tells why his son should bully his wives without reason, and that he should obtain a divorce and get girls of his choice. Though the female characters are not highlighed or spoken of highly in the text, the cliche changes when describing the heroine of the epic, Thoibi. Her reasoning, rational attitude and emotions become a hallmark of her character. When her request to Khamba for not catching the bull is dismissed by him as a trivial voice of a woman, she sharply protests, "That's a pompous masculine voice." This was one instance in which the singer expressed the voice of a woman vociferously; otherwise, on the whole, women were treated most opprobriously. He took delight in commenting upon women's weaknesses and meanness. The singer spoke from his vantage point, guided by the social construct about gender hierarchy. Allocation of inferior role and position to women, however, is not in conformity with the social and historical facts as evident in Manipuri society. The two women whom Nongban allegedly calls fools are in no way fools nor are they timid. They come to Moirang to buy fish all the way from Khuman in spite of the bull, whereas their menfolk stay indoors out of fear. This is also a sign of economic participation by women, and their role as traders. These important issues, however, failed to receive the singer's proper attention. Hence, stereotyping of women in general in such a performance situation as against the productive role of women, in short, reveals the inadequacy of a male-constructed ideology and social code. The myopia of men results in the exploitation and manipulation of women characters and the female audience as well.

Conclusion

By way of conclusion, the following observations about a performance situation of the Manipuri folk epic, *Khamba-Thoibi*, may be made: (1) the epic text alone is not self-contained: what lies behind the text counts as well, (2) the study of folklore as such cannot be one-sided; it should be holistic rather than atomistic, (3) its meaning should be explored in relation to time, situation, communication and performance, and (4) the study of folklore and writing about it must be guided by new methodologies, as Dorson puts emphatically:

> Texts and annotations will be subordinated to close analyses of group dynamics and psycho-cultural relationships. Fieldwork will become a more elaborate enterprise than the securing of verbatim texts. —1972:47

References

Biebuyck, Deniel P., 1978, 'The African Heroic Epic' in Oinas Felix J., *Heroic Epic and Saga*, Bloomington, Indiana University Press, 336-67.

Blackburn, Stuart H., 1986, 'Performance Markers in an Indian Story-Type' in Blackburn Stuart, & Ramanujan A.K., eds., *Another Harmony: New Essays on the Folklore of India*, Delhi, OUP, 167-94.

Blackburn, Stuart & Ramanujan A.K., eds., 1986, *Another Harmony.*

Bottigheimer, Ruth B., 1995, 'Gender and Folk Narrative' in *XIth Congress of the ISFNR*, Vol.II, Mysore, CIIL, 349-64.

Chatterji, Suniti Kumar, 1974, *Kirata-Jana Krti*, Calcutta, The Asiatic Society.

Dorson, Richard M., 1972, 'Introduction' in Richard M. Dorson (ed.), *Folklore and Folklife: An Introduction*, Chicago: The University of Chicago Press, 1-50.

Dorson, Richard M., (ed.), 1972, *Folklore and Folklife.*

Dundes, Alan, 1978, *Essays in Folkloristics*, Meerut, Folklore Institute.

Honko, Lauri & Anneli Honko, 1995, 'Multiforms in Epic Composition' in *XIth Congress of the ISFNR*, Vol.II, Mysore, CIIL, 207-40.

Lord, Albert B., 1981, *The Singer of Tales*, Cambridge, Harvard University Press.

Nenola, Aili., 1991, 'Folkloristics and the Genderized World', *Newsletter*, No.4, Turku: Nordic Institute of Folklore 1-7.

Oinas, Felix J., 1972, 'Folk Epic' in Richard M. Dorson (ed.), *Folklore and Folklife,* 99-115.

Oinas, Felix J., (ed.), 1978, *Heroic Epic and Saga: An Introduction to the World's Great Folk Epics*, Bloomington, Indiana University Press.

Sanatombi, S. & M. Mani Meitei, 1996, 'A Folkloristic Study on the Manipuri Folk Epic Khamba-Thoibi', *Eurasian Studies Yearbook*, 68: 133-142.

Stotter, Ruth, 1994, *About Story: Writing on Stories and Storytelling 1980-94*, California, Stotter Press.

Part IV

Regional and Cultural Dimensions

23

Nepali Oral Epic: Ramayana

C.M. Bandhu

THE ethnic composition and cultural diversity have resulted in various oral traditions in Nepal, handed down from generation to generation. Nepali, being a *lingua-franca* of this multilingual country, served as a medium of emotional unification and preserved the oral traditions including the oral epics of mythological, legendary and historical types. This paper presents a survey of different oral versions of Nepali *Ramayana* and discusses various aspects related to these.

There are at least five types of oral narratives of *Ramayana* performed in various regions of Nepal. Starting from the western part of Nepal, they are *Chait*, *Dhamari*, *Nachari*, *Sorathi* and *Balun*. The *Chait*s or *Chaiti*s are the oral narratives narrated by the ladies individually or in groups during the festivals and on auspicious occasions. The *Chait*s of classical and local deities and historical personalities have been collected and reported by Pant (1975). The *Chait*s of Sita and Hanuman are two important episodes included in his collection. Recently Bhatta (1996) has reported on a *Chait* of *Ramayana* from Baitadi, the far western district of Nepal.

Dhamari or *Dhamar* is the most popular form of oral narratives in western Nepal. The word *Dhamar* is borrowed from Indian classical music. According to Hajari Prasad Dwivedi, *Dhamari*s are devotional songs of Proto-Hindi preserved in the foothills of the Himalayas. As narratives *Dhamer*s contain stories of *Ramayana*, *Mahabharata*, as well as of local gods, goddesses and important personalities. The narratives of *Krishna Dhamari* contain words of Braj *bhasha*. It is said that during the invasion of the Moghuls the cultural life of the Indian plains was disturbed and many of the Hindus came to the foothills of the Himalayas for shelter. The *Krishna Dhamari* referred to by Hajari Prasad Dwivedi is found in the Doti region of western Nepal.

The version of folk *Ramayana* reported by Yatri (1985) is known as *Dhamari*. This is practised in several districts of western Nepal including Dailekh, Surkhet, Acham, Kalikot and Jajarkot.

Some episodes of *Ramayana* known as *Dhamari* are also reported by other scholars. The text of *Ramayana* collected and published by Yatri (1985) consists of ten episodes. An episode of Rama's marriage with Sita is performed in eastern Palpa by the Magars (Pant 1971) and it is also found in Sindhuli, east of Kathmandu, and the northern hill area of Mithila where the episodes connected with Sita's wedding are popular.

The oral epic of *Ramayana*, which is known as *Dhamari*, becomes popular as *Nachari* and *Sorathi* in central Nepal. *Nachari* is performed by the Magars – an ethnic group speaking a Tibeto-Burman language. This is also performed by the untouchables. A version of this *Nachari* is collected and reported by Sapkota (1985). The performance of *Nachari* is systematised like *Sorathi*, which is the most popular performance of the region. As we move eastwards the performance is presented as a variant of *Sorathi*, with some adaptations and changes.

Some other performances like *lila* and *charitra* are also known as *Sorathi*. Some of these performances are based on *Ramayana*. The *Dhamari* becomes *Dhamali* in the Magar community of Palpa, who perform episodes from *Ramayana*.

Balun is another art form popular among the high caste Brahmans and Chetries. This dance drama depicts the episodes of *Ramayana*, *Mahabharata* and other Hindu mythologies. The *Balun* of *Ramayana* is based on classical works and the text is available in hand-written forms as well. However, the texts found in different regions vary. Like the *Chaits* of the far west, the *Balun*s are performed by the high caste people, and they follow the classical tradition of *Ramayana* texts with least adaptations.

Creation and variation

Oral epics are handed down from generations and it is not possible to find out who created these epics. Though the professional castes such as Hudkyas and Gains also perform various epics, none of those mentioned above are performed by them. *Chait*s and *Dhamari*s are sometimes recited individually, these and other epics are performed by heterogeneous groups. *Dhamari*, *Nachari* and *Sorathi* are similar in creation and narration. They are recited by someone who knows the epics and by men and women who participate in the dance. *Dhamari*s are performed in the far western region of Nepal and reflect the vocabulary and style of the area. As they move eastwards they come closer to the standard dialect of the area. The performances of *Nachari* and *Sorathi* exhibit the characteristics of standard Nepali. They are heavily influenced by the *Sorathi* style and the Magar language. Probably, some old men who recite the epics during the performance keep handwritten manuscripts for ready reference. A manuscript of *Ghatu*, which is similar to *Sorathi*, is reported by Sapkota (1985). Handwritten texts of *Balun*s are also found in the villages. They are in the possession of literate high caste men, who recite the epic during its performance. *Balun*s on various themes have been written. They were also popular in medieval Nepali literature.

Though it is possible to locate some of the writers of *Baluns*, there is no practice of giving the names of the creator during the performance.

Adaptations

As performances like *Dhamari*, *Nachari* and *Sorathi* select local variations and adaptations of *Ramayana*, we will take these for discussion. The text of *Ramayana* collected by Yatri (1985) is taken as an illustration. This has 10 episodes, which are as follows:

(1) Ravana's return from Janakapur and the birth of Sita.

(2) Birth and growth of Rama and Lakshmana; their hunting expedition and meeting with Sita.

(3) Sita's search's for an ideal husband.

(4) Sita's wedding.

(5) Hospitality arrangements for the guests at the wedding.

(6) Lakshmana's visit to an astrologer on Rama's behest to ascertain the auspicious day for going to the forest.

(7) Abduction of Sita by Ravana.

(8) Mandodari's advice to Ravana against fighting Rama.

(9) Lakshmana's visit to a blacksmith for making bows and arrows.

(10) Moral: No one should be proud.

These episodes show the following major variations and adaptations:

1. Ravana, the king of Lanka, had come to the capital of Janaka. Janaka offered him a golden-pot full of *ghee*. He returned to his kingdom. But while he was returning, he took some young birds from their nest. When this matter was reported to Janaka, he ordered his brother to find a solution. He invited all the sixteen hundred sages of Janakapur. They decided to make a pot of gold with silver cover and collected blood in it by cutting their fingers. As Ravana was very greedy he took it happily. After he arrived at Lanka, he opened it. He threw it away as it contained blood. A fisherman found the pot. He opened the pot, found something in it, washed it with water and put it in a net without looking at what it was. Actually, the blood of the sages had turned into a baby. The baby in the net began to cry. King Janaka, who came there for bathing, lifted the girl child and brought her to his palace. She was Sita.

2. The epic narrates the birth of Rama and Lakshmana in Ayodhya. Both of them were raised with care and they grew up like the moon in the sky. They liked to go to the forest for hunting very much. One day they went for hunting and killed a

deer. After eating the deer-meat they felt thirsty and went in search of drinking water. They found a water source, where Sita had also come for a bath. Lakshmana saw her and noticed that she was very beautiful. Kings from all directions had come with their proposals to marry her. Sita was asked to choose her husband. She replied that she would marry a man who can chew 80 mounds of iron-*chiura* (powdered iron), swing an 80-mounds iron-swing, lift an 80-mounds bow and move an 80-mounds grinder. As Rama performed all these acts it was decided that Sita would be married to him.

3. Kings from all directions came to attend the marriage ceremony. They were accorded a warm welcome. Milk and rice were offered to them, soft cotton mattresses were provided for sleeping and elephants, horses and chariots were given as parting gifts.
4. One day Rama asked his brother Lakshmana to accompany him to the forest. Lakshmana wanted to know what they would eat there and where they would sleep. Rama replied that they would dig a ditch to live, eat fruits and roots and sleep on the barks and stones. Rama also asked him to go to an astrologer and fix an auspicious day for setting out to the forest. Lakshmana took a piece of gold, a pot of yogurt, and a pack of green vegetables for the astrologer. As he set forth, he asked the water carrier and cowherds for directions to the house of the astrologer.
5. Ravana, the king of Lanka came to the cottage of Sita in the forest and introduced himself as the king of Lanka who was born in the Himalayas. He began by praising Sita's beauty and finally took her away.
6. Mandodari, the wife of Ravana reported her inauspicious dream to him and requested him not to fight with Rama. Ravana assured her of his victory in the war, as he had brothers like Kumbhakarna and Vibhishana.
7. Rama asked his brother Lakshmana to call a blacksmith who would make bows of 80 mounds of iron.

Yatri (1985) thinks that some episodes are missing from the story. The epic ends with a message by Rama to Lakshmana that no one should be proud and one should have patience when in trouble.

Moving eastwards we come to Gulmi where *Ramayana* is performed as *Nachari*. *Nachari* is a dance popular among the Awadhi and Maithili speakers of Terai. In the hill area where Nepali is a dominant language, *Ramayana* is performed by the Magars. *Nachari* starts with an invocation to gods and goddesses. After the invocation the episode of fishing by Dasharatha in the sea starts. This and the next episode which describe Rama's going to the forest is reported in Sapkota's collection (1985).

Nachari shows several interesting adaptations. In this version of *Ramayana*, Dasharatha went for fishing in the sea. He was hurt by a sharp bone of a fish while tearing it. He asked his wives to pull it out from his fingers but no one could do that. Finally, Kaikeyi told the king that if Bharata, who was her own son, was given the throne, she would pull out the thorny bone. Dasharatha agreed to send Rama to the forest and give the throne to Bharata.

In the next episode Rama and Lakshmana are shown hunting in the forest. They set out a dog to chase the wild games. They see a deer and other animals, but they just let them go. Finally, they kill a rhinoceros and offer the blood of the rhino to perform their father's last rites.

Lakshmana feels thirsty after eating the raw-meat of the rhino and climbs up a tree to find a water source. He sees several ducks and cranes and guesses that there might be some water. Both the brothers head in that direction.

In the opening scene of the third episode three girls appear carrying water-pots. The girl walking in the middle is requested to give water. But she tells them that they are the daughters of untouchable castes. In reply Rama and Lakshmana say that they are also untouchables. The girl walking in the middle says that she would give them water to drink if they could swing on the rope of gold and reach Lanka. The girl is Sita. She prepares a rope of gold on which Rama swings and reaches Lanka.

Later Hanuman appears as a helper of Rama. The burning of the capital of Lanka and bringing back Sita from Lanka by Hanuman, Sita's drawing the figure of Ravana, and her exile to the forest are described in simple language by the performer to the researcher.

Nachari is known as *Sorathi* in some parts of central Nepal. *Sorathi* is not only a popular epic in Nepal but also in neighbouring parts of northern India. In central Nepal, *Sorathi* is the most popular performance which has influenced other genres as well. Thapa (1994) has reported that the epic of *Ramayana* is performed as a variant of *Sorathi* in central Nepal.

The performers

The epics such as *Chait* and *Balun* are recited by literate men of upper castes such as Brahmans and Chetris while the *Dhamari*, *Nachari* and *Sorthi* are generally practised by lower caste men. Both men and women can take part in the dances between recitations. In *Nachari*, the boys also dance dressed as girls. *Balun*s are performed as dances with men in numbers of four, eight and sixteen. The performance uses local dialects of Nepal and reflects many regional and ethnic influences.

The *Ramayana* epic in the Nepali language is found in different versions which are neither systematically collected nor studied. Some scholars and their students have done partial studies. These epic performances demand immediate attention of scholars, as they may gradually fade away.

References

Bhatta, Atma Ram, 1996, Baitadika *Pawarinik Lokagathaharuko Adhyayan ra Vishleshan*, M.A. dissertation, Tribhuvan University.

Pant, Deva Kant, 1975, *Doteli, Lok Sahitya*, Kathmandu, Nepal tatha Esiyali Adhyayan Samsthan.

Pant, Kali Bhakta, 1971, *Hamro Lok Samskriti*, Bhairahawa.

Parajuli, Motilal, 1980, *Kaski Jillaka Samajik Gathako Sankalan va Vishleshan*, M.A. dissertation, Tribhuvan University.

Sapkota, Hom Nath, 1985, *Gulmeli Lok Gatha: Sankalan, Vargikaran Va Vishleshan*, M.A. dissertation, Tribhuvan University.

Thapa, Dharma Raj, 1973, *Gandaki ko Suseli*, Kathmandu; Nepal Rajakiya/ Prajna Pratisthan.

Thapa, Dharam Raj and Hansapure Subedi, 1985, *Nepali Lok Sahitya ko Vivecna*, Kathmandu, Tribhuvan University.

Thapa, Dil Bahadur, 1994, "Gralk to Chetrama Pracalit Lok githaruko Sarvekshan ra Ashyan", Kathmandu, M.A. dissertation, Tribhuvan University.

Vatsyayan, Kapila, 1980, *Traditional Indian Theatre: Multiple streams*, New Delhi, National Book Trust.

Yatri, Purna Prakash Nepal, 1985, *Bheri Lok Sahitya*; Kathmandu, Royal Nepal Academy.

24

Important Locations (Villages) and Verbal Narratives Associated with Princess Sita in the Central Hills of Sri Lanka

H.M.D.R. Herath

Introduction

BEFORE the advent of Radio and Television, epics, folk tales and stories were very popular among the Asian communities. In spite of cultural diversities, some aspects of Indian origin or Indian culture can be clearly recognised in some of the well-known epics in the Asian continent. At the same time traditions embeded in local culture reworked the classical texts into indigenous versions. Such cross-cultural narratives overwhelmingly flourished in communities along or in the neighbourhood of silk roads.

International trade, pilgrims and travellers were responsible for the diffusion and spread of religions, and oral narratives. Thus, the unique characteristics of Indian culture including the chanted narratives of Indian origin not only spread but became popular in Greece as well as in other silk road countries. Various types of migration, trade networks, missionaries and sailors were the carriers of these narratives. Epics and episodes thus introduced into an indigenous culture were adapted and reworked according to the existing norms of a particular culture. Over a period of time they were completely assimilated into the indigeneous culture and its lore.

Some of the best known chanted narratives in Asia and particularly in the Indian sub-continent in one way or the other are directly related to the Indian motherland. Such narratives are popular in Indonesia, Burma, Cambodia, Singapore, Malaysia, Maldives, Thailand and Sri Lanka. Among these narratives, the most well-known, probably, is the Rama-Ravana legend. In this story princess Sita occupies a highly respected position. Her good qualities are appreciated to such an extent that her name is mentioned more frequently than any other character while relating or discussing this epic.

Objectives of this study

The overall objective of this study is to explore verbal narratives and important locations (villages and hills, for instance) of Sri Lanka related with princess Sita. The relationship between these narratives and India will also be examined.

Methodology

The researcher has collected chanted narratives over the last decade by combing several villages in the hill country. Later he visited geographical locations mentioned in these narratives, held discussions with the villagers and analysed data using anthropological parameters.

Findings

Rama-Sita legend is one of the most popular oral narratives among Sri Lankans, particularly those living in the central hills. When people talk about chastity, they undoubtedly talk about princess Sita as a supreme example of it. Epic of Rama-Ravana is spread all over Sri Lanka and is associated with the names of different places. These location-related stories are very specific to a given community. Most of these narratives are about female code of conduct in the area. People respectfully evoke the good qualities of princess Sita and her heroic nature and expect their ladies to possess such qualities.

Verbal narratives and geographical locations — Nuwara Eliya

Nuwara Eliya is a mountainous district in Sri Lanka, and resembles Kashmir in India. Etymologically *nuwara* means capital, *eliya* means *aloka* or light. There is an interesting story about how this location got its name. After abduction Ravana kept Sita in a hidden place. Later Hanuman came to Sri Lanka and began searching for Sita. Finally he entered Ravana's city of Badulla, where Ravana's people set fire to his tail. Hanuman then moving from place to place spread the fire and destroyed the city. The light of the fire was observed by people living in the neighbouring district. They shouted about the light in the city. The place from where people saw the light in the city was later called Nuwara-Eliya. There is no historical evidence and only an etymological explanation is available. Geographically Nuwara Eliya is the highest mountainous district in Sri Lanka and its elevation is 7200 feet above the sea level. Old folks attribute the black colour of the soil to the fire set by Hanuman in his efforts to locate princess Sita.

Valapane

In Badulla district there is an area called Valapane. The etymological meaning of *valapane* in Sinhala is *valepenawa* (weeping). When Sita was in Ravana's custody she had been weeping there. At present this site is a big village and is an electorate in the hill country. Throughout her captivity, Sita was kept hidden in a cave called Sthripura. Sita and her associates had lived in this cave. Before 1982 women used to visit this place. Recently Mahaweli-ganga, Randenigala reservoir was constructed at this location and now this area is under water.

Ravanagoda

According to oral narratives of the hill country in Sri Lanka there was an area called Kothmale. In this area there is a village called Ravanagoda. During her captivity Sita was once moved to this place. Ravanagoda means Ravana's hill. Here there is a pond called Sita Pokuna. *Pokuna* means Sita's bathing pond. At Sita Pokuna, there is a big stone called panagala which means combstone. After bathing, Sita had kept her comb on this stone. There is a spot near Ravanagoda called Kondagala. In Sinhala *konda* means *hair* and *gala* means stone. Sita once dried her hair at this place. There is a waterfall called Sita Elle situated in Nuwara Eliya district. Normally virgin ladies do not take bath at this waterfall because that place is considered harmful for ladies. It is said that women's hair grow rapidly if they take a bath there. After bathing princess Sita had sat down in the plateau called Sita Talawa. The stone plate on which she sat, still remains. From an adjoining mountain in Nuwara Eliya flows a natural waterway called Sita-Ela or Sita-stream, which is considered sacred by the Hindus. The women in the area believe that virgin ladies imbibe heroic quality by bathing here. Just after the puberty ceremony some people bring their daughters here for the first bath after the onset of menarche. The girls are believed to acquire qualities such as bravery and obedience.

Sita Eliya

Again a story that has been chanted for a long time is associated with a village at Nuwara Eliya now called Sita Eliya. During her captivity Sita was allowed to take walk here during the day time. It is also said that she had received some powerful rays from Rama at this place. *Eliya* means light. Sita Eliya is considered to be very sacred. A big Hindu temple is situated here. Almost all women after their marriage visit this place and make a vow to remain chaste like Sita Devi. They also make a vow praying for their first baby. Sita Devi is said to protect them all.

Divrumwale

This place is considered to be one of the most powerful divine places. After Rama-Ravana war Sita is said to have met Rama at this particular place. Narratives say that this place is called as Divrumwale. Etymologically the word means *divirum* (oaths of chastity). Sita remained a pure lady throughout her captivity. Ravana did not force himself on her in any way. Normally ladies in this area try to protect their chastity because they are from Divrumwale.

Ashoka Uyana

According to Nuware Eliya legends each and every village in the district in one way or the other is connected with Sita. From Divrumwale one can observe a great mountain called '*worlds-end*'. It is a mountain with a steep almost perpendicular to the ground below and has an elevation of 4000 feet from the sea level. During the British period this place was discovered by Governor Horten and is hence called Horten Plane. Here there is a very large natural *Ashoka* forest. It has only a single variety of Ashoka plants. Oral narratives maintain that thousands of years ago this garden belonged to Sita and she lived here. The adjoining forest spreads up to Matale district in the central province. Ravana had twenty-five palaces and five hundred thousand streets, which were destroyed by Hanuman in the war. According to the narratives, one of the palaces was called Laggala (Lankagala). At present in this place stands a huge mountain rock. At Matale District we can find any number of village level narratives associated with Rama-Ravana war and queen Sita which have passed on from one generation to the next over a period of thousands of years.

Great Hanuman and oral narratives

Hanuman is one of the most powerful and important persons in Sri Lankan cultural history. Even now in a number of places in the island rituals are performed and his assistance sought in predicting, forecasting and discovering unknown places and things. *Anduna*, a well-known magical chant, depicts Hanuman's divine powers and shows him as a god who protects people.

Hanuman, Rama-Ravana war, medicinal forest and oral narratives

According to Rama-Ravana legend Hanuman was a divine personality in an animal form. He was the war hero and came from India. In the war, thousands of Rama's soldiers were wounded. Hanuman wanted to provide immediate treatment to them. He went to the Himalayas and tried to choose suitable medicinal plants, but he forgot which plants were needed. After several unsuccessful trials he decided to bring a big piece of the Himalayan hill. When he approached Sri Lanka two portions fell down from his hand. One portion fell near the sea coast and the other in the middle part of the country. According to the oral tradition the first portion had fallen at the place now called Rumassala. Rumassala, near the Gall harbour in Southern Province, Sri Lanka, is completely covered by medicinal plants. Some of these medicinal plants cannot be cultivated by man due to the climate of this place; but these hill country plants grow on their own in this locality. Etymologically *rumassala* means fallen portion.

The second portion had fallen at a spot called Dolukanda (North Western Province). *Dolu-Dolan* means 'moved' and *Kanda* means 'hill'. This is a very big area having medicinal plants. This hill is now protected by the Government. This medicinal plant forest has three canopies. The ground level flora cover consists of dry-zone plant species. The middle canopy is of plants and trees normally found in an intermediate climate. Most of them are recognised medicinal plants. The topmost canopy comprises trees that normally grow in Nuwara-Eliya region. They are cold climate medicinal plants. Oral tradition in the area attributes this unique combination to the divine power of Hanuman.

People in the hill country region believe that during the war, after consuming his meals Hanuman threw away some left-over rice, which turned into small round stones. People of Nuwara Eliya, Kothmale and Valapane area make a paste from these stones and drink it as a remedy for different ailments. This is a popular remedy for the pregnant mothers.

In the up-country region, while ploughing the land farmers found egg-shaped soil pieces which are called *Sita guli*. There is a whitish substance inside them, which should be consumed since it gives protection from disease and grants long life. However, it is believed that only a man of good moral character comes across a *Sita guli*. Certainly such beliefs in getting rewards for good moral character provide inspiration and stimulus for a better society. This encourages spirituality and development of moral values much admired in Asian culture.

Rama, Ravana, and their social significance

According to oral tradition, King Rama returned to India accompanied by Sita and his army. Sometimes later he passed away and assumed his divine form of God Vishnu. God Vishnu is recognised as a custodian god who protects both Sri Lanka and Buddhism. In the southern coastal region of Sri Lanka, there is a big temple called Devundara shrine and it is dedicated to God Upulvan. Some scholars believe that both Upulvan and Vishnu refer to the same god, who provides protection. This belief is so strong that the fishing communities in the southern region perform regular rituals and seek his blessings and protection.

King Ravana is recognised as one who had expert knowledge but was stubborn and listened to no one. He owned a machine (*Dandu Monara* = wooden peacock) that could fly in the air. A place called Wariyapola (literally meaning station of the air vehicle) is said to be the location where Ravana used to stop on his way to India and back. Wariyapola is in the North-Western Province of Sri Lanka.

However, the most prominent and most referred to character in the Rama-Ravana episode is Sita. Her devotion to her husband, her chastity and moral character evoke strong emotions and deep admiration among the Sri Lankans.

Ainchali singer Nanka (Chap. 3: Molly Kaushal)

Garba Ram —The Healer Chanter (Chap. 3: Molly Kaushal)

An artist playing a musical instrument (Chap. 3: Molly Kaushal)

Cover of the chapbook of Shobha Nayaka Banjara (Chap. 4: Catherine Servan-Schreiber)

The Bhojpuri bhainsaha Banjara, source: *Indian Painting for the British* (Chap. 4: Catherine Servan-Schreiber)

Shri W. Thambalangou Singh, age: 80 years (Chap. 5: S. Sanatombi)

Shri H. Mangoljao Singh, b.1914 d.1997 (Chap. 5: S. Sanatombi)

Egg-divination (Chap. 7: Desmond L. Kharmawphlang)

Scroll of Markandeya Purana (Chap. 11: Bittu Venkateswarlu)

Scroll of Jamba Purana, A.P. (Chap. 11: Bittu Venkateswarlu)

Performance of Madelu Purana,
scroll narrative of Siricilla, Kareem Nagar Dt., A.P. (Chap. 11: Bittu Venkateswarlu)

Rukmini Kalyanam burrakatha, Satya Sai Dalam, Peddapuram (Chap. 12: Daniel Negers)

Sri Satya Haris Chandra Natakam (Chap. 12: Daniel Negers)

Bobbili Yuddham B.K. Madhurima Burrakatha Kakinada (Chap. 12: Daniel Negers)

Pancu Bhagat, Paranapur, (Chaubepur), Varanasi (Chap. 17: S.M. Pandey)

Orilal, Gujarpurava, Gonda (U.P.) died about ten years ago
(Chap. 17: S.M. Pandey)

Bobbili Yuddham B.K.
Chandana Koteswararao Dalam, Peddapuram (Chap. 12: Daniel Negers)

Pahlawan Saleh Mahmad Gorgej (left) (Chap. 19: Sabir Badalkhan)

Pahlawan Mazar Ibrahim (right) (Chap. 19: Sabir Badalkhan)

Sukanani Ojapali in action, Manasa-variety, Darrang, Assam (Chap. 20: Nabin Chandra Sarma)

Sukanani Ojapali in action,
Manasa-variety,Kamrup, Assam
(Chap. 20: Nabin Chandra Sarma)

Mare-gan in action,
Bishahari-variety, Pati Rabhas, Goalpara, Assam
(Chap. 20: Nabin Chandra Sarma)

Shrine of the deity Junjappa (Chap. 21: T.N. Shankarnarayana)

Male singer of Junjappa epic playing on *Gane*, long flute (Chap. 21: T.N. Shankarnarayana)

Bhavani (Chap. 14: Aditya Malik)

Sadu Mata and Bhagavan (Chap. 14: Aditya Malik)

List of Contributors

Sheila Asirvatham : Research Associate at the Department of Folklore, Madurai Kamaraj University, Madurai, Tamilnadu, India.

Sabir Badalkhan : Lecturer in the Department of Asian Studies, Instituto Universitario Orientale, Naples, Italy.

C.M. Bandhu : Professor in the Department of Nepali, Tribhuvan University, Kathmandu, Nepal.

Catherine Servan-Schreiber : Research Member of C.N.R.S, Centre d'etudes de L'Inde et de l'Asie du Sud (CEIAS), Ecole des Hautes Etudes en Sciences Sociales (EHESS), Paris, France.

Ajay Dandekar : Historian, National Insurance Academy, Pune, Maharashtra, India.

A.K. Das, Professor of Anthropology in the National Museum Institute, National Museum, New Delhi, India.

H.M.D.R. Herath : Senior Lecturer in the Department of Sociology, University of Peradeniya, Peradeniya, Sri Lanka.

Molly Kaushal : Research Officer, Indira Gandhi National Centre for the Arts, New Delhi, India.

Desmond L. Kharmawphlang : Lecturer at the Centre for Creative Arts, North Eastern Hill University, Shillong, Meghalaya, India.

Aditya Malik : Representative, South Asia Institute, University of Heidelberg, New Delhi, India.

M. Mani Meitei : Associate Professor in the Department of English, Manipur University, Imphal, Manipur, India.

Mahendra Kumar Mishra : Folklorist, Orissa Primary Education Programme, Bhubaneswar, Orissa, India.

Daniel Negers : Research Scholar in the Department of Social Anthropology, Paris University, France.

Richa Negi : Research Assistant, Indira Gandhi National Centre for the Arts, New Delhi, India.

S.M. Pandey : Professor in the Department of Asian Studies, Instituto Universitario Orientale, Naples, Italy.

Nicole Revel : Director of Research of C.N.R.S, Centre de Recherche sur L'Oralite (CRO), Institut National des Langues et Civilisations Orientales (INALCO), Paris, France.

S. Sanatombi : Associate Professor in the Department of Manipuri, Manipur University, Imphal, Manipur, India.

Baidyanath Saraswati : Unesco Professor, Indira Gandhi National Centre for the Arts, New Delhi, India.

Nabin Chandra Sarma : Professor in the Department of Folklore Research, Gauhati University, Guwahati, Assam, India.

William S. Sax : Professor in the Department of Anthropology, South Asia Institute, University of Heidelberg, Heidelberg, Germany.

T.N. Shankaranarayana, Director, Institute of Kannada Studies, Kuvempu University, Shimoga, Karnataka, India.

Mohan Upreti : Former Vice-President of Uttar Pradesh Sangeet Natak Academy, India.

KMA M. Usop : Professor at the Dayak Cultural Research Centre, University of Palangka Raya, Palangka Raya, Central Kalimantan, Indonesia.

Bittu Venkateswarlu : Senior Lecturer in the Department of Folk Arts, School of Fine Arts, Telugu University, Hyderabad, Andhra Pradesh, India.